Speech Acts in Argumentative Discussions

Studies of Argumentation in Pragmatics and Discourse Analysis (PDA)

This series of books on argumentation contains reports of original research on this topic as well as monographs on related topics. Contributions from linguists, philosophers, logicians, cognitive psychologists and researchers in speech communication to the fields of pragmatics and discourse analysis are brought together in order to promote interdisciplinary and international research on argumentation in natural language.

Editors
Frans H. van Eemeren
Rob Grootendorst
University of Amsterdam
Department of Speech Communication

Speech Acts in Argumentative Discussions

**A Theoretical Model for the Analysis of Discussions
Directed towards Solving Conflicts of Opinion**

Frans H. van Eemeren
Rob Grootendorst

1984
FORIS PUBLICATIONS
Dordrecht-Holland/Cinnaminson-U.S.A.

Published by:
Foris Publications Holland
P.O. Box 509
3300 AM Dordrecht, The Netherlands

Sole distributor for the U.S.A. and Canada:
Foris Publications U.S.A.
P.O. Box C-50
Cinnaminson N.J. 08077
U.S.A.

CIP-gegevens

Eemeren, Frans H. van

Speech acts in argumentative discussions: a theoretical model for the analysis of discussions directed towards solving conflicts of opinion / Frans H. van Eemeren, Rob Grootendorst; [transl. from the Dutch]. – Dordrecht [etc.]: Foris Publications. – (Pragmatics and discourse analysis; 1)
Transl. of: Regels voor redelijke discussies: een bijdrage tot de theoretische analyse van argumentatie ter oplossing van geschillen. – Dordrecht [etc.]: Foris Publications, 1982. – Also publ. as thesis Amsterdam, 1982.
ISBN 90-6765-018-8 cloth
SISO 805.9   UDC 801:162
Subject heading: argumentation; theoretical analysis.

ISBN 90 6765 018 8

© 1983 Foris Publications - Dordrecht.

Printed in the Netherlands by ICG Printing, Dordrecht.

Contents

Chapter 1. The resolution of disputes about expressed opinions   1
    1.1.   The aims of this book   1
    1.2.   Externalization of argumentation   4
    1.3.   Functionalization of argumentation   7
    1.4.   Socialization of argumentation   9
    1.5.   Dialectification of argumentation   15

Chapter 2. Argumentation as an illocutionary act complex   19
    2.1.   The basic theory of speech acts   19
    2.2.   Communicative and interactional aspects of language   23
    2.3.   Characterization of the speech act of argumentation   29
    2.4.   Points of agreement and disagreement with related views   35
    2.5.   The illocutionary act complex of argumentation   39

Chapter 3. Argumentation and the perlocutionary act of convincing   47
    3.1.   The perlocutionary act of convincing   47
    3.2.   The relation between illocutions and perlocutions   51
    3.3.   Various kinds of usage conventions   58
    3.4.   The conventionality of the illocutionary perlocution of convincing   63
    3.5.   Externalization of the perlocutionary effect of convincing   69

Chapter 4. Argumentation in discussions about expressed opinions   75
    4.1.   Problems of analysing argumentative discussions   75
    4.2.   Simple single discussions   78
         4.2.1.   Standard types of disputes and argumentative discussions   78
         4.2.2.   The resolution of simple single disputes   81
    4.3.   The structure of simple single discussions   85
         4.3.1.   The stages of the discussion   85
         4.3.2.   The structure of the argumentation   87

Chapter 5. The distribution of speech acts in rational discussions   95
    5.1.   Expressed opinions, argumentation and assertives   95
    5.2.   Illocutionary acts and the resolution of disputes   98
    5.3.   The role of speech acts at different stages in the discussion   104

5.4.   The role of usage declaratives   109
5.5.   The interpretation of speech acts   112

Chapter 6. Unexpressed premisses in rational discussions   119
6.1.   Unexpressed premisses and the co-operative principle   119
6.2.   Shortcomings in current theoretical approaches   123
        6.2.1. The Standard Logical Approach   123
        6.2.2. The Presuppositional Approach   129
6.3.   Unexpressed premisses as conversational implicatures   132
6.4.   The conditions for explicitized unexpressed premisses   137
6.5.   The explicitization of unexpressed premisses   141

Chapter 7. A code of conduct for rational discussants   151
7.1.   A general rule for speech acts in rational discussions   151
7.2.   Rules for the confrontation stage   154
7.3.   Rules for the opening stage   158
7.4.   Rules for the argumentation stage   162
7.5.   Rule for the concluding stage   173

Chapter 8. Fallacies and the code of conduct for rational discussants 177
8.1.   The treatment of fallacies in the practical literature   177
8.2.   Unexpressed premisses and the analysis of fallacies   179
8.3.   Various sorts of violation of the code of conduct   182
8.4.   The code of conduct and the analysis of fallacies   188
8.5.   Analyses of some fallacies by way of example   189

Notes   193

Bibliography   203

Index of Names   211

Index of Subjects   213

Chapter 1

The resolution of disputes about expressed opinions

1.1. THE AIMS OF THIS BOOK

People have probably always held differing opinions on countless subjects and they probably always will. Indeed, an individual may even have a difference of opinion with himself: he may, for example, return to a subject having changed his mind about it. There is nothing wrong with differences of opinion or disputes *per se*. Even if they become public they need not necessarily be a threat to world peace; they are, rather, an interesting illustration of the cultural pluriformity which exists within the microcosm.

And yet it is necessary for people to try to eliminate their differences of opinion, even if this generally means the creation of new ones to take their place. Otherwise we become intellectually isolated and can ultimately even end up in a state of spiritual and mental inertia. Every departure from the intellectual *status quo* requires the elimination of one or more differences of opinion.

For the elimination of a difference of opinion it is important that the various points of view are stated as clearly as possible. As a rule this means that the persons concerned in the difference of opinion will somehow have to *verbalize* their standpoints. In cases in which this is what actually happens, the difference of opinion is *externalized*, and in principle it is then possible for anyone to establish for himself what the dispute is about.

If those who are in dispute wish to resolve their difference of opinion they will also have to be prepared to enter into an *exchange of views* with each other regarding the expressed opinion that is at the heart of their dispute.[1] In its simplest form this means that a language user who has advanced a point of view in respect of an expressed opinion must be prepared to *defend* that standpoint and that a language user who has cast doubt upon the tenability of that standpoint must be prepared to *attack* it.

In principle, every difference of opinion has the potential to develop into a verbally externalized *dispute* about an expressed opinion. One can only speak of a fully-fledged dispute if one language user has explicitly *cast doubt upon* the other's standpoint. The interlocutors can only arrive jointly at the elimination of a difference of opinion if they allow it to develop into a proper dispute and are prepared to make a joint effort in order to *resolve* it.

A dispute, then, is not just common disagreement to be avoided if possible, but an articulated form of disunity which may be able to make a (more or less modest) contribution to intellectual progress. The primary aim of interlocutors 'embarking upon' a dispute of this kind is to resolve it, even though this may mean that as a result new differences of opinion will be called into being which in turn may become the point of departure for further disputes. Ideally, the resolution of disputes has no definite character but is an intermediate state (which is by definition temporary or provisional in nature) in a continuous process of intellectual growth.

For disputes to be resolved in a manner which is intellectually satisfactory, an exchange of views must take place between the interlocutors in the form of a *discussion*. In a discussion of this kind the discussants must advance statements *in which the standpoint under discussion is attacked and defended*. This is what we call an *argumentative discussion*.

In an argumentative discussion the participants try to *convince* one another of the *acceptability* or *unacceptability* of the expressed opinion under discussion by means of *argumentative statements*. These are designed to *justify* or *refute* an expressed opinion to the listener's satisfaction.

By advancing argumentative statements the interlocutors indicate their intention *jointly* to find a resolution of the dispute. In arguing they demonstrate their belief that the acceptability of expressed opinions does not depend on prejudices, traditions and uncontrolled emotions but on rational justifications and refutations. Prejudices and the like may of course play some part in the discussion, but it can never be a decisive one.

The crucial role assigned to argumentative language in the resolution of disputes about expressed opinions does not preclude the occurrence of other forms of language usage in argumentative discussions. For example, informative *questions*, *requests* for precization and *explanations* of unclear points may all have a particularly useful function in helping to resolve a dispute. Ultimately, however, the resolution depends on the argumentation put forward.

The language used in discussions can be studied from various angles. Ours is determined by our field of argumentation theory, and this implies that we are principally interested in aspects of the language in discussions which are relevant to the resolution of disputes about expressed opinions, and in methods which may contribute to the improvement of the practice of discussion. This *practical* and *normative* orientation is the *raison d'être* of the present work. However, it is not our intention to undertake the provision of an all-embracing and immediately applicable method for the resolution of disputes by means of argumentative discussions.

In our view it is first necessary to develop a theoretical conception of the use of language in discussions, such that it becomes possible to establish what are the principal problems that are likely to present themselves in resolving disputes and how they may be solved. This is the only way in which a proper foundation can be laid for the drafting of appropriate advice to language users.

In any event, our theoretical exposition of argumentative discussions will have to offer a solution for the following problems:

i.   The speech act theory is the best analytical instrument so far developed in descriptive interpretative pragmatics. Speech act theorists have concentrated chiefly on the analysis of illocutionary acts. Argumentation is usually deemed to fall under the heading of illocutionary acts, but in some important respects it differs from other illocutionary acts. Moreover, the conditions that have to be fulfilled for a correct performance of the speech act *argumentation* have still not been formulated anywhere. The question is, therefore, whether argumentation really ought to be treated as an *illocutionary act*, and what the *conditions* are which may be deemed to have been fulfilled if a series of utterances is regarded as an argumentation.

ii.   Speech act theorists have so far paid very little attention to perlocutionary acts. But argumentation is an attempt at convincing the listener of the acceptability or unacceptability of an expressed opinion, and *convincing* is a perlocutionary act. The relation between illocutionary and perlocutionary acts is not quite clear, so that it is also not quite clear how the performance of the speech act of *argumentation* is connected with pursuing a specific perlocutionary effect. The question, therefore, is how the *relation* between the illocution *arguing* and the perlocution *convincing* can best be characterized.

iii. In order to be able to make a responsible evaluation of contributions to a discussion, language users must be capable of analysing argumentative discussions. This requires an analytical instrument which at present is not yet available. It will have to enable us to draw up guidelines for establishing how the discussion has gone and what part each party has had in the resolution of the dispute, and can only be developed on the basis of an adequate theoretical conception of a *rational* discussion. The question, then, is what *theoretical conception of a rational discussion* can supply an instrument of analysis which will make it possible for us to draw up adequate guidelines for the *analysis of argumentative discussions.*

iv.   The contributions to the resolution of a dispute that are made in discussions in colloquial speech are not always explicit. The argumentation may contain unexpressed premises which require to be considered for a proper assessment of the argumentation. The literature has devoted attention to unexpressed premises in various ways, but the commonest approaches are unequal to the task of indicating which statement must be regarded as an unexpressed premiss in any particular argumentation. The question here, therefore, is what *approach to non-explicit language usage* will enable us to draw up adequate guidelines for the *explicitization of unexpressed premises.*

v.   Not all the speech acts performed in colloquial speech by the interlocutors in a discussion contribute to the resolution of the dispute. It is therefore necessary to establish rules for the way in which language users must behave in discussions.[2] These rules must indicate which speech acts are permitted in a rational discussion. Together they constitute a code of conduct for rational discussants. In particular, the rules must ensure that no fallacies occur in the discussion. Various authors have proposed rules furthering the rationality of discussions, but it is still not clear exactly what speech acts may be performed in a rational discussion. The question is therefore how a *code of conduct* can be formulated to ensure that in discussions about expressed opinions language users behave as *rational discussants*.

Following on from these five problems we may now formulate the aims of the present work as follows:

1.   *To clarify what sort of speech act is being performed when argumentation is advanced and what conditions may be deemed to have been fulfilled if that speech act is performed.*
2.   *To clarify the relation between the performance of the speech act of argumentation and the perlocutionary effect that the listener accepts or does not accept a given expressed opinion.*
3.   *To draw up guidelines for the analysis of argumentative discussions.*
4.   *To draw up guidelines for the explicitization of unexpressed premisses.*
5.   *To formulate rules for a code of conduct for rational discussants.*

1.2. EXTERNALIZATION OF ARGUMENTATION

Argumentative language can be made the object of study in various ways and it is possible to start from any of a number of different conceptions of argumentation. We believe that the views of argumentation that have held sway in research into the subject over the past decades are inadequate, and hope to show which conception of argumentation makes an adequate approach to argumentative language possible.

Unlike logicians, argumentation theorists concern themselves primarily with argumentation *in colloquial speech*. This means that the object of their research is not constituted from combinations of premises and conclusions formulated with the help of formal symbols whose meaning is established unambiguously beforehand, but from *constellations of statements by language users* which may in principle mean more than one thing and which must be interpreted by other language users. Another important difference is that argumentation theorists, unlike logicans, regard argumentation as a form of language which is in principle designed *to convince other language users of the acceptability or unacceptability of a given expressed opinion.* This implies that they assume that the statements constituting the argumentation have a specific *communicative and interactional function* and do not serve solely to demonstrate that a certain conclusion necessarily follows from certain premises.

These differences are not absolute. They point to a difference in orientation, but the different orientations need not necessarily be mutually exclusive. Indeed, the logical approach and the approach of argumentation theory may in principle complement one another very well. Even so, the differences in orientation do mean that the object of research is approached differently and that different priorities are established (cf. Van Eemeren, Grootendorst & Kruiger 1983, ch. 2.3). We shall therefore begin by stating which approach to argumentation we regard as the most suitable for the purposes of argumentation theory.

To be able to examine argumentation properly we must first offer some explanation of a number of fundamental terms, viz. *expressed opinion, standpoint (or point of view)*, and the expression *rational judge*.

We use the term *expressed opinion* to refer to the subject of the argumentation. Expressed opinions may refer to facts or ideas (or even entire theories), but they may also refer to actions, attitudes, and so on. They may be positive, but they may also be negative. For example, 'His resignation is inevitable' and 'His resignation is not inevitable' may both function as expressed opinions. An expressed opinion consists of the proposition (negative or otherwise) that is expressed in the speech act on which the argumentation turns.

By the term *standpoint* (or *point of view*) we mean an (externalized) attitude on the part of a language user in respect of an expressed opinion. Suppose two language users have read somewhere the statement that 'Women have a logic of their own', and that one language user agrees with this and the other does not. They might express this by saying, for example, 'I think it is true that women have a logic of their own', or 'I think it is not true that women have a logic of their own'. In that case they have advanced a standpoint (the one positive, the other negative) in respect of a positive expressed opinion. A positive standpoint expresses a *positive committedness* and a negative standpoint expresses a *negative committedness* to an expressed opinion.

By the expression *rational judge* we mean the language user regarded by the speaker as assessing or evaluating what he says. Argumentation advanced in defence of a positive standpoint is designed to *justify*, to the satisfaction of a rational judge, the expressed opinion to which the standpoint relates, and argumentation advanced in defence of a negative standpoint is designed to *refute* the expressed opinion to the satisfaction of a rational judge. Language users advancing argumentation presuppose in principle that their listeners are rational judges in the sense that they will attempt to make as adequate as possible an assessment of the acceptability or unacceptability of the argumentation, i.e. they are supposed to judge the argumentation *on the contribution it makes to the resolution of the dispute*.

One of the chief features of our approach to argumentation is the stress we place on *externalization*, i.e. on the verbal communication of the subject to be investigated. We believe that argumentation theory must concern itself with differences of opinion and with efforts to resolve disputes about expressed opinions by verbal means. This means that the argumentation theorist must concern himself with *expressed opinions* and *argumentative statements* and not primarily with the thoughts, ideas and motives which may underlie them.

We also believe that it is necessary to guard against an *internalization* of the subject of investigation, since that would return argumentation theory to philosophically extinct eras such as the 'heyday of meanings' or even the 'heyday of ideas' (cf. Hacking 1975). Such a relapse can only be avoided if it is not merely required of *language users* that they open up their 'interior' but also that the *theorist* in particular ensures that psychologizing is avoided. This means that he must start from what the discussants *say* and must concentrate on the *speech acts* performed (whether explicitly or implicitly) by language users.

For particular purposes, e.g. the discussion of aspects of meaning common to particular statements, it can sometimes be useful to refer to the 'thoughts' or 'ideas' that a speaker expresses. In that case, however, it is important to bear in mind that one is dealing with thoughts or ideas *deduced from the speaker's statements* by abstracting from a particular form of expression.[3]

Terms like *thought* or *idea* can also be considered as indicators of *psycho-pragmatic primitives*, which enable us to speak meaningfully about phenomena that are specifically connected with people. In some cases, as when referring to speech acts, it would be difficult to do without such psycho-pragmatic primitives, e.g. *intention*.[4] However, one must then be alert to the danger of *reification* and avoid investing primitives such as intention with an existence of their own and presenting them as independently operating forces.

No more than one may invest psycho-pragmatic primitives such as intention, thought or idea with an 'existence' that is independent of every verbal form of expression, may the impression be given that by postulating such primitives it is possible to reach some *revelation* of what people actually 'had in mind' by way of intentions, thoughts or ideas when they made particular statements. The content of the postulated intentions, thoughts or ideas is determined by the information *communicated* by the speaker (whether verbally or otherwise). This means that in the study of argumentation it is only permissible to use psycho-pragmatic primitives which are *directly related to statements*.

Our reason for making it a matter of principle to strive after a consistent externalization of the subject to be investigated is analogous to the reason given by Popper in *Objective Knowledge* for the verbal formulation of theories: only a *formulated* theory can be the subject of a critical discussion; a theory that is only *believed* does not lend itself for discussion (1972:31,66). To this Popper attaches consequences for his approach to problems:

> One of my principal methods of approach, whenever *logical* problems are at stake, is to translate all the subjective or psychological terms, especially 'belief', etc., into *objective* terms. Thus, instead of speaking of a 'belief', I speak, say, of a

'statement' or of an 'explanatory theory': ... and instead of the claim of the
'justification of a belief', I speak of 'justification of the claim that a theory is
true', etc. (1972:6).

We believe a similar 'objectivization' to be necessary for an approach to
problems concerning argumentation and that it must be achieved through
externalization.

Many authors writing about argumentation refer with great facility to
'thoughts', 'ideas' and 'motives' that may be attributed to language users,
without it being made clear *on what grounds* this can be so easily done. We
regard this as one of the dangers inherent in 'practicism'. If one starts
exclusively from the problems that language users perceive, or think they
perceive, in the practice of argumentation, because of the chosen perspective
one runs the risk of adopting not only the problems themselves but also,
along with them, the frequently psychologizing or otherwise subjectivistic
problem definitions of the language users.

A theorerical approach is preferable not only because we have to have a
perspective which allows us to distinguish the relevant from the irrelevant (cf.
Feyerabend 1977) but also because the problems have to be posed in a way
that is *scientifically interesting*. The externalization of the subject of investigation, as we advocate it, does not go far enough to meet this requirement
and will therefore require theoretical completion.

1.3 FUNCTIONALIZATION OF ARGUMENTATION

A second feature of our approach to argumentation is the stress we place on
functionalization, i.e. the treatment of the subject of investigation as a *purposive activity*. Since argumentation consists of making statements, we think
that theoretical thinking about argumentation should be concerned not only
with the structure of completed argumentative constellations but also with
argumentation as a verbal activity. This implies that the argumentation
theorist should regard argumentation as a *language usage process* which has
run its proper course only if certain conditions have been met in the performance of the speech act *argumentation*.

In our approach *argumentation* is not treated simply as a *product* consisting of a constellation of statements, but also as a *process*. The 'process/
product ambiguity' displayed by the word *argumentation* in colloquial
speech is deliberately preserved here. *Argumentation* refers both to the
process of making statements in order to defend a standpoint ('Don't inter-
rupt me before I've finished my argumentation') and to the product that is
the result of it ('Now that I look at it again I do see weak points in your
argumentation'). Because the process of advancing argumentation is a purposive activity, argumentation must be regarded as a form of *verbal action*.

Popper (1972:237) regards the argumentative function as the most important
function of the use of language. There is no need to go quite as fas as this to

find it strange that studies of argumentation often pay hardly any attention to the specific features of argumentation *as a form of language*. Probably chiefly due to the influence of a tradition inspired by logicians, argumentation is frequently presented solely as an abstract product quite separate from language. For this reason Fogelin speaks in this connection of argumentation 'in the logician's sense' (1978:v). In some cases this one-sided approach even seems to result in argumentation being regarded as no more than a logical deduction which, as it were, just happens to be couched in colloquial speech and is made more difficult to evaluate by the imperfections of colloquial speech. Grice calls this approach *formalistic*, characterizing it as follows:

> From a philosophical point of view, the possession by the natural counterparts of those elements in their meaning, which they do not share with the correspon- ding formal devices, is to be regarded as an imperfection of natural languages; the elements in question are undesirable excrescences (1975:42).

Haack accounts those who adhere to the opinion that the grammatical form of a 'recalcitrant' sentence in colloquial speech must be considered an indicator of its logical form, adherents of the 'misleading form thesis' (1974:53).[5] In *Philosophy of Logics* she explains what such misguided persons fail to recognize:

> Something like this: formal logical systems aim to formalise informal arguments, to represent them in precise, rigorous and generalisable terms; and an acceptable formal logical system ought to be such that, if a given informal argument is represented in it by a certain formal argument, than that formal argument should be valid in the system just in case the informal argument is valid in the extra-sys- tematic sense (1978:15).

In our view this is one of the disadvantages that are liable to result from a purely product-oriented approach to argumentation. In the 'ideal language philosophy' there is a tendency to overlook the fact that argumentation in colloquial speech is always committed and always will be committed to the specific conventions applying to ordinary everyday language. The result of this is that any approach to argumentation that is based on this philosophy and on this philosophy alone is bound to be defective.

Lambert and Ulrich point to another disadvantage that may result from a purely product-oriented approach to argumentation. They observe that one effect of the stress laid on the logical evaluation of arguments is that insuffi- cient attention is paid to the problems of recognizing and clarifying argu- mentation in colloquial language, so that, in turn, the argumentation is imperfectly understood. They therefore introduce a 'step-by-step procedure for identifying an argument in everyday discourse, extracting it, and then paraphrasing it into the formal idiom' (1980:x). It is curious, incidentally, that though they go into the matter of stylistic variation in language usage they pay no attention to the *function* of stylistic variation in communication and interaction.

A product-oriented approach to argumentation provides no insight into the conditions that have to be fulfilled for a constellation of speech utterances to count as argumentation. This is because argumentation is not treated as a form of language at all (cf. Fogelin 1978:v). In a product-oriented approach one runs the risk of becoming bogged down in 'structurism', and in our view this is a risk that can only be avoided by functionalizing the subject of investigation and treating argumentation as a *speech act*.

1.4. SOCIALIZATION OF ARGUMENTATION

A third feature of our approach to argumentation is the stress we place on *socialization*, i.e. treating the subject of investigation *communicatively and interactionally*. Argumentation is an attempt to convince a rational judge of the rightness of a particular standpoint in respect of the acceptability of an expressed opinion. A speaker engaging in argumentation addresses himself in principle to *another language user* who is supposed to assume the position of a rational judge. The language user fulfilling the communicative role of listener is in principle entitled, if he is not yet convinced, to react to the argumentation and himself act as speaker, so that a *dialogue* is initiated. In our view this means that argumentation has to be seen as part of a bilateral process.

This can also apply where only one person is involved: if a language user doubts his own standpoint and as it were tacitly disagrees with himself about the acceptability of an expressed opinion, then effectively we have *two parties* adopting different points of view in respect of an expressed opinion. This may give rise to an *interior dialogue*. Even in this special case someone has to be convinced and we may therefore speak of a bilateral or *social* process. Self-consultation in this way often takes place where it is necessary to anticipate the possible reactions of others, which makes the social nature of argumentation even more obvious.

In the case of an argumentation that is successful in all respects the listener is convinced in the sense that he either *accepts* or *rejects* the expressed opinion to which the argumentation refers. This means that in that case argumentation with convincing force constitutes a complete whole. This may consist of *pro-argumentation* and the *acceptance* of the expressed opinion or *contra-argumentation* and the *rejection* of the expressed opinion. Here two language users are involved, each of whom acts at least once as speaker and at least once as listener. A successful attempt at convincing in which this communicative role exchange takes place only once is the *smallest complete dialogic unit of argumentation where the attempt at convincing is successful*. Fig. 1.1 is a schematic representation of this minimal unit.

If language user A takes the communicative role of speaker and language user B that of listener, then in a verbally externalized discussion with success-

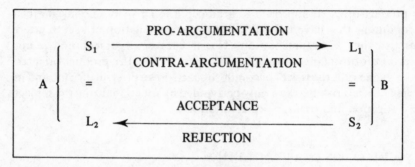

Figure 1.1. The smallest complete unit of argumentation where the attempt at convincing is successful.

ful argumentation language user B must in his turn take the role of speaker and accept or reject the expressed opinion, and language user A must take the role of listener.

In practice, of course, it will often be the case that the listener is not immediately convinced, and a series of such dialogues will then follow which may be linked to one another in a variety of ways. A discussion may contain any number of subdiscussions all containing argumentations. The main point here is that discussions may contain argumentative dialogues of greater complexity than the minimal dialogue.

Often the listener will not accept or reject an expressed opinion immediately after the very first argumentation advanced by the speaker, but will first request further argumentation (or more information). If he asks the speaker for arguments to support statements made in his original argumentation, these then function as *expressed opinions*. If he asks the speaker for arguments against objections that he has raised against the speaker's argumentation (or part of it), then those objections in turn become expressed opinions. Thus there may be all sorts of more or less complex patterns of *interrupted* dialogues, two examples of which we give in figure 1.2.

The picture given in fig. 1.2 is somewhat oversimplified and does not really express the fact that A and B are not just language users who take turns in assuming the communicative roles of speaker and listener but also *parties in a dispute* who in principle play opposing *interactional* roles in the dialogue. This is better expressed by representing the argumentation in a *dialogue tableau*. That is what we have done in fig. 1.3.

In both of the tableaux in fig. 1.3 language user A takes the interactional role of *protagonist* of a positive standpoint in respect of an expressed opinion and language user B the interactional role of *antagonist*. In these dialogues A defends a negative expressed opinion ($\backsim X$), while B expresses his doubts in respect of the acceptability of $\backsim X$.

In the third move A gives arguments for $\backsim X$. In the tableau on the left

language user A language user B language user A language user B

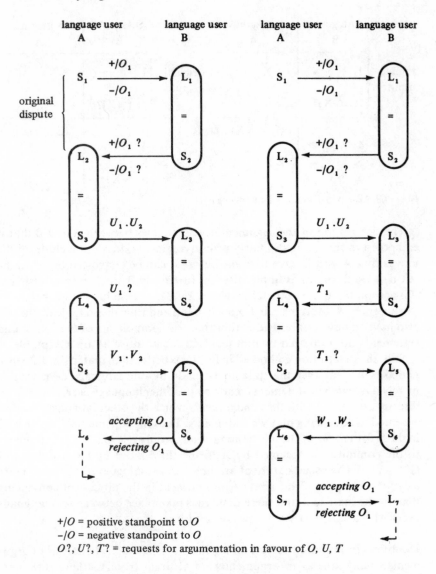

+/O = positive standpoint to O
−/O = negative standpoint to O
O?, U?, T? = requests for argumentation in favour of O, U, T

Figure 1.2. Examples of interrupted argumentative dialogues.

language user B then expresses, in move 4, his *doubt* as to the acceptability of one of the statements (Z) which go to make up A's argumentation. In the tableau on the right he makes an *objection* (in move 4) by asserting the opposite of that statement, viz. ∿ Z. In the fifth move A justifies the attacked statement in the right-hand tableau by means of argumentation: (Y⊃Z). Y. In the tableau on the left he tries to render the statement acceptable by a different method (asserting Z). Both manoeuvres are evidently sufficient to convince B of the acceptability of the expressed opinion under discussion.

Antagonist B	Protagonist A		Antagonist B	Protagonist A
original dispute { 1.	$\sim$X	original dispute { 1.	$\sim$X
2. ($\sim$X)?		2. ($\sim$X)?	
3.	(Z $\supset \sim$X) . Z	3.	(Z $\supset \sim$X) . Z
4. Z?		4. $\sim$Z	
5.	Z	5.	(Y $\supset$ Z) . Y
6. $\sim$X		6. $\sim$X	

Figure 1.3. Examples of argumentative dialogic tableaux.

The description of the argumentative dialogues between A and B that is embodied in fig. 1.3 is still fairly primitive, since it does not include all the moves that A and B have to make before B can be convinced by A. In the left-hand tableau, for example, after the fifth move B must first establish that Z is acceptable and that therefore (Z $\supset \sim$X). Z is acceptable to him, before he can accept $\sim$ X. Moreover, in both left-hand and right-hand tableaux he will also have to have established earlier that the components of the compound statements not criticized by him (e.g. Z $\supset \sim$X in move 3) are acceptable.

Still, the description embodied in fig. 1.3 is better than that in fig. 1.2, since it makes it clear that the statements made by one language user are not merely a *reaction* to statements made by the other language user, but are also directly associated with the *commitments* which the other language user has accepted in advancing his own statements. Thus the statement Z?, made by B in the fourth move of the left-hand tableau, is only relevant because it relates to the commitment accepted by A in the third move by his advancing of (Z $\supset \sim$X).Z. The social nature of argumentative dialogues is expressed more clearly in the role of this kind of commitment in the process of convincing than in the mere fact that these dialogues take place between two language users who act alternately as speaker and listener.

Doubtless in imitation of common practice in the logical analysis of arguments, many studies of argumentation abstract from the language users involved in the argumentation and hence from their communicative and interactional roles. Argumentation is then treated not as an attempt at convincing others of a particular standpoint, but as an autonomous and abstract pattern of depersonalized propositions. Like most logicians, the representatives of this view ignore the various communicative and interactional roles that are presupposed in argumentation and automatically regard it as a *monologue*.[6] In this way argumentation is stripped of its social character.

Perelman and Olbrechts-Tyteca (1971), who have made an influential contribution to the study of argumentation, appear at first sight to elect, in their

New Rhetoric, for a dialogic approach to argumentation. On closer inspection, however, their contribution is not dialogic, because the (universal) audience that is supposed to guarantee rationality is composed of a sometimes imaginary company of *passive listeners* offering no verbal opposition at all. This quasi-social treatment of argumentation predominates in literature on argumentation in which a *rhetorical* perspective is chosen.

Theoretical studies of argumentation in which the subject is considered as part of a bilateral process have been supplied by Naess (1966) and Crawshay-Williams (1957). Barth and Krabbe (1982) draw on their insights (and on those of the 'Erlangen School' of Lorenzen et al.) to develop a dialogic theory of argumentation. In the dialogic view argumentation is regarded as part of a discussion between language users that is calculated to resolve a dispute about an expressed opinion.

In the dialogic logic the *expressed opinion* takes the place of the *conclusion* in monologic logic. The *premisses* of monologic logic become *concessions* (or *hypotheses*) by the *opponent* of the expressed opinion in dialogic logic. Concessions are statements made by the opponent at the beginning of the dispute which he is prepared to defend if they are attacked, so that the *proponent* can employ them in his defence of the expressed opinion. This initial situation in the dialogic logic differs from what we, allying ourselves with argumentative practice, regard as the norm.

For didactic reasons the proponent P and the opponent O are often given namens like *Peter, the Pope, Olga* and *Otto*, but this is misleading, for they are only *roles* in a dialogic game.

If one starts solely from the dialogic division of roles it is less easily apparent that the initial situation in a dispute as it is taken for their starting point by dialogic logicians, *differs* from what is normal. Moreover, there is also a risk of becoming bogged down in an *abstract* form of socialization. At this abstract level it is perhaps no great surprise that the *opponent* should make certain concessions in advance, but when one remembers that the dialogic logicians equate these in principle with the *proponent's argumentation* it assumes a more curious aspect. If one imagines a dispute about an expressed opinion between A and B, it seems rather strange if A simply takes over B's argumentative statements.

We believe that in practical argumentation one language user is unlikely simply to take upon himself an obligation to defend statements which are in principle *the other language user's premisses*. As a rule the initial situation that the dialogic logicians take as their starting point will, in our view, be *preceded* by an earlier one which may or may not lead to it.

The point here is that the dialogic logicians' initial situation relates to the defensibility of an expressed opinion *in relation to a particular constellation of argumentative statements*, while as a rule the testing of this defensibility will not occur until the moment at which the interlocutor refusing to accept the expressed opinion *has*, in the meantime, accepted the argumentative statements. If he does *not* accept one or more of these statements, the person who is arguing has chosen a point of departure which in principle itself requires further argumentation.

The initial situation chosen by the dialogic logicians to be their starting point therefore lies as it were *a stage further* than our initial situation. The interlocutors have then decided to test the defensibility of the expressed opinion in relation to the argumentation advanced by each assuming a different dialogic role and jointly establishing whether the expressed opinion, given a certain dialogic standardization of language or terminology, is or is not tenable by an opponent who judges the statements made in the argumentation to be acceptable. In fig. 1.4 we illustrate the two initial situations by means of example (left, our initial situation; right, the dialogic logicians' initial situation).

B	A		O	P
1.	$A \to C$		1. $A \to B$	
2. $(A \to C)$?			2. $B \to C$	
— — — —	— — — — — —		3.	$A \to C$
3.	$(A \to C) . (B \to C)$		4. $(?) A/3$	
4. ...			— — —	— — — — —
			5.	...

Figure 1.4. Two views of the initial situation in a dispute.

A's argumentation can be regarded, if desired, as a component of the expressed opinion (which is then more complex) in P. In principle this presents no problem, since every combination of argumentation and an expressed opinion can be rewritten as a compound statement in the form of an implication in which the argumentation acts as the antecedent and the expressed opinion as the consequence. At a later stage, of course (following the rule system of dialogic logic), the same initial situation evolves as that taken by the dialogic logicians as their starting point (according to dialogic logic the opponent of an implication must hypothetically assert the antecedent of the implication) (cf. Kamlah & Lorenzen 1973:210). This is illustrated in fig. 1.5.[7]

We have preferred a dialogic approach to argumentation because we believe monologism to be an obstacle standing in the way of progress towards gaining insight into the way in which language users use their language argumentatively in communicating and interacting with other language users. In our opinion this dialogization must start with a socialization of the subject to be investigated, and it is for this reason that we see no benefit in approaches to argumentation which totally ignore the language users involved in the argumentation. If it is to be possible to develop an adequate theory of argumentation, it seems to us, it will always be necessary to start from *language users in a dialogue situation*.

O	P
1.	$[(A \to B) . (B \to C)] \to (A \to C)$
2. (?) $[(A \to B) . (B \to C)]$	$[\![P$ is obliged to defend $A \to C]\!]$
3.	$A \to C$
4. (?) A/3	
5.	. . .

Figure 1.5. Reconstruction of argumentation as a concession.

1.5. DIALECTIFICATION OF ARGUMENTATION

A fourth feature of our approach to argumentation is the stress we place on *dialectification*. If a language user advances argumentation in defence of a standpoint he advances a constellation of statements calculated either to justify or to refute an expressed opinion. In the first case we speak of *pro-argumentation*, and in the second of *contra-argumentation*. In either case the language user addresses another language user who is supposed to adopt the position of a rational judge and who reacts to the argumentation critically, so that a critical discussion ensues.

Although it need not necessarily be the case that in a critical discussion both language users have committed themselves to an expressed opinion positively or negatively (one of them may merely have expressed doubt), as a rule it will be so. In that case two opposing standpoints are adopted. A resolution of the dispute acceptable to both language users can only be achieved if both are able and allowed to advance their argumentation. This means that in critical discussions it must in principle be possible for both pro-argumentation and contra-argumentation to be put forward. The literature on argumentation generally focuses attention exclusively on pro-argumentation and tacitly ignores contra-argumentation.

The attention that has been paid to argumentation exclusively as an attempt at justification can perhaps be explained by the biased orientation of many argumentation theorists towards logic. This is, at least, the explanation suggested by Fogelin (1978:v). However, if this explanation is at all correct, we believe that at the very most it is a matter of an *imperfect* imitation of logicians, since the principle of falsification and the attempt to refute expressed opinions that are its concomitants are anything but strangers to logic. For example, Purtill makes it clear right at the beginning of his book *Logic* that logic relates both to attempts at justification and attempts at refutation:

> Logic is the science that studies and evaluates kinds of arguments. By *argument* is meant not just a quarrel or a disagreement, but rather the attempt to give reasons or evidence for accepting a statement as true *or rejecting it as false* (1979:2; our italics).

One of the dangers of regarding argumentation exclusively as an attempt at justification is that a link can easily arise in people's minds between argumentation theory and *justificationism* or *letzt Begründung philosophy*. As long as one's starting point is the notion of the 'sufficient reason' one relies, as Albert (1963) puts it, on an *authoritarian scheme of justification*. Albert believes that the philosophies both of classical rationalism and of classical empiricism, in which individual intuition and observation respectively are regarded as sufficient grounds for justification, are guilty of this. In his view a concealed dogmatic remnant of these justificatory philosophies still plays an important role in our thinking today.

If, in their *New Rhetoric*, Perelman and Olbrechts-Tyteca provide an accurate description of the means of persuasion that are effective in practice, then we have confirmation of Albert's assertion about our thinking today,[8] since according to them theories can in practice be vindicated sufficiently by appealing, for example, to 'the structure of reality'. Albert, on the other hand, believes he is able to observe that those engaged in the sciences are gradually beginning to break away from the notion of sufficient foundation, so that it will be possible for a consistent Popperian criticism to develop.

Of course, it need not necessarily always be the case that authors who refer only to *justification* in their definitions of argumentation are automatically adherents (consciously or unconsciously) of justificatory philosophy. It may also be the case that they simply equate defending a point of view in respect of an expressed opinion with defending a *positive standpoint*, i.e. with *justifying* an expressed opinion. This would mean that they ignored the possibility of a *negative standpoint* in respect of an expressed opinion being defended so that the argumentation is calculated to *refute* that expressed opinion. However, this view of argumentation is at the very least one-sided and incomplete, and it may, moreover, have the same undesirable consequences as a view of argumentation that *does* spring from justificationism.

Justificationism, of whatever hue, can never escape the so-called *Münchhausen trilemma*[9]. In our view the danger of that can best be avoided by adopting a Popperian critical-rationalist standpoint and assuming the *inherent fallibility* of human reason while elevating the notion of *critical testing* to the status of a guiding principle for the solution of problems. This critical-rationalist attitude implies that one must further the creation of a *dialectic* in the Socratic sense of the word.

The idea that the Socratic dialectic is a model for rationality has been propagated in every conceivable way by Popper. It now looks as if increasing numbers of writers are taking the same line (though they do not always draw the right conclusions from this). Albert stresses that the dialectical method makes possible a comprehensive critical rationalism which is not subject to restrictions and which constitutes a *general* alternative to classical methodology (1967).

Argumentation theorists, too, have recently begun to call for a *dialectical* approach (cf. Wenzel 1979:85), as distinct from the *logical* and *rhetorical* approaches. Its proponents believe that logical and rhetorical starting points must be combined in a specific manner.

The logical approach to argumentation has traditionally concentrated on argumentation as a *product*, attention being focused primarily on the *validity* of arguments in which a conclusion is deduced from one or more premisses. The rhetorical approach, on the other hand, concentrates on argumentation as a *process*, stressing the *effectiveness* of the activities developed in the argumentation in connection with the gaining of *approbation*.

The question is now what a dialectical approach to argumentation implies. According to Wenzel, an advocate of this approach, the term *dialectic* has traditionally been linked with the notion of 'a structure of discourse marked by critical intention'. In his opinion, following on from this notion, argumentation must be regarded as 'a systematic management of discourse for the purpose of achieving critical decisions' (1979:84). In his view the dialectical approach to argumentation is designed to establish *how debates must be conducted for the critical testing of expressed opinions* (1979:93).

We too regard argumentation as a part of a critical discussion about an expressed opinion. By a *critical discussion* we mean a discussion between a protagonist and an antagonist of a particular standpoint in respect of an expressed opinion, the purpose of the discussion being to establish whether the protagonist's standpoint is defensible against the critical reactions of the antagonist.

The argumentation advanced by the protagonist in defence of his standpoint may be either pro-argumentation or contra-argumentation in respect of the expressed opinion to which his standpoint relates. In the former case he tries to justify the expressed opinion and in the latter he tries to refute it. In either case the antagonist may in turn react critically to the protagonist's argumentation. This means that the protagonist will have to continue his attempt at justification or refutation with further pro- or contra-argumentation. This too may elicit a critical reaction from the antagonist, and so on. In this way an *interaction* is created between the speech acts performed in the discussion by the protagonist and those performed by the antagonist.

We believe this interaction to be an essential feature of a dialectical process of convincing. However, it will only be able to lead to a resolution of the dispute at the centre of the discussion if the discussion itself is adequately *regimented*. This means that in a dialectical theory of argumentation it will be necessary to propose rules for the conduct of argumentative discussions.

The regimentation achieved by these rules will have to meet two comprehensive conditions: it must further the resolution of the dispute and be acceptable to the discussants, and it must apply to all speech acts which may have to be performed in the course of the discussion to bring about a resolution of the dispute at the centre of the discussion. The rules must promote the conclusion of the discussion with an unambiguous result, the rapid reaching of that result, the consideration of all possibilities, the lucidity of the discussion and a step-by-step approach to the resolution of the dispute. This means that the rules must be *realistic, dynamic, radical, orderly* and *systematic* (cf. Barth & Krabbe 1982:ch. 3).

These rules can only lead to the resolution of the dispute if the language users concerned try to achieve that aim by conducting an argumentative discussion in which they adhere to them. This means that language users wishing jointly to resolve a dispute must take not only a *critical* but also a *co-operative* attitude. With this in mind we may formulate the following *norm of rationality*:

> *A language user taking part in an argumentative discussion is a rational language user if in the course of the discussion he performs only speech acts which accord with a system of rules acceptable to all discussants which furthers the creation of a dialectic which can lead to a resolution of the dispute at the centre of the discussion.*

We shall term a *rational discussion* only one conducted by language users adopting a rational attitude in the sense just described. We prefer a dialectical approach to argumentation, which improves the chances of such rational discussions taking place, to any form of justificationism. The crux of a dialectical approach is that argumentation is regarded as an attempt to defend a standpoint in respect of an expressed opinion against the critical reactions of a rational judge in a regimented discussion.

In accordance with the externalizing, functionalizing, socializing and dialectifying approach to argumentation, which we shall elaborate in the following chapters, we can now summarize our view of argumentation in the following definition:[10]

> *Argumentation is a speech act consisting of a constellation of statements designed to justify or refute an expressed opinion and calculated in a regimented discussion to convince a rational judge of a particular standpoint in respect of the acceptability or unacceptability of that expressed opinion.*

Chapter 2

Argumentation as an illocutionary act complex

2.1 THE BASIC THEORY OF SPEECH ACTS

The speech act theory offers the most effective theoretical framework for the functional analysis of language currently available, but argumentation has hitherto not been analysed as a speech act. An additional complication here is that it has not yet even been established whether argumentation is actually, like those speech acts for which analyses are already available, an *illocutionary* act. Moreover, speech acts are generally analysed from the point of view of the speaker, whereas in the context of resolving disputes we are interested precisely in what conditions the *listener* regards as fulfilled when he treats a constellation of statements as argumentation. We have therefore made it one of our aims to clarify what sort of speech act is performed when argumentation is put forward and what conditions may be deemed to have been fulfilled when that speech act is performed (*objective 1*).[11]

This implies that we have to try to solve two problems. We shall start from the 'standard version' of the speech act theory. This means that the theoretical framework within which we shall argue consists of the basic theory of speech acts whose foundations Austin laid in *How to Do Things with Words* and which was elaborated further by Searle in *Speech Acts*, partly on the basis of his own insights. *Speech Acts* is the common point of departure for many studies of speech acts. Like some other authors, we shall incorporate modifications where that is necessary to our purpose.

Like Austin, Searle assumes that language can be regarded as a form of *verbal acting*. He distinguishes (in a classification slightly different from that used by Austin) three sorts of speech act which are in principle performed whenever a speaker utters a sentence: 1. an *utterance act* (the bringing forth of certain speech sounds, words and sentences), 2. a *propositional act* (referring to something or someone and predicating some properties of that thing or person), and 3. an *illocutionary act* (investing the utterance with a communicative force of promise, statement of fact, and so on). Besides these acts, when uttering a sentence the speaker can also perform a *perlocutionary act* (bringing about certain effects, such as shock and boredom).[12]

In *Speech Acts* Searle stresses that the utterance act, propositional act and illocutionary act are not spatio-temporally discrete and independent acts but mutually interdependent *sub-acts* of the complete speech act which are performed simultaneously:

> I am not saying, of course, that these are separate things that speakers do, as it
> happens, simultaneously, as one might smoke, read and scratch one's head
> simultanously ... Nor should it be thought from this that utterance acts and
> propositional acts stand to illocutionary acts in the way buying a ticket and
> getting on a train stand to taking a railroad trip. ... utterance acts stand to
> propositional and illocutionary acts in the way in which, e.g., making an 'X' on a
> ballot paper stands to voting (1970:24).

However, it is confusing that Searle refers both to the third speech act
(allocating an illocutionary force) and to the speech act that is formed by the
three sub-acts together as an *illocutionary act*. It is likewise confusing that he
also uses this term as a synonym of *speech act*, so that it is unclear to what
extent a *perlocutionary act* (to which he makes no further reference) can also
be part of the complete speech act that is performed with the utterance of a
sentence. This vagueness also occurs, for example, when in his article 'What
is a Speech Act?' Searle informs us that the title of the article might equally
well have been 'What is an Illocutionary Act?' (1971:39).

To remove any chance of such obfuscation here, we shall make the
terminological (and conceptual) distinctions represented in fig. 2.1.

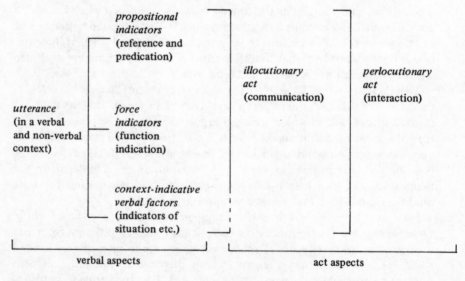

Figure 2.1. Analytical reconstruction of a 'complete' speech act.

We shall elucidate these distinctions further as our argument unfolds. In the
first instance we shall confine ourselves to a discussion of some insights
regarding *illocutionary acts* that are relevant to our purpose and which Searle
advances in his basic theory, which relates to *explicit* illocutionary acts.

Searle expands further on Austin's idea that language is a form of verbal
action which is only 'happy' if certain sorts of condition have been met and
that this is true both of *performative* speech utterances, which were originally

the only speech utterances which Austin regarded as having the nature of an act, and of *constative* speech utterances, which are characterized by the possession of a certain truth value. He regards it as an essential feature of every specimen of verbal communication that a speech act is performed by the utterance of a sentence:

> To put this point more precisely, the production of the sentence token under certain conditions is the illocutionary act, and the illocutionary act is the minimal unit of linguistic communication(1971:39).

According to Searle, performing illocutionary acts means performing an activity which is subject to a set of rules in rather the same way as is the playing of a game like soccer. Just as the rules of soccer make it possible for the players to 'be off-side' or 'score a goal', so the rules governing illocutionary acts make it possible for language useres to 'give a promise', 'express their approval' or 'criticize a statement'. The rules are *constitutive*, not merely *regulative*. In principle they take (or can be reduced to) the form '*X* (the speech utterance) *counts as Y* (the illocutionary act)'. Searle's central hypothesis is that the semantics of a language can be regarded as a series of systems of constitutive rules and that illocutionary acts are acts performed in accordance with those constitutive rules.

Because we ourselves are full-fledged language users, Searle believes we know the rules obtaining in our own language for the performance of illocutionary acts and we ought therefore in principle to be capable of explicitizing those rules. To illustrate this he formulates the rules for the use of the force indicator formed by the *performative formula* 'I promise' - a formula that may be used to perform the illocutionary act *promise*. He does so by deducing these rules from the *conditions that must be fulfilled when a promise is given.* Here he distinguishes several sorts of condition: *general conditions* (which apply to all illocutionary acts and may therefore be unstated when a specific illocutionary act is analysed), *preparatory conditions* (which indicate the required point of departure), *propositional conditions* (which relate to the 'content' of the speech utterance being invested with a particular communicative force), *sincerity conditions* (which relate to the intention that a speaker performing a particular illocutionary act may be regarded as having, and which therefore might perhaps have been more aptly called *responsibility* or *liability conditions*), and *essential conditions* (which relate to the quintessence of the illocutionary act concerned and have to do with the 'sense' or interactional purpose of the act). The conditions formulated for an illocutionary act must be such that each of the conditions is a *necessary* condition and the conjunction of the conditions is a *sufficient* condition for the performance of the illocutionary act concerned and such that observing that a speaker has performed that illocutionary act entails this conjunction (1971:47).

In fact, Searle's chief concern in *Speech Acts* is to establish the conditions applying to such illocutionary concepts as 'promises', though he himself stresses that he is formulating *semantic rules* for the use of (explicitly performative) expressions such as 'I promise'. This has to do with the fact that he confines himself to *explicitly performed* illocutionary acts (which he regards as justified by the 'principle of expressibility') and believes that the performance of illocutionary acts is bound not only by *intentions* but also by *semantic conventions*. According to him the speaker performing an illocutionary act is trying to achieve the effect that the listener understands which illocutionary act the speaker is performing, by making him recognize his intention to achieve that effect by using verbal means which (in accordance with the rules governing the use of these means) *are by convention used to achieve that effect*.

Without wishing to move onto the problem of the precise delimitation of semantics and pragmatics (which in our view has no intrinsic interest anyway), we believe we may nevertheless say that the understandability of illocutionary acts in colloquial speech depends strongly on *pragmatic* conventions. One indication of this is that *implicit* and *indirect* illocutionary acts are as a rule understood perfectly and the speaker can also assume in principle that they will be understood, so that it is plausible that other conventions besides strictly semantic ones will (also) play a role. In the context of argumentation we shall be returning later to such non-explicit cases.

It is conspicuous that in his later publication 'A Taxonomy of Illocutionary Acts', in which he lays the foundations for a system of classifying illocutionary acts, Searle advances as his first objection to Austin's earlier attempt at classification the contention that Austin's lists constitute not a classification of illocutionary *acts* but of English illocutionary *verbs*: 'Austin seems to assume that a classification of different verbs is *eo ipso* a classification of kinds of illocutionary acts, that any two non-synonymous verbs must mark different illocutionary acts' (1979:9). 'But there is no reason to suppose that this is the case', observes Searle quite rightly. The correspondence between illocutionary *acts* (or conditions for their performance) and illocutionary *verbs* (or the semantic rules for their use) need evidently not be regarded as so rigid as he once suggested.

For our purposes it is interesting that in 'A Taxonomy of Illocutionary Acts' Searle tries to make a consistent classification of *functions* of language usage by dividing illocutionary acts into *categories*. Taking as his chief criteria for classification the *illocutionary purpose* or *point* of the act (corresponding to the essential condition), the *correspondence direction* of the act or *direction of fit* (which has to do with the relation between words and the world) and the *state of mind* expressed by the speaker in the illocutionary act (corresponding to the sincerity condition), he distinguishes five *basic functions* that language can fulfil: we can use language to (1) say how something is, (2) try to get people to do something, (3) commit ourselves to doing something, (4) express sentiments or attitudes, and (5) bring about changes in reality. The merit of this classification, to which we shall return later, is chiefly that, even though some aspects of the classification are debatable, it becomes clear that language can fulfil a *finite* and *determinate* number of functions.

We shall take Searle's basic theory of illocutionary acts as our starting point when we come to our functional analysis of argumentation. First, however, we shall have to add to it (and amend it) in such a way that it becomes possible to arrive at a closer definition of the speech act *argumentation* and to formulate the conditons that have to be met if advancing a constellation of utterances is to be a correct performance of that speech act, since the problems presenting themselves here include the fact that in the form determined by Searle the theory applies exclusively to individual sentences and not to larger units of text (such as argumentation), and the fact that Searle confines himself to cases in which the illocutionary force is expressed explicitly in a performative formula (which in principle is not the case in argumentation). Before we try to solve these problems, we shall pay attention to *interactional* aspects of language which are disregarded by Searle, who deals exclusively with *communicative* aspects. We believe that it is necessary to analyse the speech act of argumentation both as to its communicative and as to its interactional aspects.

2.2. COMMUNICATIVE AND INTERACTIONAL ASPECTS OF LANGUAGE

Language users performing speech acts do not, in principle, do so with the sole intention of making the persons to whom they address themselves understand what speech act they are performing: rather, by means of those speech acts they hope to elicit from their listeners a particular response (verbal or otherwise). This means that their language must serve not only a *communicative* but also an *interactional* purpose. Translated into terms of the speech act theory, the communicative aspects of language are expressed in attempts to bring about *illocutionary* effects and the interactional aspects in attempts to bring about *perlocutionary* effects. Searle's basic theory, on the other hand, applies only to *illocutionary acts*, *perlocutionary acts* being disregarded.

As Wunderlich has rightly observed, the performance of speech acts cannot be treated as one-way traffic between a speaker and a listener; rather, a speech act only acquires significance for the further progress of the communication when the listener takes some notice of it (1972:22). We believe that a person performing a speech act not only wishes his words to be *understood*, but also certainly wants them to be *accepted*, even though, in connection with the presuppositions and consequences attached to his speech act (in anticipation of further precization or reasoning), this acceptance may in the first instance be no more than acceptance 'on approval'. According to Wunderlich, indeed, a speech act is essentially aimed at making the listener accept its content, and the speech act cannot be regarded as happy as long as it has not been accepted, because until then it has no relevance for the listener (1972:22).

It is not, of course, the case that the listener always reacts perfectly explicitly and indicates *expressis verbis* whether or not he has understood and accepted the speech act, and indeed as long as this does not give rise to problems there is no need for him to. If there are no indications to the contrary, a speaker may normally assume that the listener who *fails to understand* or *refuses to accept* a speech act will, in ordinary conversation, give some indication of this fact to the speaker (indeed he must, if he does not wish the communication to degenerate into *pseudo-communication*).

It is then possible for two sorts of dialogue to be initiated. If the listener fails to understand, he can indicate the necessity of explication by requesting clarification or further information and the speaker will be obliged to express what he wishes to say more clearly or more explicitly, so that in principle an *explicative dialogue* develops. If the listener does not accept what has been said, he can indicate the necessity of problemization by expressing his doubts or issuing refutations, and the speaker (assuming that he wishes to stand by his words) will attempt to justify or defend what he has said, so that in principle a *problemizing dialogue* develops.

In ordinary conversational situations some speech acts by speakers are specifically calculated to elicit from listeners certain verbal (and possibly also non-verbal) responses in which they indicate understanding and (in particular) acceptance. In our view this applies pre-eminently to the argumentation advanced during a discussion or debate. This means that to a certain extent arguments in debates are designed to achieve precisely defined *verbally externalized illocutionary and perlocutionary effects* that are immediately related to the speech acts performed and must be distinguished from the more comprehensive effects (often difficult to establish exactly and sometimes not becoming evident until much later) of speech acts on the further behaviour, thought processes and emotional life of discussants; these effects sometimes also being referred to as *perlocutionary effects*.

In order to distinguish between the perlocutionary effect of *acceptance* and the broad range of further consequences attendant on a speech act in practice (varying from a furious look to the start of a new life), we introduce a terminological and conceptual distinction between *inherent* perlocutionary effects and *consecutive* perlocutionary consequences. Inherent perlocutionary effects consist exclusively of the *acceptance of the speech act by the listener* and consecutive perlocutionary consequences comprise *all other consequences of the speech act*. To the extent that these effects or consequences are ones which the speaker is consciously trying to achieve with his speech act, we may also term inherent perlocutionary effects *minimal* and consecutive perlocutionary consequences *optimal*. This terminology expresses the fact that with his speech acts the speaker in any case ('minimally') wishes to achieve the perlocutionary effect of *acceptance*, but that as a rule he will only regard the result as completely satisfactory ('optimal') if he also succeeds in bringing about other consequences lying in the extension of acceptance. However, as long as we do not approach language from any one specific angle we use the more neutral terminology uncommitted to the specific points of view of speaker and listener as regards the success or failure of the speech act.

If the communication and interaction go reasonably well, the illocutionary effect of *understanding* will in principle be a *necessary* condition for bringing about the inherent perlocutionary effect of *acceptance* and consecutive perlocutionary consequences, but in neither case is it a *sufficient* condition. In practise, however, there is no certainty that the communication and interaction will go smoothly, so at this stage we shall disregard this point. The distinctions we draw are illustratd in fig. 2.2 with reference to examples.

speech act	communicative aspects		interactional aspects		
	illocution	illocutionary effect	perlocution	inherent perlocutionary effect	consecutive perlocutionary consequence
example 1	*advising*	understanding the advice	*cheering up*	accepting the advice	enrolling for a new course
example 2	*arguing*	understanding the argumentation	*convincing*	accepting the argumentation	desisting from opposition to a point of view
example 3	*requesting*	understanding the request	*persuading*	accepting the request	abandoning the intention to leave
example 4	*informing*	understanding the information	*instructing*	accepting the information	henceforth using contraceptives
example 5	*warning*	understanding the warning	*alarming*	accepting the warning	keeping mouth shut

Figure 2.2. Illustration of communicative and interactional aspects of language.

Since both the achievement of the illocutionary effect 'understanding' and the achievement of the perlocutionary effect 'acceptance' can be assumed to be among the *speakers' intentions*, in ordinary conversations between language users, and since speakers try to achieve both these effects by means of (the same) *speech utterances*, we are dealing here with two different sorts of verbal action (one communicative and one interactional), both of which are in principle part of a complete speech act and therefore must be included in an adequate theory of speech acts. That is why it is regrettable that Searle pays no attention to perlocutionary acts (for reasons which will be discussed below).

By contrast, in *How to Do Things with Words* Austin does go into the matter of perlocution, albeit that he does so solely in order to obtain greater clarity about illocutions (1976:103). In his introduction of the concept of *perlocution* he elects for an extremely broad definition:

> There is yet a further sense . . . in which to perform a locutionary act, and therein an illocutionary act, may also be to perform an act of another kind. Saying something will often, or even normally, produce certain consequential effects upon the feelings, thoughts, or actions of the audience, or of the speaker, or of other persons: and it may be done with the design, intention, or purpose of producing them . . . We shall call the perfomance of an act of this kind the performance of a 'perlocutionary' act, and the act performed, where suitable . . . a 'perlocution' (1976:101).

Examples of perlocutionary acts given by Austin include *informing, alarming, persuading* and *convincing*.

Austin's characterization of the *locutionary* act as 'the act *of* saying something', of the *illocutionary* act as 'the act done *in* saying something', and of the *perlocutionary* act as 'the act done *by* saying something' does provide some clarification of the *nomenclature*, but (as Austin himself admits) fails to offer a watertight *criterion* for distinguishing between the various sorts of act. Even the correspondence between a perlocutionary verb preceded by 'trying to ' (e.g. 'trying to convince') and an illocutionary verb (e.g. 'arguing') fails to provide a suitable criterion, he says, because equivalence of this kind is not always present, besides which illocutionary verbs can also be preceded by 'trying to' (e.g. 'trying to argue'). Rather, it is characteristic of the difference between illocutionary and perlocutionary acts that in them the speaker hopes to achieve *different sorts of effects*.

An illocutionary act is 'happy' if with his speech utterance the speaker achieves the effect that the listener *understands* the illocutionary force and the propositional content of the utterance. In Austin's terminology:

> Generally the effect amounts to bringing about the understanding of the meaning and of the force of the locution. So the perfomance of an illocutionary act involves the securing of *uptake* (1976:117).

A perlocutionary act is 'happy' if *another* desired effect on the listener is brought about (later Austin says hardly anything about effects on the speaker or other persons referred to by him), but the nature of this effect may vary considerably from perlocutionary act to perlocutionary act. Ultimately, Austin considers that the most important difference between illocutionary and perlocutionary effects is that the former can be achieved solely by *conventional verbal means* and the latter cannot. We shall return to this question in chapter 3.

In effect, Austin uses the denominator *perlocutionary effect* as a waste basket to cover the most disparate and dissimilar consequences of language. It is therefore useful to make certain distinctions. In the first place it is important to distinguish between consequences which occur accidentally and effects that are *intended* by the speaker. In conformity with the tradition in the social sciences we reserve the term *act* for conscious, purposive activities founded, unlike 'mere behaviour', on rational considerations. This means that bringing about completely *unintended* consequences cannot be regarded as *acting* and thus that there can be no question of the performance of perlocutionary acts. A rough-and-ready criterion for distinguishing between the performance of perlocutionary acts and the bringing about of unintended consequences is whether the speaker can reasonably be asked to *provide his reasons* for causing the effect or consequence in question. We shall refer to a *perlocutionary act* only where that is possible.

In the second place we think it is important to draw a distinction between effects or consequences of speech acts that are *not* brought about on the basis of *understanding of an illocutionary act* and effects or consequences where this *is* the case. There are various sorts of examples of non-illocutionary perlocutionary effects or consequences. For example, a pupil may flinch simply because his teacher shouts at him, regardless of the content and force of what is shouted. In that case his fright stems solely from the manner in which the speech act is *uttered*, and we refer to an *utterance perlocution*. However, he may also jump because he hears his name linked with that of someone with whom he is in love, without his already having sufficiently woken from his daydreams to recognize the illocutionary act. In that case he is startled by the *proposition* (or part of it) that is expressed in the speech act, and we refer to a *propositional perlocution*. It is further possible, for example, for him to be startled by a civilized, anti-authoritarian teacher suddenly launching into a tirade of screamed orders in the middle of a dictation (without the pupil being *au fait* with what is happening). In that case it is the *force* of the speech act that startles him, and we refer to a *force perlocution*. And finally it is, for example, possible for the pupil to be startled by the teacher, having made an admission to him during a confidential conversation, suddenly addressing him as 'mister' so-and-so. In that case it is not immediately apparent what the precise cause of his surprise is, but it seems clear that yet other factors play a part here than the *utterance act* or the *propositional act* in the sense in wich they are treated in the speech act theory,nor does the pupil's surprise depend simply on the completed *illocutionary act*. To the extent that this is a matter of *verbal* causes (so that it may be a case of a perlocutonary act) one might in such circumstances speak of a *contextual perlocution* (to be further specified according to the dominant factor), but we believe that there is little point in a further classification of this kind unless it serves well defined purposes.

Here we shall concern ourselves exclusively with *illocutionary perlocutions* realized on the basis of the understanding of an illocutionary act. These are also the same perlocutionary acts which are more or less automatically regarded by Searle, who makes no distinction between illocutionary perlocutions and other sorts of perlocutions, and by many other authors (whose views we shall turn to later) as the 'normal' cases. This emerges, for example, in the way in which Searle introduces perlocutionary acts and in the examples he gives there:

Correlated with the notion of illocutionary acts is the notion of the consequences or *effects* such acts have on the actions, thoughts, or beliefs, etc. of hearers. For example, by arguing I may *persuade* or *convince* someone, by warning him I may *scare* or *alarm* him, by making a request I may *get him to do something*, by informing him I may *convince him* (*enlighten, edify, inspire him, get him to realize*). The italicized expressions above denote perlocutionary acts (1970: 25).

Third, we regard it as desirable to distinguish between effects or consequences of speech acts which may be brought about by way of *a rational decision by the listener* and effects or consequences that are wholly divorced from rational decision-making. To Searle, the performance of perlocutionary acts always consists of using illocutions to bring about effects on the actions, thoughts, beliefs etc. of the listener, but he makes no distinction between effects in whose bringing about the listener can play an *active role* and effects where this is not the case. One of several disadvantages to this is that the listener is always deemed to play a purely *passive role* and no account is taken of the *interactional aspect* of language. This conflicts with what often actually happens (or ought to happen) with perlocutions in practice and easily leads to a view of conversations in which a conversation is reduced to a flow of one-way traffic. In most conversations between language users - certainly, in our opinion, in discussions designed to resolve disputes - the listener is expected to decide on rational grounds whether or not he should allow the perlocutionary effect desired by the speaker to be brought about, i.e. whether or not he regards the performance or non-performance of the act required of him (verbal or otherwise), the endorsement of a point of view, and so on, as acceptable. As the degree increases to which externalization (of thoughts, feelings etc.) takes place in the conversation in verbal acts, it will become apparent from the listener's reactions to what extent the speaker has succeeded in his perlocutionary purpose; indeed, the listener may even be expressly required to give reasons as to why the intended perlocutionary effect has not been brought about ('You're just going to have to tell me why you won't do it', or: 'So why are you still not convinced?').

We shall concern ourselves here exclusively with perlocutionary acts whose success is in principle partly dependent on *rational considerations on the part of the listener*. For example, perlocutions designed to influence uncontrollable emotions or to bring about thought associations will be disregarded. Moreover we shall confine ourselves as far as possible in our argument to a specific acceptability perlocution which is of especial interest to us in connection with argumentation: the perlocutionary act of *convincing*. To conclude this review of perlocutions the distinctions we have drawn are reproduced schematically in fig. 2.3.

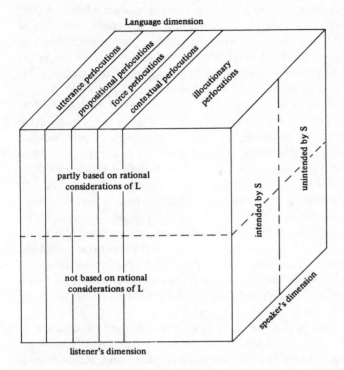

Figure 2.3. Perlocution cube: a survey of perlocutionary distinctions.

2.3. CHARACTERIZATION OF THE SPEECH ACT OF ARGUMENTATION

We shall now try to place argumentation in the theoretical framework of the speech act theory just outlined. This means that we shall have to describe argumentation as a specific sort of speech act. Our hypothesis is that in the *communicative* sense argumentation is a form of language use corresponding to the forms of language use characterized in the speech act theory as *illocutionary* acts and that as regards its *interactional* aspects argumentation is linked with the *perlocutionary* act of *convincing*. In this chapter we shall examine the communicative aspects of the speech act *argumentation* and in the next chapter we shall return to the interactional aspects.

Before we concern ourselves with the difficulties observed earlier of characterizing argumentation as an illocutionary act, we must first establish the extent to which the term *argumentation* is an adequate label for the speech act that we wish to discuss here. This is because the word *argue* already has a specific commonly accepted meaning in colloquial speech (just as have related words such as *argument*), and there is no automatic guarantee that this meaning corresponds in every respect to the meaning that we wish to give the term *argumentation*. Let us therefore look first at some lexicographical descriptions of words in colloquial speech that are relevant for us here. The *Concise Oxford Dictionary* describes *argumentation* as 'methodical reasoning; debate', *argument* as (among other things) 'reason advanced (*for, against,* proposition or course); ... reasoning process; debate; summary of subject-matter ...' and *to argue* as 'prove, indicate ..., maintain by reasons ...' (Fowler & Fowler 1959:60). And *Webster* defines *argumentation* as '(1) reasoning; the act of forming reasons, making inductions, drawing conclusions, and applying them to the case under discussion, (2) argument; debate, (3) writing or speaking that argues ...', while *argument* is described as (among other things) '(1) a reason or reasons offered for or against a proposition, opinion, or measure ..., (2) the offering of such reasons; reasoning; (3) a debate or discussion in which there is disagreement ...' and *to argue* (transitive and intransitive) is given such definitions as 'to offer reasons in support of or against a proposition, opinion, or measure', 'to dispute', 'to present objections', 'to debate or discuss; to treat by reasoning', 'to try to prove; contend', 'to indicate or give evidence of' and 'to persuade by giving reasons; as to *argue* a man into a different opinion' (Webster-McKechnie 1979:100). We believe this list makes it clear that observations relating to *argumentation* or related words are in principle quite usable for our purposes, though of course we shall have to decide from case to case whether such observations are indeed applicable if we use the term *argumentation* in the sense in which we mean it.

Our conclusion must be that the meaning we attach to the term *argumentation* certainly does not conflict with the meaning that such words as *argue*, *argument* and *argumentation* have in colloquial language and, indeed, that if one digs down a little deeper one finds that our meaning is even confirmed by ordinary idiom, but that we nevertheless give the word *argumentation* a more explicit and more 'worked out' or 'developed' meaning than it has in everyday language. This means that we can use the term *argumentation* to denote the speech act *argue*, in the meaning that we wish to give that speech act, without fear of 'wrong' connotations due to its meaning in colloquial speech.

One of the speech act theorists of the Anglo-American school to devote attention to argumentation is Austin, albeit that he leaves it at the observation that 'he argued that ...' is an *illocutionary* act that must be distinguished from the *locutionary* act 'he said that ...' and the *perlocutionary act* 'he convinced me that ...' (1976:102). Many authors appear to regard this as going without saying, for both Searle (1970) and Cohen (1973) simply call *argumentation* an illocutionary act and *convincing* a perlocutionary act without any further ado. Unlike Austin they also point out explicity that there is a special relationship between arguing and convincing.

None of these three authors gives reasons as to *why* he regards argumentation as an illocutionary act (and Searle and Cohen provide no information as to exactly what the special relationship between arguing and convincing consists of). Though we agree with Austin, Searle and Cohen that argumentation has to be treated as an illocutionary act, we believe that characterizing it in this way nevertheless presents certain important problems and is therefore not as much a foregone conclusion as they suggest.

The problems presented by the characterization of argumentation as an illocutionary act become abundantly evident if one takes Searle's basic theory as one's starting point. Searle's theory relates to illocutionary acts and the verbal means by which they are performed. According to him, the characteristic grammatical form of the illocutionary act is 'the complete sentence' (1970:25). Because he starts from the 'principle of expressibility' he regards it as reasonable to restrict his analysis of illocutionary acts to sentences in which the illocutionary force *is expressed explicitly and unambiguously by means of a performative formula*. However, one preliminary problem which presents itself with the analysis of argumentation is that the argumentative force of a sentence is seldom, if ever, expressed by an (explicit) performative formula.

Arguing language users will not as a rule introduce their argumentation with the phrase 'I argue', and the mnenomic suggested by Austin for recognizing illocutions, which entails being able to say 'I hereby X' (where X represents the name of the illocutionary act) will not work at all for argumentation. However, this is true of other illocutionary acts too, and in that sense too it is merely a coincidental fact that probably has more to do with specific language conventions in a particular linguistic community than with a distinctive feature of illocutionary acts. In any event it is perfectly possible to say 'this, then, is my argumentation', and second and third parties can in exactly the same way say of someone's words that he 'argued' as they can in other cases say that he 'promised', 'asserted' or 'advised'. Moreover a speaker *can*, if he wishes, introduce his argumentation with the words 'my argumentation is as follows' (or an equivalent formulation), when the words that follow actually do constitute his argumentation and, if the illocutionary act is successful, can be understood as such by the listener (just like other illocutionary acts). There are also various *illocutionary indicators*, such as the words *because* and *for*, which can make it clear to the listener that the speaker's utterances are to be regarded as argumentation. All in all, then, there are no real grounds for deducing that *arguing* is not an illocutionary act from the circumstance that 'I argue' is not a practical performative formula.

More essential problems arise from the manner in which Searle characterizes the relation between *illocutionary acts* and (grammatical) *sentences*. According to him the complete sentence is the characteristic grammatical form of the illocutionary act and in all the illocutionary acts that he analyses there is a one-to-one relation between the utterance of a particular sentence and the performance of a particular illocutionary act. If the conditions for the correct performance of the speech act concerned have been fulfilled, the utterance of one sentence amounts to asking a question, the utterance of another sentence amounts to the making of an assertion, and so on, and conversely it holds good that a question may be asked by uttering one sentence, an assertion made by uttering another sentence, and so on. In the case of argumentation, however, this one-to-one correlation presents problems on at least three counts.

(1) The first difficulty is that in principle a completed argumentation consists of more than one statement, so that the speech act of *arguing can consist of more than one sentence.* Even the simplest argumentation for or against an expressed opinion contains, if it is made fully explicit, at least two statements (cf. the *datum* and the *warrant* in Toulmin's model). Each of these statements can be expressed in a separate sentence and if this happens there is no one-to-one correlation between what Searle calls the illocutionary act of *arguing* and one particular sentence.

At this point it should be noted that it is of course possible in the case of *other* illocutionary acts too for two or more sentences to make up a single illocution. Thus a number of sentences together can form a single statement or piece of information and a recommendation or piece of advice can be so complicated that it is difficult to express in a single sentence. Though it is not our purpose here to stress the differences between argumentation and other speech acts, we do want to point out that there still seems to be a distinction between an argumentation consisting of more than one sentence and, for example, a statement consisting of more than one sentence. A person sending a telegram containing the information 'Father dying. Mother not too well either' is in fact making *two* statements of fact, even though they are probably so closely interdependent that together (at a 'higher' level) they constitute a single complete whole. But the person who adduces the argumentation 'I hear William comes from the north. Those northerners have always been dark horses' to justify the expressed opinion 'William is a dark horse', though he may also be making two statements is in fact only advancing a single argumentation, since neither of the individual statements can stand as a complete argumentation on its own.

(2) The second difficulty (already hinted at in the 'dark horse' example) is that with each of the statements which together constitute the argumentation the speaker is performing an illocutionary act that is different from the illocutionary act of *argumentation*, so that the sentences uttered in an argumentation in fact *have two illocutionary forces simultaneously.* For example, a statement that is part of the argumentation may at the same time be an assertion, a statement of fact, a supposition or some other specific illocutionary act from the category of *assertives* which Searle distinguishes in his classification of illocutionary acts. What this then boils down to is that these assertives are part of a greater complex of statements, which we earlier labelled a *constellation*, and which forms the illocution of *argumentation*. However, this means that there is yet another respect in which there is no question of the one-to-one ratio between sentences and illocutionary acts that Searle took as his starting point.[13]

It should be noted here that this breakdown of the one-to-one correlation makes it tempting to regard argumentation as an *indirect speech act*, since the statements have the double illocutionary force regarded by Searle as typical of indirect speech acts (1979:31). Clearly, however, this would be an over-hasty conclusion. With indirect speech acts the correspondence between sentence and illocutionary act is only disrupted *at this specific point* and not at the two points at which, as we demonstrate in this section, it is broken in argumentation. Indirect speech acts do not, like argumentation (see point 1), have to consist of more than one statement (indeed they generally do consist of only one statement) and they are not, like argumentation (see point 3), linked in a specific manner with another statement (or collection of statements). Moreover the double illocutionary force has a highly *specific function* which it does not have, or at least does not have to have, in argumentation (in principle argumentation too can be indirect). In indirect speech acts the literal meaning only determines the 'secondary' force, while the primary force (because, say, of conventions of politeness) is not made known overtly but can be inferred from the literal meaning by means of idiomatic and other conventions. In the case of argumentation there need not be any question at all of any such ambiguity.

(3)The third difficulty, just hinted at, is that advancing a constellation of statements can only be regarded as a performance of the speech act *argumentation* if the sentences uttered stand in a particular relationship to *another* sentence (or collection of sentences) whose utterance counts as the advancing of an *expressed opinion*, so that the sentences uttered in an argumentation *must be linked to another sentence in a special manner*. That sentence may (in the form of a *conclusion*) follow the sentences that go to make up the argumentation, but it may also precede it (in the form of a *claim*) and in practice it is also possible for it not to be uttered explicitly at all; but in no case can statements act as argumentation in isolation from a sentence which has the function of an expressed opinion. This means that no constellation of statements can ever independently constitute the illocution of *argumentaton*, so that the one-to-one ratio between sentences and illocutionary acts is absent in yet another respect.[14]

Here it should be observed that the expressed opinion (in the form of a claim or conclusion) is regarded by some authors as *part* of the argumentation. In that case at least the third of the problematical points we have listed appears to be removed. We believe, however, that it is wrong to count the expressed opinion as part of the argumentation, since this would not only go against ordinary idiom, in which one might very well say, for example, 'I share your view but I think your argumentation is feeble', it would also - and this is a more essential objection - make it impossible to distinguish properly between the various functions of the statements made in a discussion and show up in the analysis that, for example, the pro-argumentation of one of the discussants and the other's contra-argumentation are not two independent entities having nothing in common, but two speech acts acting one upon the other and both relating to the same expressed opinion.

Thus there are in argumentation at least three important problems relating to the one-to-one relation between sentence and illocutionary act which accord-

ing to Searle is characteristic of illocutions. But does this observation necessarily mean that it must be considered undesirable, wrong or even impossible
to regard argumentation as an illocution? It does not. It depends whether the
problems can be satisfactorily solved. In our view this is possible if one
distinguishes between illocutionary forces *at sentence level* and illocutionary
forces *at a 'higher' textual level*.

The basic theory of speech acts, as developed by Searle as a further
extension of the ideas of Austin, relates exclusively to *minimal units of
communicative language* corresponding to the linguistic units which in (sentence) grammar are called *sentences*. We refer to these minimal communicative units as *elementary illocutions*. However, in communication between
language users it is possible to distinguish larger units too which act in the
same way as the elementary illocutions. These larger communicative units
correspond to the linguistic units which are usually called *sequences* in (text)
grammar and which consist of combinations of sentences. These larger
communicative units we refer to as *compound illocutions* or *illocutionary act
complexes*.[15]

We believe that argumentation can be treated as an illocutionary act
complex. This act complex is composed of elementary illocutions which
belong to the category of the *assertives* and which at the sentence level
maintain a one-to-one ratio with (grammatical) sentences. The total constellation of the elementary illocutions constitutes the illocutionary act complex
of *argumentation*, which at a higher textual level maintains, as a single whole,
a one-to-one ratio with a (grammatical) sentence sequence. The compound
illocutionary act of *argumentation* does not, therefore, stand in a one-to-one
ratio to individual sentences, but to a combination of sentences ordered into
a sequence. This means that the one-to-one correspondence between *functional* units and *linguistic* units, which seems to us to be the quintessence of
Searle's view, is preserved, and there is no good reason for regarding it as
undersirable, mistaken or even impossible to treat argumentation as an
illocution.

On the contrary, in this way the functional correspondence between
argumentation and speech acts like promises, statements of fact and assertions is more clearly expressed than in any other way. Just as promises are
constituted at sentence level by (with due regard to the conditions applying)
uttering a particular sentence, argumentations are constituted at a higher
textual level by (with due regard to the conditions applying) uttering a
particular sequence of sentences. Even if the fact that an element of it remains
'unexpressed' or 'suppressed' means that linguistically speaking the argumentation appears to consist of only one sentence, this does not present a
problem. In that case the utterance of the one sentence means that at the
sentence level an assertion (for example) is made, while at the higher textual
level an argumentation is performed.

Introducing the distinction between elementary illocutions at sentence
level and compound illocutions at a higher textual level means that it is now
possible properly to draw in to our analysis of argumentation the special

relation which exists between *argumentation* and the statement that we have called the *expressed opinion*. If the analysis had to concentrate exclusively on (elementary) illocutions at the sentence level this would, it is true, be able to account for the fact that by uttering particular sentences speakers can make *assertions, statements of fact*, and so on, but it would not be possible to explain why in uttering those sentences they are in some cases at the same time advancing *argumentation* and in other cases at the same time pro-pounding *expressed opinions*. In an analysis that can also take account of compound illocutions at a higher textual level it is possible to give both sorts of explanation. Moreover - and this is perhaps even more important - this subtler and more comprehensive analysis also offers better opportunities of at the same time giving a satisfactory characterization of the relation between argumentation and an expressed opinion, since the expressed opinion, which at sentence level might, say, be an assertion, may at the higher textual level be regarded as a claim or conclusion which (on this textual level) is linked through a justification or refutation relations to the constellation of assert-ives that constitute the argumentation. Figure 2.4 is a schematic representa-tion of the various levels and relations that we distinguish in argumentation.

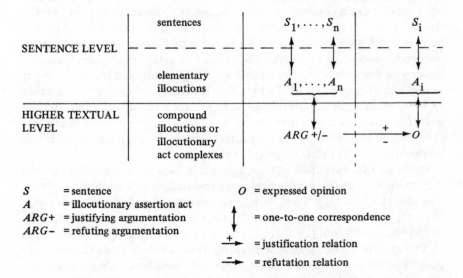

S = sentence
A = illocutionary assertion act
$ARG+$ = justifying argumentation
$ARG-$ = refuting argumentation

O = expressed opinion
= one-to-one correspondence
= justification relation
= refutation relation

Figure 2.4. Analytical reconstruction of the compound illocution argumentation.

2.4. POINTS OF AGREEMENT AND DISAGREEMENT WITH RELATED VIEWS

Our view that argumentation can be regarded as an illocutionary act com-plex at a higher textual level, performed by advancing a sequence of *as-sertives* at the sentence level which at the higher textual level is linked in a particular manner to an expressed opinion, is related to views formulated by various other writers. To some extent these views correspond to our own but are presented in only a very rudimentary form and do not lead to a precise characterization of argumentation. Others, while related to our own, nevertheless also differ from it in various important respects. We shall examine examples of both categories.

A view which has clear points of correspondence with our own is that recently propounded by Wunderlich, viz. that argumentation is one of the 'typical complex speech units' that 'may be composed of more elementary speech acts' (1980:295, 311). Wunderlich's reference to the component illocutions as *elementary speech acts* corresponds almost exactly to our own convention of calling the illocutionary acts that at the sentence level go to make up an argumentation *elementary illocutions*. Unfortunately Wunderlich's observations of 'complex speech units' do not go much further than his remark that one speech act 'may convey another speech act' and that some speech acts 'are identifiable only on the basis of their position in a sequence', the latter point being again slightly different from what we mean when we characterize argumentation as a compound illocution (Wunderlich 1980:311).[16]

It is notable that Searle accords to some assertives the extra feature that 'they mark certain relations between the assertive illocutionary act and the rest of the discourse or the context of utterance' (1979:13). He is referring here to members of the category of *assertives* that Austin has called *expositives* and which according to Austin are used 'in acts of exposition involving the expounding of views, the conducting of arguments, and the clarifying of usages and of references' (1976:161). Searle regards the connective function of some illocutions - he mentions for example *concluding*, *deducing*, and *objecting* - as a possible criterion for the classification of illocutionary acts (1979:6). This is another way of approaching the problem, though our approach might in principle produce the same result.

Searle devotes very little attention to argumentation, but he does observe that there is a connection between argumentation and certain *assertives*. Thus he remarks that 'I am simply stating that *p* and not attempting to convince you' *is* acceptable and that 'I am arguing that *p* and not attempting to convince you' is not (1970:66). One might deduce from this that he judges argumentation to consist of *assertives*, but that he believes these *assertives* to possess an additional feature that distinguishes them from other *assertives*. It is our view that he rightly couples argumentation to embarking on an attempt to convince (see chapter 3), but it will have become clear in the previous section that *this* (both in our own conception of it and in Searle's) cannot be a sufficient ground for characterizing argumentation as a special sort of illocutionary act.

Fogelin, too, appears to hold a view which broadly coincides with our own. Without himself remarking on the fact, in *Understanding Arguments* he draws a distinction between an argumentative force at a higher textual level and illocutionary forces at sentence level. According to him 'statements' are the most characteristic ingredients of argumentation, but 'arguments . . . are not used to make statements' (1978:34). The different levels that we distinguish find expression in his observation 'Although an argument is (typically) constructed from statements, the argument itself, *taken as a whole*, is not a statement' (1978:34; our italics). But otherwise Fogelin has nothing to say on the subject.

There are also authors who, like us, believe that besides illocutionary acts there are also larger units of language use to be distinguished, but who have a rather different view of these larger units from our own. This is true of both Van Dijk and Quasthoff. Both are concerned with sequences of speech acts, but in neither case do these sequences coincide exactly with the sequences that we call *compound illocutions*. We shall try to outline the main differences briefly.

Van Dijk uses the term *macro-speech acts* to refer to sequences of speech acts which have an *overall unity* (1978:66). This 'overall unity' implies that the macro-speech act consists of a group of speech acts which are in some way related and thus constitute a whole. This looks like our concept of 'compound illocution', but Van Dijk goes on to comment: 'Thus we can *overall* issue a request or a protest *in a letter* which itself consists of *all sorts of other* speech acts, e.g. assertions, questions, suggestions etc.' and 'A *speech* can thus *have the overall function* of a statement, an accusation or a threat' (trans. fr. 1978:67; our italics). The examples make it clear that, after all, what Van Dijk means by *macro-speech acts* is not the same as what we mean by *compound illocutions*. Later we shall try to identify the differences more closely.

Quasthoff uses the term *action schema* ('Handlungsschema') to refer to verbal activities such as telling a story or joke, issuing an invitation, reporting an event, and so on (1978:7). Following Kallmeyer and Schütze (1976:16 ff.) she requires of the performance of an action schema that (1) there be a beginning and an end recognizable to the participants, (2) that the participants be in a position to anticipate the schema, (3) that the schema be accepted as a mutual obligation, and (4) that there be a sequence of necessary steps known to the participants 'in terms of mutually shared expectations'. Following Wald (1978) she adds to these the requirement that (5) 'the speaker who initiates the action schema is considered to be the "principal speaker" and continues to hold the floor throughout the entire action schema' (1978:7).

In Quasthoff's view argumentation is not an illocution but an action schema. She defines argumentation as 'a form of verbal interaction [which] is more than a sequence of basic speech acts like statements and justifications. The basic speech act relates to the whole of the complex action "arguing" in the same way that "toasting a piece of bread" relates to "making breakfast"' (1978:6-7). The (standard version of the) speech act theory 'implicitly suggests a consideration of isolated basic acts' and therefore does not in her opinion do justice to argumentation (1978:6). In itself we regard this as an accurate observation, but the consequence, as we have already indicated, need not necessarily be that the theoretical framework of the speech act theory must be abandoned altogether. Moreover, because of the risk of theoretical fragmentation which would cause us to lose sight of the similarities and links between *elementary* speech acts at sentence level and *compound* speech acts at a higher textual level, we regard this conclusion as highly undesirable.[17]

The most essential objection to both Van Dijk's and Quasthoff's approach is, however, that they mix up two types of theorization. The terms *macro-speech act* and *action schema* are used not only to refer to the functional language use units that we call *compound illocutions* but also to refer to the institutional language use units which Wunderlich (1980:296) calls *discourse types* and which we have earlier described as *text genres* (Van Eemeren & Grootendorst 1982a:6). However, text genres are formed by 'speech events' such as sermons, speeches, interrogations and discussions which themselves consist of illocutions (compound or otherwise) (cf. Gumperz 1972 and Hymes 1962 and 1967). This means that the theoretical concepts of 'text genre' and 'illocution' do not coincide, even though in practice it may happen, as in a prayer or in congratulation, that a 'speech event' consists of only one (compound) illocution. Quasthoff increases still further the confusion that can easily arise here by calling the compound illocution of *argumentation* a closed *thematic unity* (1978:8).

More important than any 'quantitative' differences between illocutions (both elementary and compound) and text genres are the qualitative differences between them. Text genres are institutional units, more or less determined by tradition, which are primarily linked to specific *socio-cultural contexts* and not to particular intentions of language users. Thus pleadings in court and political speeches are forms of language use which have evolved within particular legal and political institutions and traditions, whereas prayers for example are linked to a religious context. Illocutions are *functional* units, determined by pragmatic rules, which are primarily linked to specific *intentions of language users* and not to particular socio-cultural contexts. This means that *text genre* is a term relating in principle to the social organization of language use in certain language usage situations, while the term *illocution* relates in principle to the way in which language users use verbal means to inform one another of particular intentions.

Naturally in some circumstances it may be useful to link the social organization of language usage and an analytical reconstruction of language usage functions, but in that case it must of course be done in a theoretically responsible manner. Thus it may happen, for example, that a particular text genre is dominated by utterances all having one specific function, and in that case forms of language use belonging to that text genre can be more closely characterized by analysing the illocutionary force of the language used. This makes it easier to point accurately to the differences between, say, such text genres as informative discussions and argumentative discussions.

When characterizing different sorts of discussion in terms of characteristic illocutions one has to bear in mind, as indeed one must when describing other sorts of text genre too, that it will not usually be the case that a particular text genre contains only illocutions from one and the same illocutionary category, let alone that the variation is confined to only one illocution. Even in the most strictly regimented discussions on *expressed opinions*, for example, there will as a rule be not only *expressed opinions* and *argumentations*, but also illocutions like *questions* (which belong to the category of the *directives*) and *definitions* (belonging to the category of the *declaratives*). If this is not the case the rules regimenting the discussion will hardly be of any practical significance.

The coexistence of different sorts of illocution in discussions about expressed opinions is one of the reasons why the study of *argumentation* in discussions is only a *part* of the investigation necessary if one is to be able to draft an adequate theory of discussion. For that, the entire speech act arsenal that is important for the resolution of disputes about expressed opinions must be drawn into the theorization (see chapter 5).

The disregard for the qualitative differences between text genres (such as the various sorts of discussion) and compound illocutions (such as argumentation) which occurs in Van Dijk and Quasthoff can easily lead to the different sorts of task that have to be carried out for the drafting of an adequate theory of discussion failing to be distinguished properly so that the theorization is left incomplete and indequate.

2.5. THE ILLOCUTIONARY ACT COMPLEX OF ARGUMENTATION

We have already characterized argumentation as an illocutionary act complex composed of elementary illocutions. The component elementary illocutions belong in principle to the category of the *assertives* and together constitute an illocutionary constellation standing in a justifying or refuting relation to an expressed opinion (which consists of statements acting as a claim or conclusion). In this section we shall submit the illocutionary act complex of *argumentation* to a closer analysis. We shall begin with a statement of the purpose of our analysis.

Our objective is to give an analysis of the speech act *argumentation* which accords with Searle's basic theory of illocutionary acts and with the definition of the term *argumentation* which we gave in chapter 1. We shall formulate the conditions that the listener considers to have been fulfilled if he regards a constellation of utterances as an attempt at the justification or refutation of an expressed opinion. Since it is not clear in advance what sort of condition we intend to formulate, we must first explain exactly what analytical purpose we wish to achieve and what choices we shall be making in its achievement

It is not our intention here to provide a survey of the various 'moves' made by language users advancing and interpreting argumentation. This means that we shall make no attempt to give an empirical description of the way in which language users argue in practice, nor shall we try to arrive at an analytical reconstruction of the interpretation process. Both sorts of investigation are necessary, we believe, but they can only usefully be performed if a theoretical conception has first been developed of the place occupied by argumentation in the resolution of disputes about expressed opinions. We shall turn our attention to this subject in chapters 4 and 5.

Here we shall try to answer the question of *what it means* if language users consider a sequence of utterances to be *argumentation*. That implies that we shall have to clarify what conditions a happy performance of the illocutionary act complex of *argumentation* has to fulfil and what the consequences are if the performance of the illocutionary act complex fails to meet one or more of these conditions. To this end we shall formulate, on the basis of the day-to-day experience that we as language users have of argumentation, the constitutive conditions that have to be fulfilled for a happy performance of that speech act.

According to Searle's basic theory a speaker performs illocutionary acts by expressing in speech utterances his intention to assert something, promise something, and so on, in such a way that the listener can recognize the speaker's intention. In our view this also applies to illocutionary act complexes like *argumentation*. The constitutive conditions of the illocutionary act complex of *argumentation* that we wish to describe are conditions that must be fulfilled if a complex of utterances is to count as argumentation. This means that they are on the one hand conditions that the speaker must fulfil if by uttering a complex of utterances he wishes to perform the compound illocution of *argumentation*, and on the other hand they are conditions that the listener may regard as having been fulfilled when he decides to treat a complex of utterances as *argumentation*. In other words, they are conditions which in principle *have consequences for both speaker and listener*.

One complication here is that it is necessary to make a distinction between a *correct* performance of illocutions and an *incorrect* one. It may happen, for example, that although a speaker explicitly promises the listener that he will do something for him, he has in fact no intention of doing it, or knows that in fact the listener would prefer him not to do it. In either case, the performance of the illocutionary act is incorrect. In the first instance a condition is violated which is called the *sincerity condition* in Searle's basic theory, and in the second instance the speaker offends against a *preparatory condition* for correct promising. Even so, the listener may (i.e. is entitled to) regard the utterance as a promise, and he is therefore also entitled, generally speaking, to hold the speaker to his promise. For both speaker and listener the utterance has all the consequences attaching to a promise, and that being so one might with some justification maintain that that speaker has succeeded in performing the illocutionary act *promise*. This is all the more defensible an attitude if one takes into account the fact that the listener need not be aware that the speaker has failed to fulfil these conditions (and the listener may also overlook the fact that he thinks that he alone knows that he would prefer the promised action not to be carried out).

These examples (to which many more might be added) make it clear that although an illocution may be recognized (e.g. the listener knows that the speaker intends to perform a particular illocution), it need not necessarily have to be entirely correct, so that it would be a good idea to distinguish between the constitutive conditions of a *recognizable* performance of illocutions and the constitutive conditions of a *correct* performance of illocutions. In our view, the constitutive conditions for a *happy* performance of illocutions will have to comprise the constitutive conditions for both a recognizable performance and a correct performance.

The observation made by Bach and Harnish, among others, that we can only speak of a *succesful communication* (interactional aspects of language being disregarded for the time being) if the intention expressed by the speaker in his utterance 'is identified by means of recognizing the reflexive intention to express it' (1979:xv) requires, we believe, the rider that this only applies if the illocution concerned *has also been correctly performed*. A listener who fails to notice (and in some cases he *cannot*) that an illocution has been incorrectly performed because certain necessary conditions have not been met, will certainly attach to that illocution the same consequences (for both himself and the speaker) as he would to an illocution that had been *correctly* performed, but it would scarcely be possible to maintain that the communication had been perfectly succesful.

If, as we do, one wishes to approach verbal communication not as something seen from the sole perspective of the speaker, but as a bilateral process in which the listener's perspective is also significant, then we believe it is necessary to accept the restriction we have imposed. It accords not only with the ideal norms that have to be applied in connection with the efficacy of using language, but also with the norms applied by the majority of ordinary langage users. However critically he may approach the task of interpreting speech utterances, the listener cannot always uncover the fact that an illocution is defective, whereas if he knew that the performance of the illocutionary act was incorrect he would not regard the communication as completely successful. This means that in such a case someone setting himself up to be 'impartial' *cannot automatically call the communication successful*.

We do not agree with Searle when he appears to equate the 'happiness' of communication with the fulfilment of correctness conditions which are coupled exclusively to the speaker. In our opinion the recognizability of illocutions for the listener must be incorporated into the happiness conditions. This is something that Searle does only to a very limited extent.

Searle's correctness conditions for the illocutionary act *promise*, for example, relate exclusively to the speaker's intention and the impression that the speaker has formed of the listener's preferences and expectations. If the listener *recognizes* the speaker's utterance as a promise, he knows what intention he may attribute to the speaker and what preferences and expectations the speaker attributes (or may be deemed to attribute) to him. One important complication, however, is that Searle's correctness conditions in no way guarantee that the listener *can actually recognize* a promise as a promise. This means that an illocutionary act that meets Searle's correctness conditions cannot automatically be regarded as 'happy'.

Searle bypasses this problem by confining himself to illocutions which are expressed *explicity* in a *performative formula*. If certain 'normal input and output conditions' have been met (viz. that speaker and listener speak the same language, that the utterance is worded in that language, that the utterance may be treated at face value, etc.), then recognition ought indeed to present no problem. But in ordinary idiom the illocutionary force of utterances is often not expressed explicity, and in that case the listener can only recognize the illocutionary force if other recognition conditions have also been fulfilled (these may also be fulfilled in the case of explicit illocutions), but Searle says nothing about this.

Since speech acts are units of language use whose functionality is determined by the (verbal and non-verbal) context of which they are a part, the illocutionary force that speech acts may have depends on *the place they occupy in the context in which they are performed*. This means that in the case of non-explicit illocutions one recognition condition is that the listener, given the overall purpose of the discourse, is able to determine which illocutionary acts may be relevant at that moment in that context, since then, using maxims for the conduct of discourse such as those explicitized by Grice (1975), he can determine what the actual illocutionary force is (cf. chapter 6). If, using the maxims, the listener succeeds in establishing the illocutionary force of a speech act, then, irrespective of the degree to which the correctness conditions have been fulfilled from the point of view of the speaker, he may hold the speaker to all the consequences attendant on the performance of the illocutionary act concerned.

According to Searle, no 'genuine' promise is made where the correctness conditions that he lists for the speaker have not been fulfilled. According to us, however, a listener may in certain circumstances hold the speaker to his promise even where not all these correctness conditions have been fulfilled. This may be demonstrated, for example, by reference to the *sincerity condition*. If the speaker makes a promise, then, regardless of his intention on that point (i.e. irrespective of whether the sincerity condition has actually been fulfilled), he takes upon himself a certain responsibility to which the listener can hold him. And this is why, as we observed earlier, we believe it might have been better to call the sincerity condition the *responsibility condition* or *liability condition*.[18]

In our opinion the communication is only completely successful if the sincerity condition *has* been met. This means that for a 'happy' communication both *recognition conditions* and *correctness conditions* must be fulfilled. However, these conditions do not automatically coincide, and in any event they must, with a view to a satisfactory analysis of verbal communication, be clearly *differentiated*.

We shall now formulate the conditions that a listener may regard as having been fulfilled when a speaker performs the illocutionary act complex of *argumentation.* We shall assume that the *recognition conditions* have been met and that the listener has indeed *understood* that the speaker wishes to advance an argumentation. This means that we shall be concentrating on the *correctness conditions* of argumentation. Since a complex of speech utterances may act not only as *pro*-argumentation but also as *contra*-argumentation, we shall have to formulate the correctness conditions for both.

The situation that we take as our starting point is that a speaker S has put to a listener L a number of statements which belong to the category of the *assertives* and which together constitute a constellation of statements S_1, S_2 $(,\ldots, S_n)$ which acts as *pro-argumentation* or *contra-argumentation* for an expressed opinion *O*. This means that those conditions must be fulfilled which in Searle's basic theory of illocutionary acts are called the *propositional content condition* and the *essential condition*. In the case of the illocutionary act complex *argumentation* the *propositional content condition* is the same for both pro-argumentation and contra-argumentation. This condition may be formulated as follows:

> The constellation of statements $S_1, S_2 (,\ldots, S_n)$ consists of assertives in which propositions are expressed.

The *essential condition* for the illocutionary act complex *argumentation* is different for pro-argumentation and contra-argumentation. For *pro-argumentation* it may be formulated thus:

> Advancing the constellation of statements $S_1, S_2 (,\ldots, S_n)$ counts as an attempt by S to justify O to L's satisfaction, i.e. to convince L of the acceptability of O.

For *contra-argumentation* the essential condition may be formulated as follows:

> Advancing the constellation of statements $S_1, S_2 (,\ldots, S_n)$ counts as an attempt by S to refute O to L's satisfaction, i.e. to convince L of the unacceptability of O.

If S performs his argumentation in a recognizable manner, this automatically means that the propositional content condition and the essential condition for pro- or contra-argumentation have been fulfilled. If the *propositional content condition* is not met, this means either that S has expressed *no proposition whatsoever* or that he *has* expressed a propostion, but *not with an assertive illocutionary force*. In the first of these cases the statements he has made are 'empty' and there is nothing at all for L to assess. In the second case the statements made by S may be orders, requests, questions, and so on, but not part of an argumentation (for more complex cases see chapter 5). In that case L would be able to assess the acceptability of the *order*, the *request*, the *question*, and so on, but not the acceptability of an *argumentation*.

If the *essential condition for pro-argumentation* is not met, then advancing the constellation of statements is not an attempt to *justify O* to L's satisfaction, so that L *cannot recognize* the constellation as pro-argumentation. If the *essential condition for contra-argumentation* is not met, then advancing the constellation of statements is not an attempt to *refute O* to L's satisfaction, so that L *cannot recognize* the constellation as contra-argumentation. In either case, of course, it is not only possible for S to have performed one or more illocutionary acts at the sentence level, it is also possible that at a higher textual level he has performed an *illocutionary act complex* (he may, for example, have *provided elucidation*), but in such a case he will not have performed the illocutionary act complex *argumentation*.

S may succeed in performing the illocutionary act complex *argumentation* in a recognizable manner, but this does not automatically mean that he has also performed that compound illocution *correctly*. However, L is nevertheless *entitled to assume* that the illocutionary act complex *argumentation* has been correctly performed, and even if this is not actually the case, the consequences for both S and L may therefore be precisely the same as if it had been.

To be able to say that the illocutionary act complex *argumentation* has been correctly performed, we must first establish that certain additional *correctness conditions* have been fulfilled; these correspond to Searle's *preparatory conditions* and *sincerity conditions*. We shall indicate what preparatory and sincerity conditions must always be fulfilled for a correct performance of the illocutionary act complex *argumentation*. If at the same time the necessary recognition conditions have been met (and hence also the propositional content condition and the essential condition), then we have listed all the conditions that we believe have to be fulfilled for pro- or contra-argumentation to be *completely 'happy' at the communicative level*.

We shall begin with a formulation of the preparatory conditions and the sincerity conditions for the correct performance of a *pro-argumentation*.

Preparatory conditions

1. *S believes that L does not (in advance, completely, automatically) accept the expressed opinion O.*
2. *S believes that L will accept the propositions expressed in the statements S_1, S_2 (,..., S_n)*
3. *S believes that L will accept the constellation of statements S_1, S_2 (,..., S_n) as a justification of O.*[19]

Sincerity conditions

1. *S believes that O is acceptable.*
2. *S believes that the propositions expressed in the statements S_1, S_2 (,..., S_n) are acceptable.*
3. *S believes that the constellation of statements S_1, S_2 (,..., S_n) consttutes an acceptable justification of O.*[20]

The preparatory conditions and sincerity conditions for the correct performance of a *contra-argumentation* can, we believe, be formulated as follows.

Preparatory conditions

1. *S believes that L accepts (for the time being, in whole or in part, more or less) the expressed opinion O.*
2. *S believes that L will accept the propositions expressed in the statements S_1, S_2 (,..., S_n).*
3. *S believes that L will accept the constellation of statements S_1, S_2 (,..., S_n) as a refutation of O.*

Sincerity conditions

1. *S believes that O is unacceptable.*
2. *S believes that the propositions expressed in the statements S_1, S_2 (,..., S_n) are acceptable.*
3. *S believes that the constellation of statements S_1, S_2 (,..., S_n) constitutes an acceptable refutation of O.*

That all of these conditions must be fulfilled for a correct performance of the illocutionary act complex *pro-argumentation* or *contra-argumentation* can be made plausible by indicating the consequences of one or more of these conditions *not* being fulfilled. Argumentation is then always to a grater or lesser extent *defective* ('unhappy'), though the nature of the defectiveness is not the same in all cases.

If the *first preparatory condition* is not met, in the case of pro-argumentation this implies that S believes that L accepts (in advance, completely, automatically) the expressed opinion O, and the same applies, *mutatis mutandis*, in the case of contra-argumentation. It follows from this that in that case the performance of the illocutionary act complex *argumentation* is *superfluous*. And in that case, S's performance of that illocutionary act complex is in fact a waste of time and effort and both S and L know beforehand that it is.

If the *second preparatory condition* is not met, this implies, whether the argumentation is pro-argumentation or contra-argumentation, that S *does not believe* that L will accept the propositions expressed in statements S_1, S_2 (,..., S_n), or even that S *believes that L will not accept* those propositions. In either case S assumes in advance that his statements will not convince L, and that renders the performance of the illocutionary act complex *argumentation* *pointless* from S's point of view. Whether it is really pointless or not is determined by the correctness of his assumption, and that depends on L.

If the *third preparatory condition* is not met, this implies in the case of pro-argumentation that S *does not believe* that L will accept the constellation of statements S_1, S_2 (,..., S_n) as a justification of O, and in the case of contra-argumentation it implies that S *does not believe* that L will accept that constellation of statements as a refutation of O. It may even mean that S *believes that L will certainly not accept* the constellation of statements as a justification or refutation of O. In either case, performing the illocutionary act complex of *argumentation* is again *pointless* from S's point of view. The defectiveness here means that S accepts in advance that his argumentation *lacks cogency*. Here again, it depends on L whether this is in fact the case.

If the *first sincerity condition* is not met, this implies in the case of pro-argumentation that S *does not believe* that O is acceptable, or even that S *believes that O is unacceptable*, and in the case of contra-argumentation it implies that S *does not believe* that O is unacceptable, or even that S *believes that O is acceptable*. In all these cases S behaves as if there is a dispute between L and himself regarding O, whereas in fact there is no such dispute. This means that S (if, at least, he acts as if he is serious) leaves L under the misapprehension that there is a dispute. In that case S is guilty of *misleading* L. However, whether or not L is aware of having been misled, he is always entitled to hold S to his statements.

If the *second sincerity condition* is not met, this implies, whether the argumentation is pro-argumentation or contra-argumentation, that S *does not believe* that the propositions expressed in the statements $S_1, S_2 (, \ldots, S_n)$ are acceptable, or even that S *believes that these propositions are unacceptable*. This means that he is deliberately furnishing L with inaccurate information, and this form of misleading implies that performing the illocutionary act complex of *argumentation* must be regarded as *cheating*. Whether or not he is aware of this deception, L is always entitled to hold S to his statements.

If the *third sincerity condition* is not met, this implies in the case of pro-argumentation that S *does not believe* that the constellation of statements $S_1, S_2 (, \ldots, S_n)$ constitutes an acceptable justification of O, or even that S believes that that constellation of statements *does not constitute any justification of O* at all, and in the case of contra-argumentation the same applies, *mutatis mutandis*, to the refutation of O. In the case of pro-argumentation S present as an acceptable justification something that he himself believes not to constitute an (acceptable) justification, and in the case of contra-argumentation he presents as an acceptable refutation something that he himself believes not to constitute an (acceptable) refutation. This means that in such cases he is guilty of a form of misleading and that performing the illocutionary act complex of *argumentation* must here be regarded as an attempt at *manipulation*. Whether or not he is aware of this attempted manipulation, L is always entitled to hold S to his pretence of justification or refutation.

The defectiveness occurring as a result of the non-fulfilment of *preparatory conditions* may all be ranked under the common heading of *inexpediency*, and the defectiveness arising as a result of the non-fulfilment of *sincerity conditions* under the common heading of *untruth*. Different forms of inexpediency or different forms of untruth can of course occur together, and inexpediency and untruth can also occur in combination, but need not. To be able to indicate more precisely all the things that can go wrong in the performance of the illocutionary act complex of *argumentation*, however, it will be useful to distinguish clearly between the various possibilities.[21]

Chapter 3

Argumentation and the perlocutionary act of convincing

3.1. THE PERLOCUTIONARY ACT OF CONVINCING

The performance of the illocutionary act complex *argumentation* is not only intended to make the listener understand that the speaker is trying to justify or refute a particular opinion, it is also designed to convince the listener of the acceptability or unacceptability of that opinion. This means that an analysis of the speech act *argumentation* must concern itself with both the communicative and the interactional aspects of this form of language use. Therefore we shall now, having analysed the communicative aspects in chapter 2, examine the interactional aspects. We have made it our purpose to clarify the relation between the performance of the speech act *argumentation* and the perlocutionary effect that the listener accepts or does not accept a particular expressed opinion (*objective 2*).

In formulating the *essential condition* that we believe must be fulfilled if a complex of speech utterances is to count as a pro-argumentation or contra-argumentation, we have already explicitly linked the illocutionary act complex *argumentation* with the perlocutionary act of *convincing*. That there is a link between that illocution and that perlocution is not disputed in the speech act theory. True, neither Austin nor Searle are particularly concerned with argumentation, but they do emphatically point out the connection with convincing. Searle distinguishes the illocutions of *asserting, stating* and *affirming* from the illocutionary act *argumentation,* for example, by observing that they, unlike the last illocution, 'do not seem to be essentially tied' to attempting to convince (1970:66). At the same time he points out, as we have already observed, that 'I am simply stating that *p* and not attempting to convince you' is acceptable, but 'I am arguing that *p* and not attempting to convince you' is not.

Likewise T. Cohen, who unlike Austin and Searle *has* been especially concerned with perlocutions, recognizes a constant link between the illocution *argumentation* and the perlocution *convincing*. He refers to an *association* between arguing on the one hand and convincing or persuading on the other; this association then implies that the illocution and the perlocution 'belong together' and that the perlocution is brought about through the illocution. According to him the relationship between arguing and convincing is 'tidy and obvious' (1973:499). The idea that there is a link between arguing and convincing is confirmed by the definitions of the words *convince* and *persuade* in the dictionaries we cited in chapter 2. The *Concise Oxford Dictionary* defines *persuade* as 'convince (person, oneself, of fact, that thing is so); induce (person to do, into action)' (Fowler & Fowler 1959:889), *Webster* as '(1) to cause (someone) to do something, especially by reasoning, urging, or inducement; to prevail upon, (2) to induce (someone) to believe something; to convince' (Webster & McKechnie 1979:1339), while the two dictionaries define *convince* as 'firmly persuade' (1959:263) or 'to persuade or satisfy by evidence or argument; to overcome the doubts of; to cause to feel certain' (1979:400). Webster adds by way of explanation: 'To *convince* a person is to satisfy his understanding as to the truth of a certain statement; to *persuade* him is to influence his feelings or will'.

The definitions given in the dictionaries raise the question of whether it is really necessary to differentiate between convincing and persuading. We believe that there is no need for an explicit differentiation, since the way in which we shall be using the term *convince* is fairly specific and immediately makes clear what senses of the words *convince* and *persuade* as used in colloquial idiom are covered by our term and which are not, so that no confusion can arise. What we understand by *convince* is: *to use pro-argumentation to induce a listener to accept an expressed opinion, or to use contra-argumentation to induce a listener to reject an expressed opinion.*

The difference in meaning between the words *convince* and *persuade* in colloquial speech appears to be chiefly: (1) that persuading is primarily aimed at influencing the actions (or will to act) of the listener ('persuade *to*') and convincing at influencing his points of view ('convince *of*'), (2) that the quality of the argumentation plays a less important role in persuading than in convincing ('He managed to persuade me, but his argumentation did not convince me'), and (3) that persuading is more directly linked with the personal interests of speaker and listener than convincing is. These three points are furthermore closely interrelated. Indeed, they are not clearly differentiated in the dictionaries.

For our purposes this difference between convincing and persuading is not important. The first point of difference is removed when one realizes that attempts to influence someone's actions (or will to act), too, always have a certain underlying opinion, and this can be expressed in the form of an expressed opinion. If this is useful for some well defined purpose, it will always be possible to distiguish between argumentation relating to expressed opinions about actions and argumentation relating to other sorts of expressed opinion. Here we refer, for example, to the distinction between *practical argumentation* about normative statements relating to actions and *theoretical argumentation* about descriptive statements relating to facts, a distinction drawn by Wunderlich (1976:257) and others.

The second and third points of difference become doubtful as soon as the word *persuading* appears in the dictionary definitions of *convince*, and vice versa. But even assuming that these differences do in fact exist in colloquial idiom, they are still not relevant to our purpose here. The degree to which the attempt at influencing is linked with the self-interest of speaker and listener does not, after all, play a part in our definition of *convincing*. Moreover, the extent to which the quality of the argumentation plays a part is always dependent on the qualities of the listener and the manner in which he utilizes those qualities. At best, therefore, it is only possible to establish whether a particular attempt at influencing must be labelled an *attempt to persuade* or an *attempt to convince* by judging each case on its merits (and, moreover, not until it has finished). When it comes to characterizing the perlocutionary purpose of argumentation this difference is irrelevant. In short, we believe that all relevant aspects of the senses in which the words *convince* and *persuade* are used in colloquial speech are embodied in our definition of *convincing*.

In our definition we have linked convincing to the performance of the illocutionary act complex *argumentation*, and this coupling is supported by the dictionary definitions just cited. Yet it is still possible to wonder whether this coupling actually exists in all practical cases. After all, it is sometimes possible to convince someone of something without uttering a single word, perhaps by merely showing him something. Thus by showing a listener a set of fingerprints a speaker can convince him that he has justly accused a particular person of a crime. However, quite aside from the question of whether or not it is rather uncommon in colloquial speech to refer to the showing of fingerprints as an *attempt to convince*, it should be noted that even in cases like this *a form of argumentation underlies the convincing*, even if here the argumentation is not formulated aloud.

A person showing another person a set of fingerprints in order to justify, to that person's satisfaction, the expressed opinion that a certain person is guilty of some crime, will in principle be attempting to convince the other person with the (unexpressed) argumentation 'These fingerprints were left by the culprit, they are X's fingerprints, therefore X is the culprit' (or a variant of this). Showing the fingerprints is not, *in itself*, sufficient to convince the other person. He will only be convinced when he links his observation with an interpretation corresponding to the argumentation just reconstructed. This is also apparent even if he is not at firstly entirely convinced, in which case he will probably request argumentation, perhaps for the unexpressed premiss (which would then be 'degraded' to an expressed opinion) 'These fingerprints were left by the culprit'. This request for argumentation might also be made indirectly by advancing a counter-argument such as 'But they might be someone else's fingerprints'.[22]

Now that we have made it plausible that convincing is always linked with argumentation and have defined the illocutionary act complex of *argumentation* (in our formulation of the essential condition) as an attempt to convince, one might ask oneself to what extent convincing has to do with a *different* act (or a *different aspect* of the complete speech act) from that involved in arguing. Unlike some other authors (to be discussed in section 3.2), we believe that here we are indeed dealing with *two distinct* acts (or aspects of the complete speech act), viz. an *illocution* (the communicative aspect) in the case of *argumentation* and a *perlocution* (the interactional aspect) in the case of *convincing*.

Our chief argument for this is that arguing and convincing, just like other illocutions and perlocutions, have *different happiness conditions*. *Argumentation* is happy (as an illocutionary act complex) if the speaker has performed the illocution correctly and achieved the effect that the listener *understands* that the speaker has advanced a pro- or contra-argumentation, i.e. has tried to convince him, using verbal means, of the acceptability or unacceptability of a given expressed opinion. *Convincing* is happy (as a perlocutionary act) if the speaker has achieved the effect that the listener *accepts* the expressed opinion to which the speaker's argumentation relates (in the case of pro-argumentation) or *rejects* it (in the case of contra-argumentation).

For an expressed opinion to be acceptable to the listener, different conditions must be fulfilled from those that have to be fulfilled for a correctly performed argumentation to be understandable to the listener. In the latter case, the conditions that have to be met relate chiefly to the adequacy of the *communication* between the language users and in the former case they relate chiefly to the adequacy of the *interaction* between them. In our view these differences render it necessary to differentiate between the acts of *arguing* (illocution) and *convincing* (perlocution) in the analysis of the complete speech act.

This distinction is an extension of a distinction known to every language user from everyday speech. Every language user knows that arguing does not have to be the same as convincing: the argumentation may succeed while the attempt to convince fails. The differences between the *illocution* of argumentation and the *perlocution* of convincing find expression in the second and third preparatory conditions of the illocutionary act complex of *argumentation*. Both conditions are formulated (both for pro-argumentation and for contra-argumentation) from the point of view of the *speaker*. In both cases the point at issue is nothing but the *attitude that the speaker attributes to the listener* with regard to the acceptability of the propositions expressed in statements $S_1, S_2 (, \ldots, S_n)$ or of the justificatory or refutatory potentiality of that constellation in respect of the expressed opinion O. For the *illocutionary act complex* to be perfectly successful it is *sufficient* (assuming of course that the other conditions obtaining have been met) that these two conditions be fulfilled, but for the success of the *perlocutionary act* this is *insufficient*.

The perlocutionary act *convince* can only succeed if the listener actually subscribes to the attitude attributed to him by the speaker or at least if he wishes to tie himself down to that attitude. If this is true for both of the conditions named, then in principle all the conditions have been fulfilled which must be fulfilled for the perlocutionary act *convince* to be successful (though this does not necessarily imply that we have an indication of *when* this will be the case). The differences between the illocutionary act complex *argumentation* (or the happiness conditions for it) and the perlocutionary act *convince* (or the happiness conditions for it) arise from possible discrepancies between the attitude ascribed to the listener by the speaker and the attitude that the listener actually subcribes to (or pretends to subscribe to).

3.2. THE RELATION BETWEEN ILLOCUTIONS AND PERLOCUTIONS

We have made it clear in the foregoing that we regard illocutions and perlocutions as two distinct aspects of the complete speech act, with the illocutionary act relating to the communicative aspect expressed in the attempt to achieve understanding and the perlocutionary act relating to the interactional aspect expressed in the attempt to achieve acceptance. So far, however, we have given no characterization of the way in which illocutions and perlocutions are related. We shall attempt to do so in this section.

Since the literature on speech acts contains a variety of views on the relation between illocutions and perlocutions, we think it might be helpful if we set out our own view on the matter by means of a critical discussion of the views of others. We shall start with the points of view adopted by Holdcroft and Sadock, who deny that illocutions and perlocutions are different sorts of act, so that their stance is radically different from that of Austin and Searle and from our own.

Like Searle (and the majority of the other authors who have written on the subject of perlocutionary acts since Austin), in *Words and Deeds* Holdcroft confines himself, though without actually using the term, to *illocutionary perlocutions*. He does not go so far as Max Black (1963), who regards illocutionary perlocutions as the only sort of perlocution, but like Ted Cohen (1973) he does regard them as the *normal* sort:

> The root idea of a perlocutionary act is of an act which when performed by saying something can be redescribed as the performance of an illocutionary act with certain consequences (1978:20).

Moreover Holdcroft appears to suggest that perlocutions are really a *special sort of illocution*, distinguished from other illocutions chiefly by the special nature of their consequences. To be able to speak of *perlocutionary* acts it is not sufficient, according to Holdcroft, for illocutionary acts to have consequences: *specific* consequences have to occur (1978:21). He shifts the problem of the distinction between illocutions and perlocutions from one that has to do with the differing nature of *two acts* to one that has to do with the differing nature of the *consequences of a single sort of act*.

Sadock, in *Toward a Linguistic Theory of Speech Acts* (1974), also reduces illocutions and perlocutions to a single sort of act. However, unlike Holdcroft, he does not regard perlocutionary acts as a special sort of illocutionary act but, quite the contrary, considers illocutionary acts to be a special sort of perlocutionary act. According to him, illocutionary acts have all the features of perlocutionary acts, whereas the converse does not hold:

I suggest, then, that an illocutionary act is a special kind of perlocutionary act,
with characteristics that distinguish it from all other kinds of perlocutions ...
(1974:153).

According to Sadock, the distinguishing characteristic of illocutions is that
the consequence, unlike that of other perlocutions, depends solely on the
meaning of the utterance. He therefore refers to 'sense perlocutions'
(1974:153).

With this Sadock adds nothing to earlier observations by Austin, who (like
Holdcroft later) remarks that illocutions and perlocutions can both have
consequences, that these consequences differ and that the consequences of
illocutions depend on the meaning of the utterance (*locutionary act*) whereas
those of perlocutions do not. However, an important difference is that
Austin regards illocutions and perlocutions as different acts and Sadock (and
Holdcroft) do not. But we can see no advantage in Sadock's (and Holdcroft's) view. The fact that both illocutionary and perlocutionary effects are
the consequences of *utterances* is in itself insufficient reason to regard the acts
by which those effects are caused as one and the same kind. There is,
however, a sufficiently good reason for differentiating between the two, viz.
that the *happiness conditions* for the two sorts of act are not identical.

We can illustrate this with an example. When an illocutionary perlocution
is performed, an illocution is also performed by means of *the same* utterance.
Thus the utterance of a threat (illocution) is at the same time an attempt to
intimidate the listener (perlocution). Yet this does not necessarily mean that
the one act automatically succeeds or fails if the other succeeds or fails. For
example, the listener may realize perfectly well that the speaker's utterance is
designed to be treated as a threat ('happy' illocution) without his being
impressed by it ('unhappy' perlocution). Thus the happiness conditions for
the perlocutionary act *intimidate* and the illocutionary act *threaten* are *not
identical*.

In this chapter we describe a situation that looks very much like that which
occurs in *indirect speech acts*, and it might therefore help to clarify matters if
we paid some attention to these. We shall do so by starting from a speaker
who says 'Could you pass me the salt?', not meaning it to be a simple *question*
but also a *request*. This is an example of an *indirect speech act*, because 'one
illocutionary act is performed indirectly by way of performing another'
(Searle 1979:31). This utterance has two illocutionary forces, so that *two acts*
are performed *in a single utterance*. In this respect illocutionary perlocutions
resemble indirect speech acts.

Indirect speech acts and illocutionary perlocutions also appear to resemble each other in that the two acts that are performed concurrently are
not performed in complete isolation from one another but *are related in a
specific way*. Furthermore in either case it is true that the success or failure of
the one act *does not necessarily go hand in hand with the success or failure of the
other*. For example, the listener may interpret the utterance 'Could you pass

me the salt?', intended to be a request, as a question (in which case he would have understood the *secondary* illocutionary force) and content himself with the answer 'Yes', without realizing that the speaker (also) intended the utterance to be a request (the *primary* illocutionary force).

A crucial difference between indirect speech acts and illocutionary perlocutions is that indirect speech acts are performed by means of *two illocutions*, whereas illocutionary perlocutions are performed by means of *one illocution and one perlocution*. The only consequence that is required for the 'happiness' of an indirect speech act (as an illocution) is that the listener should recognize both of the two illocutionary forces (and the propositional content) and thus *understand* the illocutions, whereas *more than this* is necessary for an illocutionary perlocution to be 'happy'. This implies that the happiness conditions are different and means that illocutionary perlocutions cannot simply be regarded as indirect speech acts but must be seen as separate (albeit related) phenomena of language usage.

In passing it should be noted, of course, that in practice it is possible for *combinations* of indirect speech acts and illocutionary perlocutions to occur. A single utterance, for example, may have two illocutionary forces and one perlocutionary effect. Thus the sentence 'It's nearly two o'clock' can be uttered with the intention of giving the listener a fright (perlocutionary effect) while the primary illocutionary force is that of a warning and the secondary illocutionary force that of a statement of fact.

Our view that illocutions and perlocutions are distinct kinds of act that are related in a particular way is supported by T. Cohen (1973). Cohen wonders 'whether the illocution is instrumental in the production of the perlocution' (1973:494). He believes that in illocutionary perlocutions (which he calls *direct* perlocutions) the perlocution *is associated with* the illocution (1973:496). According to him this would be the case, for example, in *intimidate* (associated with *threaten*), *alarm* (associated with *warn*) and *convince* and *persuade* (both associated with *argumentation*). He defines an *associated perlocution* as a perlocution brought about by means of an illocution that 'it belongs with' (1973:497).

The association, according to Cohen, extends over two levels: the level of *the relation between perlocutions and illocutions in general* and the level of *the specific constraints which perlocutions may impose on the performance of illocutions*. By the first of these he means that the perlocution is 'something like the rationale' for the illocution: 'It constitutes a general reason, a reason *überhaupt*, for performing the illocution'. In (yet) other words: 'It gives the illocutionary act, considered as an act of a kind, a point' (1973:500). By the specific constraints that perlocutions may impose on the performance of illocutions he means the fact that in any given case it must be possible (or at least it must appear possible to those concerned) for the associated perlocution to occur. It is as it were in the nature of the illocution to bring about the perlocution and if it is clear that the perlocutionary effect cannot occur, then the illocution is 'in some way and to some degree abortive (or, we might say, the illocutionary force is to some degree unactualized)' (1973:500).

According to Cohen the general and particular relation that may exist between perlocutions and illocutions does not necessarily imply that the success of the perlocution is a *condition* for the success of the illocution: 'there is arguing which doesn't persuade and threatening which doesn't intimidate' (1973:500). However, the particular relation does imply that there must at least be a *possibility* that the intended perlocutionary effect will occur. If the perlocutionary effect *has already been actualized*, so that the perlocution is no longer 'open', there is no point in the illocutionary act: 'I can't argue the point with you if you're already persuaded, or warn you of a danger to which you're already alerted, or point out something you already see', or at least not if we both know that you're already persuaded, alert, or aware (1973:501).[23]

Unfortunately Cohen does not clarify what he means by the *rationale, point* or *purpose* of an illocution, and it is only from his examples that we can deduce what he means by 'open' perlocutions, but we believe this defect can be compensated for by linking *rationale, point* and *purpose* with the *essential condition* and 'open' with the *preparatory conditions* of illocutionary acts. What Cohen means by the first three terms appears to correspond to what Searle, in 'A Taxonomy of Illocutionary Acts'means by the *point* or *purpose* of an illocutionary act. The point or purpose corresponds to the essential condition for the relevant illocutionary act.

The 'openness' of the perlocution, which Cohen regards as a condition of the success of the illocution, corresponds to a general preparatory condition applying to a wide variety of types of illocution and acknowledged as such by Searle. According to him an illocutionary act is defective if what has to be achieved by fulfilling the essential rule has already been achieved. If this general preparatory condition is not met, Searle believes that many illocutionary acts are pointless (1970:59).

Cohen takes the view that even in clear cases of associated perlocutions one cannot automatically speak of a *means-end relation* between illocution and perlocution (1973:501). If our interpretation of his key terms is correct, then the question arises: why not? And hanging together with this question is another: *are all illocutionary acts associated per se in one way or another with trying to achieve perlocutionary effects?* Cohen allows for the possibility that this question has to be answered affirmatively, but Searle does not.

Searle turns emphatically against the (somewhat more powerful) proposition that the fact that every illocutionary act has a purpose or point implies that every illocutionary act 'has a definitionally associated perlocutionary intent' (1979:3). Assertions and promises, for example, he believes not to be attempts to bring about perlocutionary effects on listeners. This point of view accords with that of Austin (1976:126). The implication is then naturally that there cannot be any association between an illocution and a perlocution. *Request, ask* and *order* are according to Austin and Searle illocutions that *do* have a perlocutionary effect and that may be regarded as *means to a perlocutionary end.*

If Austin and Searle are right, there would appear to be absolutely no reason for making a categorical objection, as Cohen does, to the means-end characterization. But Cohen's standpoint is that *all* illocutions are associated with the bringing about of perlocutionary effects and the means-end characterization *does not apply in all cases*. He considers it misleading – perhaps Austin and Searle are the victims of this – that suitable terms are not available to denote all associated perlocutions, but it would certainly be mistaken to deduce from this that no perlocutionary effect was linked with the illocutions in question. For example, the illocution *promise* is associated, says Cohen, with such perlocutionary effects as 'the recipient's feeling gratified in some way, his attributing to the speaker an intention to do what is promised, and his acting in ways commensurate with and dependent on the speaker's doing what is promised' (1973:499). All these can be placed under the heading of *accepting* a promise, so that we have an example of an association between an illocution and a perlocution, even though the association is not as 'tidy and obvious' as in *argue/convince* and *threaten/intimidate* (1973:499).

But Cohen's analysis of *promise* does make it clear why he regards the means-end relation as not an appropriate general characteristic of the association between illocutions and perlocutions. The acceptance of a promise is not, after all, the illocutionary purpose formulated in the essential condition of the illocution *promise*. The means-end characterization is *adequate in some cases* (e.g. *order*) *and not in others* (e.g. *promise*), so that it cannot be regarded as a *general* characterization.

Cohen's suggestion that the acceptance of a promise should be regarded as the perlocutionary effect of the illocution *promise* seems to us to be sensible, but we also believe that the way he looks at it requires correction and augmentation on two points. In the first place, in the way he uses the term *accept* it has too much of an *all-embracing content*. According to him a listener who accepts a promise fulfils the following conditions: (1) he feels gratified in some way, (2) he attributes to the speaker an intention of doing what is promised, and (3) he acts in ways commensurate with the speaker's doing what is promised.

This description of the listener's state of mind is not inaccurate, but in our opinion only (1) can be considered a *perlocutionary effect* of promising, since (2) is an *illocutionary*, not a *perlocutionary* effect of promising (a listener who does not attribute the relevant intention to the speaker has, as is clear from the conditions applying to this illocution, *failed to understand* that the speaker has promised him anything), and (3) is itself (unless the scope of the term *perlocutionary effect* is stretched to unmanageable proportions so that it is no longer used in the sense indicated earlier) not a perlocutionary effect, but at most a *consequence* arising out of the perlocutionary effect *accept*.

With regard to the feeling of gratification (1), which is associated with the acceptance of the promise, we must make another observation. This has to do with the way in which Searle incorporates this perlocutionary aspect into his conditions for the *illocutionary* act *promise*. He regards it as one of the preparatory conditions of the illocutionary act *promise* that the speaker promises something regarded as desirable by the listener. In explanation of this he observes that for a promise not to be defective 'the thing promised must be something the hearer wants done, or considers to be in his interest, or would prefer being done to not being done, etc.' (1970:59). Apart from the surprising (and in Searle's scheme inconsistent) exchange of the speaker's and the listener's perspectives which occurs in this condition, it does indeed seem to us correct to call a promise defective if this condition is not met, but we consider it misguided to place this condition *at the illocutionary level*.

At the illocutionary level a promise is 'happy' *if the speaker believes* (or at least may be deemed to believe) that the thing promised is something that the listener regards as desirable (and of course if the other conditions for the illocution *promise* have also been met). If the listener attributes this belief to the speaker on the grounds of the utterance, then he *understands* that the speaker has made him a promise and that he has not, for example, issued a warning or threat. And if the listener *actually does regard as desirable* the thing that the speaker has promised, then the speech act is also 'happy' *at the perlocutionary level*. In that case the listener will *accept* the utterance and, as Cohen puts it, will feel in some way *gratified*.

Our second observation regarding Cohen's thinking here relates to the fact that he gives the impression that the perlocutionary effect *accept* can occur *only with certain speech acts*. Perhaps this idea arises easily because in the case of a *promise* the interaction seems to have been fully concluded once the listener has accepted, whereas for example in the case of speech acts in which a *question* is asked, a *request* made or an *order* given, certain (speech) acts on the part of the listener must follow the acceptance. In this respect promises are on a par with, for example, *statements of fact, assertions* and *expressions of thanks*, where the interaction is in principle over as soon as acceptance has taken place on the part of the listener. In such cases this acceptance implies that the listener indeed believes that the speaker can prove the truth of the proposition expressed or regards the thing for which he expresses his gratitude as something in his own interest. In the case of these speech acts, just as with promising, the conditions for this acceptance correspond to conditions that Searle (1970:66-7) regards as being among the conditions for the 'happiness' of the *illocution* but which in our opinion are conditions for the success of the *perlocution*.

It is not absolutely certain that Cohen believes *acceptance* to be a perlocutionary effect that occurs *exclusively* in illocutions such as *promise, assert, state* and *thank*, but in the first instance it certainly looks as if he does, for he calls the pair *promise/assure oneself of acceptance* 'another example of an illocution and its associated perlocution', alongside the pairs *warn/alarm, argue/convince* and *threaten/intimidate*. Thus *accept* is here presented as a special kind of perlocutionary effect (1973:499). Yet he also allows for the possibility that *accept* is a *general* perlocutionary effect capable of occurring with *any* illocution. At least, he calls *promise/assure oneself of acceptance* an example of 'a rambling general description of effects characteristically realized by an illocution' (1973:501).

Cohen does not elaborate on this suggestion, which is of course open to other interpretations, but we believe that *accept* can indeed be treated as a *general perlocutionary effect* that is one of the goals of *all* speech acts. As we have indicated in section 2.2, it is necessary to differentiate between perlocutionary effects that are partly dependent on the rational considerations of the listener and those that are not. We shall reserve the term *accept* for the first kind of perlocutionary effect, the occurrence of which requires a decision on the part of the listener.

In the case of illocutionary acts such as *promise*, which are characterized by an essential condition in which *no goal to be achieved with the listener is indicated*, the perlocutionary effect *accept* is in principle the *only* one to be aimed at and the only one to be called – in our terminology – an *inherent* perlocutionary effect. In the case of illocutionary acts such as *order*, characterized by an essential condition in which *a goal to be achieved with the listener is indicated*, the perlocutionary effect *accept* always *precedes* any further consequences (such as the performance of the act by which the order is executed), which – in our terminology – are called *consecutive* consequences. In all cases in which the occurrence of a consecutive consequence depends partly on rational considerations on the part of the listener, there is always a perlocutionary effect *accept* associated with an illocutionary act.

In practice acceptance often remains *implicit*, unlike non-acceptance. As a rule the speaker is entitled to infer from the absence of any explicit reaction on the listener's part that the listener has accepted his speech act. Nevertheless the listener is in principle always able to give some *explicit* sign of his acceptance. This may be done *verbally* (e.g. by an explicit declaration of agreement with a promise) but it may also be done *non-verbally* (e.g. by carrying out an order). In cases in which *verbal externalization* is necessary for the sake of clarity, the listener – acting in turn as speaker – will utter one of the available 'acceptance formulas', in which case he will say something like 'I accept ...' or 'O.K.'

By uttering a formula of acceptance the listener himself performs an *illocutionary act*, viz. that of *acceptance*, which in its turn entails certain interactional obligations in respect of his further behaviour (verbal or otherwise). For example, a person who has explicitly accepted a *promise* cannot subsequently simply turn round and say that the acts by which the promise is fulfilled are not to his liking, and a man who has explicitly accepted an *order* can subsequently be required to carry it out. The obligations arising out of the illocutionary act of *acceptance* are similar to those incurred by a speaker by the performance of the illocutionary act of *promising*. *Verbal externalization* of acceptance (or non-acceptance) by the listener means that the mutual obligations between the interlocutors are firmly and clearly established.

3.3. VARIOUS KINDS OF USAGE CONVENTIONS

Before we attempt a more specific characterization of the relation between the illocution *argumentation* and the perlocution of *convincing*, we must distinguish between various kinds of *conventions* in language usage, since the concept of 'convention' will play an important part in that characterization and there is still a great deal of uncertainty as to its meaning. The term *convention* is used variously by various authors, and even if one establishes the meaning of the term in one particular way it always turns out to be necessary to differentiate between different sorts of convention. We shall begin, therefore, by indicating how we use the term *convention*, and will then clarify what kinds of language usage conventions have to be differentiated for our purposes.

Before we start, however, it should be noted that empirical research has so far failed to provide much information about the conventions that play a part in the use of language, so that it is impossible to state with certainty how far the sorts of convention that we differentiate analytically have a well-defined analogue in the reality of language usage. In this respect we have little to add to authors who have expressed the opinion that language usage conventions are 'highly diverse in nature' and have to do with 'divergent aspects of language usage'.

A second introductory remark that we should like to make is that a not insignificant element in the controversies surrounding the conventionality of language usage that have been conducted in the literature has been the inability of some contestants to recognize that the meaning they attach to the term *convention* need not necessarily be regarded as its only possible or 'real' meaning. Many disputes about conventionality appear to be founded on not much more than *verbal disagreement*. Thus we believe that there is no fundamental difference of opinion underlying the difference described by Wunderlich (1972:15) between his own conception of the conventionality of speech acts and that adhered to by Searle or Strawson. In order to avoid such apparent antitheses we stress that we do not assert that the meaning we shall attach to the term *convention* is the only possible or 'genuine' one. We shall define the term *convention* in the way that is most adequate *for our purposes*, and this means that we shall simply *stipulate* what we mean by it.

We assume in our definition of convention that people communicating with one another have formed a more or less common picture of the framework within which their communication and interaction take place. The result of this 'social construction of reality', as Berger and Luckmann (1971) call the formation of this picture, is not of course, as Elias rightly stresses (1970), perfectly monolithic and static, but nevertheless sets up a more or less fixed pattern of *reciprocal expectations* as to the actions of those involved in the communication and interaction. We suppose that these mutual expectations in one way or another constitute part of the cognitive equipment available to language users in verbal communication and interaction. We believe that these expectations on the part of language users are an appropriate starting point for a definition of the concept of 'convention' that is adequate for the study of verbal communication and interaction.

That the expectations of language users are assumed in the definition of the concept of 'convention' means a stressing of the *intersubjective* nature of conventions, and one of the advantages of that is that conventions of language usage are not isolated from the language users and reification is avoided. In this way it is possible to express the fact that the regularities in language usage to which conventions relate are not simply statistical or 'immanent' regularities but socially relevant regularities which – because they correspond to the expectations of language users – must in principle be capable of being *recognized* with the aid of the cognitive equipment available to the language users who share the conventions.

The conventions to which we refer here are pre-eminently *social* conventions. They are shared by a community of language users and have to do with expectations held in common by the members of the community in respect of regularities in language users. Since it has to be possible for language users to *anticipate* these regularities, and since in some sense the regularities *must serve the purpose* aimed at, our definition of the concept of 'convention' must take account not only of the *expectations* of language users in respect of regularities in usage, but also of *actual* regularities and of *norms* relating to those regularities.

We believe the following definition of 'convention' to fulfil the stated conditions.

A *language usage convention* exists in the usage of the members of a community of language users if:
1. *the language of the members of the community displays a certain regularity which occurs in strictly delineated cases;*
2. *the members of the community expect these regularities to occur in those cases;*
3. *the members of the community prefer the regularity to occur in those cases because it solves a problem of communication or interaction.*

Condition 1 expresses the *factual* aspect of conventions, condition 3 the *normative* aspect, and condition 2 the *social* nature of conventions. If only condition 1 is fulfilled, the regularity is in principle no more than a statistical fact; if only condition 2 is fulfilled, then there is a collective expectation that is unfounded; and if condition 3 is the only one to be fulfilled, then there is an unfulfilled social desire. If both condition 1 and condition 2 are met, but not condition 3, then there is a 'natural' peculiarity in the usage that is acknowledged by the language users, if both conditions 2 and 3 are fulfilled but not condition 1, then this is a case of 'wishful thinking', and if conditions 1 and 3 are fulfilled but not condition 2, then the ideal communication and interaction take place as it were 'over the head of the language users'.

Our view of language usage conventions leans heavily on the definition of the concept of 'convention' given by Lewis:

> A regularity R in the behavior of members of a population P when they are agents in a recurrent situation S is a *convention* if and only if, in any instance of S among the members of P,
> 1. everyone conforms to R;
> 2. everyone expects everyone else to conform to R;
> 3. everyone prefers to conform to R on condition that the others do, since S is a coordination problem and uniform conformity to R is a coordination equilibrium in S (1977:42).

This definition, which Lewis first formulated in 1969 in *Convention*, has been adopted by various authors as the starting point for discussions on the conventionality of language. However, Lewis's definition was designed with 'games of pure coordination' in mind, and this finds expression in the third condition. Some writers, such as Wunderlich (1972), wishing to apply the definition to language or language usage, content themselves with taking over the passage 'everyone prefers to conform to R' and *simply omit* the rest of condition 3.

This we regard as misguided, since that way the *ratio* of the condition is lost and the concept of 'convention' then also applies in the case of a blind preference for regularity or conformism to regularity. One of the disadvantages of this is that the term *convention* can then be applied to the more or less ritual aspect of certain forms of usage (e.g. the recitation of the formula of baptism) and to the communicative and interactional aspects associated with the specific intentions of language users that are characteristic of the performance of speech acts. Thus the confusion that has often governed discussions on the conventionality of language or usage in the past is given a further boost.

We have advanced our definition of language usage conventions in order to be able to make a distinction between various kinds of regularity which may occur in the use of language. Regularities fulfilling not only the first condition of the definition but also the second and third we call *conventionally determined*. We regard it as mistaken to call *the regularities themselves*, as Lewis does, *conventions*.

According to our definition of usage conventions, in precisely circumscribed conditions usage will display regularity which is preferred by the members of the community of language users and which is also expected by them. This expectation may be the result eighter of the language users' *past experience* or of an explicit *agreement* arrived at by them (or by others before them). For a description of usage conventions their genesis is not in the first instance of particular relevance, but we mention these two possibilities here because later on we shall be concerning ourselves with the problems of *renewing* (for precisely circumscribed purposes) existing conventions relating to discussions. Conventions that prove to exist in a community of language users without there having been any explicit agreement involved in their creation may be described, in order to distinguish them from ones which *are* founded on a specific agreement, as *semi-conventions*.

In connection with the various kinds of problems that are solved by the regularities to which conventions relate, we distinguish between *communicative* language usage conventions and *interactional* language usage conventions. Communicative usage conventions have to do with regularities in the performance of *illocutions* and the interactional usage conventions are concerned with regularities in the performance of *perlocutions*. In the case of the first, the conventions are designed to solve *problems of comprehensibility*, and in the case of the second they are designed to solve *problems of acceptability*.

Both communicative and interactional conventions of language usage are in principle 'informal' *conventions of usage*, which have to be distinguished from the 'formal' *conventions of language* that are the subject of study in the syntactic and semantic branches of linguistics (which have until recently been isolated from the pragmatic branch). *Conventions of language* have to do with formal linguistic features (of language in general or one specific language in particular) which are connected with the combinability of language elements and the meaning of linguistic constructions. This means that the conventions in this case are primarily connected with regularities in the (extrinsic) *form* of speech utterances. *Conventions of usage* have to do with informal features (of verbal communication and interaction in general or of particular genres of them) which are connected with the illocutionary and perlocutionary effects of language usage. This means that the conventions in that case are primarily connected with regularities in the (intrinsic) *function* of utterances.

This distinction between conventions of language and conventions of usage appears to correspond in its general tenor to a distinction that has been made by Searle in his more recent work:

> It is by now, I hope, uncontroversial that there is a distinction to be made between meaning and use, but what is less generally recognized is that there can be *conventions of usage that are not meaning conventions* (1979:49; our italics).

The distinction to which we refer is expressed even more clearly by Morgan in 'Two Types of Convention in Indirect Speech Acts':

> In sum, then, I am proposing that there are at least two distinct kinds of convention involved in speech acts: *conventions of language* ... and *conventions in a culture of usage of language* in certain cases ... The former, *conventions of the language*, are what make up the language, at least in part. The latter, *conventions of usage*, are a matter of culture (manners, religion, law ...) (1978:269; our italics).

Human languages, we suppose, were evolved primarily (though not through any conscious process of construction) in order to make more complex (verbal) communication and interaction between people possible. It would therefore seem natural when studying languages to start from socio-cultural functions that have to be fulfilled by language usage, even though there may be important methodological reasons for not taking this as one's starting point in certain circumstances. We believe that in any event the functions of usage should be the starting point in any investigation of illocutions and perlocutions. The verbal means of expression available in a particular language for 'realizing' these functions are secondary in importance. This means that when we study illocutions (and perlocutions) we choose a route that is, as it were, diametrically opposed to the route taken by Searle in *Speech Acts*.

When establishing the communicative conventions that make an utterance count as a *promise*, Searle starts from promises expressed by means of *a (literally meant) utterance of the explicit performative formula 'I promise.'* From this starting point he then attempts to formulate the *semantic* rules applying to the use of this performative formula. Quite apart from the question of how the listener is supposed to tell whether the speaker *means his utterance literally*, the problem arises of how one is to offer an explanation of cases in which the speaker *does not express* the illocutionary force he intends *explicitly* in the utterance and yet the listener still understands that what the speaker is saying is a promise.

In our opinion this can only be explained satisfactorily if one assumes that the listener knows what is meant by 'promise', i.e. is familiar with the conditions that have to be fulfilled for the illocutionary act *promise*. Only if this is true will he be able to determine whether those conditions have been met and hence whether he can regard the speaker's utterance as a promise. If the speaker expresses his promise by means of an *explicit performative formula* (and if there is no reason to suppose that he does not mean his utterance literally) this means that he is as it were giving it to the listener on a plate, since thanks to a *convention of language* (in which the use of the verbal symbols concerned is linked to a particular illocution) the illocutionary force of the utterance is *formally established* in the explicit performative formula.

It seems to us that making a promise by saying 'I promise' is a special 'actualization' of this illocutionary act which is only possible thanks to the general *conventions of usage* applying to the making of promises. Without a knowledge of these conventions of usage it is impossible for the listener, even in the case of a promise issued explicitly, to comprehend what the speaker's utterance implies. A speaker making a promise by means of an explicit performative formula fulfils the *recognition conditions* only *in a special manner*, namely solely by means of a convention of language.

In 'A Taxonomy of Illocutionary Acts', first published six years after *Speech Acts*, Searle rightly warns (in his discussion of Austin's taxonomy) against simply equating illocutionary *acts* and illocutionary *verbs* (1979:9). However, in *Speech Acts* he treats explicit performative formulas as if they were the illocutionary acts 'proper', whereas we believe these formulas to be no more (and no less) than special forms of expression that have evolved in a particular language for particular illocutions and which in a sense 'parasitize' the general conventions of usage applying to illocutions (which may also be made recognizable in other ways).

3.4. THE CONVENTIONALITY OF THE ILLOCUTIONARY PERLOCUTION OF CONVINCING

In section 3.1 we indicated that arguing and convincing are an illocution and a perlocution that are very closely related. In section 3.2 we then gave a characterization of this relation, and in section 3.3 we went on to consider the various kinds of convention in language usage, drawing a distinction between communicative conventions of usage (which in principle have to do with regularities in the performance of illocutions) and interactional conventions of usage (which in principle have to do with regularities in the performance of perlocutions). The question now facing us is to what extent the relation between the illocution *argumentation* and the perlocution *convincing* can be described as *conventional*.

We believe that the conventionality of *illocutionary perlocutions* can have a bearing on at least three aspects: (1) the *illocution* by means of which the illocutionary perlocution is performed, (2) the *association* between the illocution and the perlocution, and (3) the *perlocution*. Since the conventionality of illocutions has already been the subject of numerous studies and is virtually beyond dispute, and since we have already demonstrated that the association between arguing and convincing is conventional, we shall now concentrate on the conventionality of the perlocution *convince*. We shall turn first to the conventionality in general.

Austin and Searle are of the express opinion that perlocutions are *never* conventional, whereas Cohen, on the contrary, allows for the possibility that they *are* conventional. However, a not inconsiderable difficulty that presents itself when one tries to assess the standpoints of these writers is that by taking care to avoid any explanation of what they mean by *convention*, Austin and Cohen maintain what Morgan ironically refers to as a 'hallowed linguistic tradition' (1978:279). Searle treats conventions as conventions of language which determine the meaning of explicit performative formulas. Beyond the observation that unlike illocutions they are not conventional, he pays no attention to perlocutions.

Austin examines perlocutions only in order, by way of a characterization of the distinction between perlocutions and illocutions, to obtain greater insight into the *illocution*. It is his view that ultimately the distinction between illocutions and perlocutions must be sought not so much in the different natures of the effects produced (whether intentionally or not) as in the *verbal* and *conventional* character which he says that illocutions possess in contrast to perlocutions.

In Austin's view the success of illocutions always depends on the *locutionary* act, whereas this is never exclusively the case with perlocutions.

According to him the effects of perlocutions can also be achieved without a locutionary act. However, this view of things is somewhat too unsubtle. According to Austin illocutions like *inform, reckon, state* and *argue* can indeed only be performed by *verbal* means, but *order* can also take place merely by the making of a simple gesture, *warn* by a shaking of the head, *protest* by throwing tomatoes, and so on (1976:119-120). Irrespective of the question of whether or not certain perlocutions can only be brought about by verbal means, this means that in any event 'verbal' as a criterion for drawing distinctions is not necessarily adequate.

Combined with the criterion of 'conventionality', Austin believes, the verbal nature of illocutions *would* be able to constitute a usable criterion for making the distinction, for perlocutions are certainly *not* conventional (whether or not they are brought about by verbal means), whereas the illocutionary force of the utterance 'may ... be said to be *conventional* in the sense that at least *it could be made explicit by the performative formula*' (1976:103; our italics). Thus he regards the use of language for *argumentation* or *warning* as conventional in this sense, but not the use of language for *convincing* or *alarming* (1976:103).

Unfortunately, as Strawson has rightly observed (1964), it is far from clear exactly what Austin means here. The suggestion is that illocutions are only conventional in so far as they are performed by means of explicit performative formulas, which are themselves conventional because their meaning is determined by *conventions of language*. However, this conflicts with (*inter alia*) Austin's assertion that performatives can be correctly performed only if a *generally accepted conventional procedure* exists which has a particular *conventional effect* (1976:26). Moreover, in this assertion Austin appears to be assuming a 'wider' conception of conventionality which apparently corresponds to the definition we have given of a *convention of usage*. Later observations by Austin, such as 'it is difficult to say where conventions begin and end' (1976:119) are also more easily reconcilable with this latter view of conventions.

If the 'strict' interpretation of convention as *convention of language* prevails, Austin is not really claiming that *illocutions* are conventional but that *locutions* are conventional.

Due to the vagueness of his conception of convention Austin has in effect shifted the problem of the distinction between illocutions and perlocutions to the problem of defining the concept 'convention'. If convention is taken in the strict sense of *convention of language* then there is little to object against in Austin's claim that perlocutions are *not* conventional, though it then remains the question whether illocutions *are* (and, if they are, whether they are *in all cases*). If convention is taken in the wider sense of *convention of usage*, there is no doubt but that illocutions are conventional, but there is then also no reason to presume that perlocutions are in all cases *not* conventional. In that case Cohen may be right when he says that perlocutions may be just as conventional as illocutions:

> What needs to be shown is that within a total speech act the perlocution has some
> claim to be counted as a conventional constituent, perhaps as much claim as the
> illocution (1973:500).

We shall continue by starting from the definition of *convention* that we gave
in section 3.3, and will try to use that definition to establish the extent to
which perlocutions can be conventional. This means that we take a wider
conception of conventionality as our starting point than Searle and (according to the 'strict' interpretation favoured by many authors) Austin. Whether
our conception of conventionality coincides with Cohen's is uncertain,
because although he makes a major issue of the conventionality of perlocutions he nowhere indicates what he means by conventionality. In any event,
he does not appear to mean the same by *conventions* as Searle.

   Cohen believes that in the case of associated perlocutions there must be a
possibility of the desired perlocutionary effect occurring. The presence or
absence of this possibility, like the actual *occurrence* of that effect (which is
what conventionality is really about), does not depend directly on the
meaning of the sentence uttered. In other words the conventions that might
perhaps play a part in these associated perlocutions cannot be identical to
conventions of language in the Searlean sense.

Schlieben-Lange (1975a:89) likewise believes that perlocutions certainly do
not fall beyond the scope of conventionality, and she provides rather more
information about her conception of conventionality. In *Linguistische Pragmatik* she discerns in perlocutionary acts, alongside a form of conventionality connected with the fact that *sanctions* are associated with attempts to
achieve some perlocutionary goals, *procedures* which have been 'conventio-
nalized' in a particular way. In her article 'Perlokution' she adds to these:

> Conventions in the sense that the procedures are to a certain extent socially
> firmly established and unified and because of this fact are also correctly inter-
> preted (trans. fr. 1975b:323).

The procedures to which Schlieben-Lange refers correspond to the regularities in usage referred to in our definition of convention; in a speech act
context these (to go along with Schlieben-Lange's terminology) may also be
called illocutionary *action schemata*. In the case of associated perlocutions
these are then the action schemata of a particular illocution. Because the
associated perlocution *argue/convince* has our special interest in this book,
we shall concentrate further on the action schemata of the illocutionary act
complex of *argumentation*. The question we shall have to answer is how far
the action schemata used in the illocutionary act complex of *argumentation*
turn the perlocution *convince* into a conventional act.

For the perlocutionary act *convince* to be successful, the illocutionary act
complex *argumentation* must not only be understood by the listener (illocutionary effect), it must also have the consequence that the listener accepts (in

the case of pro-argumentation) or rejects (in the case of contra-argumentation) the expressed opinion to which the illocution refers. In section 3.5 we
shall go into this perlocutionary effect more deeply and define it more closely
in a manner satisfactory for our purpose. Here all that concerns us is the
observation that the perlocutionary act *convince* is designed to make the
listener accept or reject a particular expressed opinion and that pro-argumentation is a means of achieving the former and contra-argumentation is a
means of achieving the latter, so that when determining the conventionality
of the perlocution *convince* we must establish to what extent it is possible in
pro-argumentation to use action schemata which *by convention* bring about
the perlocutionary effect that the listener accepts the expressed opinion and
in contra-argumentation action schemata which *by convention* bring about
the perlocutionary effect that the listener rejects the expressed opinion.

We shall call the action schemata used in an argumentation *argumentation
schemata*. In the case of pro-argumentation the argumentation schemata are
justificatory argumentation schemata and in the case of contra-argumentation they are *refutatory* argumentation schemata. A justificatory argumentation schema consists of a *particular kind of constellation* of statements
relating to an expressed opinion, a constellation which is designed to justify
that expressed opinion (cf. the *modus ponens* form of reasoning in propositional logic). A refutatory argumentation schema consists of a *particular kind
of constellation* relating to an expressed opinion, this time a constellation
designed to refute the expressed opinion (cf. the *modus tollens* form of
reasoning in propositional logic).

The question is now when an argumentation schema may be regarded as
conventional. In our definition of convention we named three conditions
which have to be fulfilled before we can say that convention of usage exists.
Before we go through these conditions one by one in connection with
convincing, let us first outline the initial situation. A speaker S tries to
convince a listener L of the acceptability or unacceptability of the expressed
opinion O by means of the constellation of statements $S_1, S_2 (, \ldots, S_n)$, which
constitutes an illocutionary act complex of *argumentation*. For the sake of
simplicity we shall assume that the argumentation is part of a discussion
serving the interactional purpose of obtaining a resolution of a dispute
involving S and L concerning an expressed opinion O.

The *first condition* that has to be fulfilled by the action schema of the
constellation of statements $S_1, S_2 (, \ldots, S_n)$ according to our definition of
convention, is that this argumentation schema represents a *regularity* in the
usage of the members of the community of language users, of whom S and L
are two. Since so far no theory of argumentation has been developed to
provide a satisfactory and complete description of the argumentation schemata used in particular communities of language users, it is far from possible
in every case to tell whether this condition has been met or not.

In spite of this, however, there are a number of argumentation schemata that can easily be demonstrated as being used in a particular community, such as the best known valid argument forms (or colloquial variants of them) in propositional logic. Nor is it implausible that the argumentation schemata discerned by Perelman and Olbrechts-Tyteca (1971) should be actually used regularly in practice. However, because of the imperfections in the way Perelman and Olbrechts-Tyteca define and classify them, it is not such a simple matter to demonstrate this (cf. Van Eemeren, Grootendorst & Kruiger 1983, ch. 5). But for our purposes this is no great obstacle, since it is at any rate clear that argumentation does contain a number of argumentation schemata that occur regularly.

The *second condition* that has to be fulfilled by the action schema of the constellation of statements S_1, S_2 $(, \ldots, S_n)$ according to our definition of convention is that the occurrence of the argumentation schema is *expected* by the members of the community of language users. To a certain extent this will always be the case. If we do not interpret *expect* so narrowly that it means 'predict', and if we allow for expecting not implying that the language users consciously await a particular schema, then it might be maintained that language users trying to resolve a dispute about an expressed opinion by means of argumentation are prepared (by the nature of the discussion and their experience of argumentation) for the use by their co-discussants of particular argumentation schemata, so that in that sense they expect the use of those argumentation schemata.

Support for this proposition may be found (for example) in the fact that language users sometimes (successfully) *anticipate* the argumentation of others, and in the fact that descriptions of argumentation schemata, even if they are as defective as those given by Perelman and Olbrechts-Tyteca, in very many cases possess a high degree of *recognizability*. However, it is also necessary to remark that in discussions in colloquial speech (in contrast to the regimented discussions such as described by writers like Lorenzen, Lorenz, Barth & Krabbe and other dialecticians[24]) there is usually not, as the second condition demands, a possibility of indicating in what case *a particular argumentation schema* may be expected and in what case another one. In any event we think it is permissible to conclude that the use of argumentation schemata to some extent accords with language users' expectations.

The *third condition* that has to be fulfilled by the action schema of the constellation of statements S_1, S_2 $(, \ldots, S_n)$ according to our definition of convention is that the members of the community *prefer* to use this argumentation schema in cases in which it will resolve a particular interactional problem. As we have already observed, far from all the argumentation schemata used in a community of language users have been satisfactorily and fully described, but this does not alter the fact that language users wishing to resolve an interactional problem such as a dispute about an expressed opinion will always have to prefer sound argumentation schemata. Thus the answer to the question of whether the third condition has been fulfilled in a given case depends on how the language users concerned judge the soundness of the argumentation schema used in the illocutionary act complex.

Of course, an argumentation schema that one group of language users regards as sound may be regarded as unsound or even as a *fallacy* by another group of language users. This means that the two groups judge the problem-solving capacity of the argumentation schema concerned differently. In such a case one might also say that the two groups of language users start from different *conceptions of rationality*. If differences of this kind occur in respect of more than one point, one might even ask oneself whether, as regards argumentation, the two groups must not be treated as two different *communities*.

It is not necessarily the case that the norms applied by language users in practice when evaluating argumentation display more differences than similarities. In practice, language users turn out to be more often in agreement than in disagreement as regards the question of whether a particular argumentation is sound or not, at least in so far as their judgement relates to the argumentation schema used. We believe that we may draw the conclusion that it is always true that members of a community of language users wishing to resolve a dispute about an expressed opinion – irrespective of whether they are acting as speaker or listener – will prefer argumentation schemata that are adequate to solve the interactional problem concerned, and that in many cases they will also agree about which argumentation schemata meet this criterion.

To summarize we must conclude that it is impossible to make any *final* pronouncement about the conventionality of the perlocution *convince*. There are still too many uncertain factors for that. However, we can say that in any event the perlocution *convince* may be regarded as conventional in the sense that in the attempt to achieve the perlocutionary effect of the listener being convinced of the acceptability or unacceptability of an expressed opinion argumentation schemata are employed which meet all three of the stated conditions for conventionality. These argumentation schemata do, after all, constitute *regularities* in the usage of language users trying together to resolve a dispute, the language users *expect* these argumentation schemata to be used and they would *prefer* to resolve disputes with their help.

Whether the perlocutionary effect that the listener is convinced of the acceptability or unacceptability of the expressed opinion to which the argumentation relates actually occurs, depends on various factors, one of which is the listener's assessment of the *soundness* of the argumentation schema being used in the argumentation. Here there is an important problem, because it is not yet clear precisely *which* argumentation schemata are regarded as sound by language users or (seen from a normative angle) which argumentation schemata *ought* to be regarded as sound. What *is* clear, however, is that the soundness of argumentation schemata is also to some extent conventionally determined or must at least be partly tied to conventions, so that the occurrence or non-occurrence of the perlocutionary effect of a listener being convinced by a particular argumentation is also dependent on conventions.[25]

3.5. EXTERNALIZATION OF THE PERLOCUTIONARY EFFECT OF CONVINCING

In the preceding sections we have tried to make it plausible that *convincing* is in principle a conventional perlocution designed to use certain argumentation schemata to convince the listener of a particular point of view in respect of a particular expressed opinion, i.e. of the acceptability or unacceptability of that expressed opinion. However, we have not yet indicated exactly what this perlocutionary effect entails. In this section we hope to clarify this point by reference to a *happy* illucutionary perlocution of *arguing/convincing*.

It is not our intention simply to equate the acceptance or non-acceptance of an expressed opinion with 'being convinced' in the full psychological sense of the term. *Acceptance*, to us, is not a state of mind to be compared with a belief in its complexity and intensity. The acceptance or non-acceptance of an expressed opinion is a perlocutionary effect intended by the speaker, brought about by means of an illocutionary perlocution, and based partly on rational considerations by the listener. This perlocutionary effect is inherent in the success of the illocutionary perlocution of *arguing/convincing*. It amounts to no more nor less than *agreeing* to the point of view defended in the argumentation. Thus our term *accept* has a lesser extension than the expression 'be convinced' may have in colloquial idiom, and it is free of any psychological (and philosophical) connotations. In figure 3.1 we try to illustrate the relationship between 'accept/not accept' and 'hold a conviction' figuratively.

Nor is it our intention to treat the acceptance or non-acceptance of an expressed opinion solely as an 'inner' matter that is the listener's business, as the term *acceptance* might perhaps suggest. In this respect the term *accept* already has something to offer that *be convinced* does not have. The latter expression can only relate to *states of mind*, which by their very nature are not observable and can only be expressed by indirect means. A listener accepting or not accepting an expressed opinion can express this directly by acting in his turn as speaker and performing the illocutionary act of *accepting* or *rejecting* (the expressed opinion).

It is, of course, possible for the listener to show that as a result of the speaker's argumentation a certain conviction has arisen in his mind, and this can be an *optimal* consequence desired by the speaker. In that case the consecutive consequence of the speaker's speech act might then be that the listener makes a certain choice, manifests a particular attitude or displays a certain 'involvement'. By contrast, a conviction or belief, which is more than and goes deeper than the *acceptance* or *rejection* of an expressed opinion, *cannot be turned into a fact* by uttering a performative formula like 'I hereby accept'.

One important reason for seeking *externalization* of convincing effects is that by making his *acceptance* or *rejection* known, a person who accepts or rejects an expressed opinion explicitly makes it plain that he *regards himself as committed*, positively or negatively, to that expressed opinion. In interac-

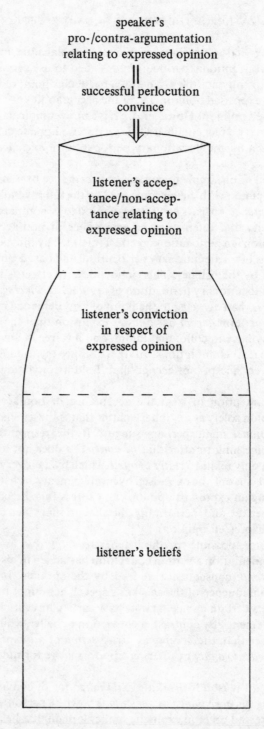

Figure 3.1. Acceptance/non-acceptance as the cream on the milk.

tion that does not involve a lack of commitment, such a plain statement is a great advantage, even though acceptance, as Popper (1972:142-3) has stressed in connection with scientific theories, must in principle never be regarded as an unshakeable and everlastingly valid datum, automatically precluding all further discussion of the expressed opinion concerned. Nevertheless, until or unless he revokes his standpoint a person who has *expressis verbis* accepted or rejected an expressed opinion *can always be held* to that acceptance or rejection. This is true (assuming at least that he was not acting under duress) even if 'in reality' he is not (in whatever sense) convinced (or gives others the impression that he is not).

Acceptance or rejection of an expressed opinion may be entirely by non-verbal means (e.g. by nodding or shaking the head), but it may also be by verbal means *by performing the illocutionary act of accepting or rejecting*. Where verbal externalization is to be consistent this last *must* happen, because only then is it unambiguously clear to what a person is committed.

The utterance by which the listener (now acting as speaker) makes known his acceptance or rejection has the illocutionary force of a *commissive*, since the illocutionary purpose of *accept* and *reject* is of course to *commit* the speaker positively or negatively to the propositional content of his utterance, the direction of fit is *from-world-to-words* and the sincerity condition relates to the speaker's *intention* (cf. Searle 1979:14-15).

In the last lecture in *How to Do Things with Words*, Austin, who like us regards *accept* as an illocution, ranks acceptance with the *expositives*, but he also observes of this category that some of the illocutions included in it might equally justifiably have been placed in other categories. According to him, *accept* (and some other illocutions) might also have been considered for the category of the *commissives*, which includes, for example, *promise* (1976:162). We find this latter classification more satisfactory because *accept* has in common with *promise* and other commissives that the illocutionary purpose is in a specific manner *to commit the speaker to a particular proposition*.

The way in which this committedness is brought about can best be illustrated by listing the conditions applying to the illocutions *accept* and *reject*. The *propositional content condition* we believe to be that the speech utterance in which the acceptance or rejection is expressed must have as its propositional content the opinion to which the argumentation relates. The *essential condition* is that the utterance must count as an acceptance or rejection of the expressed opinion, i.e. as an expression of agreement with the standpoint of the person advancing the argumentation and hence as an expression of the success of the attempt to convince.

The correctness conditions for acceptance and rejection are, *mutatis mutandis*, the same. The *preparatory condition* is that the person performing the illocution must believe that the person performing the illocutionary act complex of *argumentation* is thereby making a serious attempt to convince him of the acceptability or unacceptability of an expressed opinion, in other words that the essential condition for the performance of that illocution has been fulfilled. In these cases the *sincerity conditions* decree that the speaker believe that the propositions expressed in the argumentation are acceptable, that the argumentative constellation is a justification or refutation of the expressed opinion and that on these grounds the expressed opinion must be accepted or rejected, as the case may be.

The committedness created by a happy performance of the illocutionary perlocution *argue/convince* leading to the performance of the illocution *accept* or *reject* is founded on the assumption that the correctness conditions have been met, in exactly the same way as in the case of the illocutionary act complex *argumentation*. With all illocutions, the sincerity conditions see to it that the speaker can be held to the responsibility that he has taken upon himself with his utterance. Whether he realy believes it is in the present context not relevant. If the recognizability conditions have been fulfilled, the speaker can be held liable for the illocution concerned, and this implies that the listener is entitled to assume that the preparatory condition and sincerity conditions have been met. The performance of the illocution of *acceptance* or the illocution of *rejection* always endows the listener with certain rights and imposes upon the speaker certain obligations. The chief of these, in this case, is that the listener may hold the speaker to his standpoint regarding the expressed opinion.

One might say that the listener who, following a successful performance of the illocutionary perlocution *argue/convince*, takes his turn to act as speaker and performs the illocution of *acceptance* or *rejection, may be deemed*, on the grounds of the sincerity conditions applying to those illocutions, to have a certain 'conviction', since his listener (the original speaker) is entitled to reprove him on anything he may then say or do that is contrary to his professed standpoint. Thus the *consequences* of performing the illocution *accept* or *reject* are more clearly defined than those of holding an 'uncommitted' belief. Another important difference is that the acceptance or rejection of an expressed opinion consists exclusively of the verbal externalization, that is to say *making known*, of agreement with the point of view defended in the argumentation in respect of an expressed opinion, and does not necessarily presuppose a particular state of mind.

We consider the perlocutionary effect *acceptance* or *rejection* of the successful associated perlocution *argue/convince* to be exclusively a form of agreement with the point of view defended in the argumentation, and assume further that this agreement is expressed verbally by the performance of the illocution of *acceptance* or *rejection* (of the expressed opinion to which the point of view relates). Fig. 3.2 sets out the links between the occurrence of these two perlocutionary effects and the performance of the illocution *pro-argumentation* or *contra-argumentation* where there is a successful performance of the illocutionary perlocution *argue/convince*.

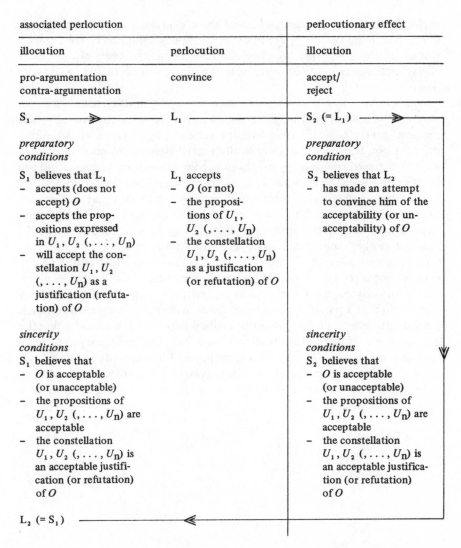

associated perlocution		perlocutionary effect
illocution	perlocution	illocution
pro-argumentation contra-argumentation	convince	accept/ reject

$S_1 \longrightarrow\!\!\!\!> \quad L_1 \longrightarrow \quad S_2 (= L_1) \longrightarrow\!\!\!\!>$

preparatory conditions

S_1 believes that L_1
- accepts (does not accept) O
- accepts the propositions expressed in $U_1, U_2 (,\ldots, U_n)$
- will accept the constellation $U_1, U_2 (,\ldots, U_n)$ as a justification (refutation) of O

L_1 accepts
- O (or not)
- the propositions of $U_1, U_2 (,\ldots, U_n)$
- the constellation $U_1, U_2 (,\ldots, U_n)$ as a justification (or refutation) of O

preparatory condition

S_2 believes that L_2
- has made an attempt to convince him of the acceptability (or unacceptability) of O

sincerity conditions

S_1 believes that
- O is acceptable (or unacceptable)
- the propositions of $U_1, U_2 (,\ldots, U_n)$ are acceptable
- the constellation $U_1, U_2 (,\ldots, U_n)$ is an acceptable justification (or refutation) of O

sincerity conditions

S_2 believes that
- O is acceptable (or unacceptable)
- the propositions of $U_1, U_2 (,\ldots, U_n)$ are acceptable
- the constellation $U_1, U_2 (,\ldots, U_n)$ is an acceptable justification (or refutation) of O

$L_2 (= S_1) \longleftarrow\!\!\!\!<$

Figure 3.2. A successful illocutionary perlocution argue/convince with verbally externalized convincing effect.

If there were no consensus at all in a community of language users in respect of the soundness of argumentation schemata, i.e. the argumentation schemata that can help to solve the interactional problem brought about by a dispute about an expressed opinion, then it would never be possible to reach a solution of the problem, since the speaker would then not know how to move the listener to perform the illocutionary act *accept* or *reject*, and the listener would not know in what circumstances he had to perform one or other of those acts.

In practice, however, we find that in many cases language users are in fact perfectly capable of bringing disputes about expressed opinions to a resolution. Assuming that these are not simply phoney solutions arrived at by a wholly irrational process, we conclude that the performance of the illocutionary act of *acceptance* or *rejection* is in practice subject to certain conventions.

It is evident, too, that language users engaging in discussion with one another also assume in principal that the acceptance or rejection of expressed opinions on the basis of argumentation is bound by certain conventions: if they did not, they would automatically regard attempts to resolve disputes about expressed opinions by means of argumentation as pointless, and the practice of discussion does anything but provide grounds for supposing that this is what happens. However, it is also easily established that the conventions governing the acceptance or rejection of expressed opinions not only often remain implicit but are also far from always clearly laid down, while in some cases they appear not to be shared by all language users. As far as argumentative conventions are concerned, perhaps we ought to distinguish between separate sub-communities within a community of language users.

It frequently happens that speakers (and their supporters) believe they may claim that a particular expressed opinion must be accepted or rejected, whereas the listeners believe that this claim is unjustified. We believe that the only way of improving this situation is for argumentation theory to provide language users with the tools by which they will be enabled to identify and solve the problems that present themselves in the resolution of disputes about expressed opinions. In the following chapters we shall try to make a contribution to this.

Chapter 4

Argumentation in discussions about expressed opinions

4.1. PROBLEMS OF ANALYSING ARGUMENTATIVE DISCUSSIONS

Besides the illocutionary act complex of *argumentation* an argumentative discussion may also contain a wide variety of other speech acts. It is far from always immediately obvious what contribution these speech acts make to the resolution of the dispute at the heart of the discussion. This can only be established through an analysis of the discussion. However, in the practice of argumentation such an analysis presents certain difficulties, and we shall therefore have to indicate how these may be adequately solved. We shall make it our purpose to draw up guidelines for the analysis of argumentative discussions (*aim 3*).

We approach argumentation in the functionalizing, externalizing, social-izing and dialectifying way introduced in chapter 1. Every discussion in which argumentation is employed in an attempt to resolve a dispute about an expressed opinion we regard as an *argumentative discussion*.

While it is true that the speech act *argumentation* plays a crucial role in argumentative discussions, it is not the only speech act capable of being performed in such discussions, nor is it the only one capable of contributing to the resolution of the dispute at the heart of the discussion. This means that in order to be able to carry out a proper analysis of an argumentative discussion one has to have an insight into the moves that have to be made for the resolution of disputes and into the nature of the speech acts that may play a part in this.

The *first* problem that has to be solved for the analysis of argumentative discussions is that a discussion may centre on *a dispute of greater or lesser complexity*. In the simplest case the dispute relates to a single expressed opinion concerning which only one standpoint has been advanced. Doubt must then be cast on this standpoint, otherwise there is no dispute. Things immediately become more complicated as soon as one language user ad-vances one point of view regarding the expressed opinion and the other language user then puts forward a different point of view regarding the same expressed opinion.

More complicated still are cases in which more than on expressed opinion is being discussed. It may be that these expressed opinions have absolutely nothing to do with each other, in which case we are actually dealing with separate disputes which as it were just happen to present themselves for discussion simultaneously. However, it may also be the case that the expressed opinions (or some of them) are related in some way: for example, one expressed opinion may be a denial of another. Furthermore it is also possible that the language user who takes a positive attitude to one expressed opinion takes a negative attitude to another, and that the converse is true of another language user. In such cases we refer to a complex dispute.

Disputes can vary in complexity in various ways, and depending on the complexity of the dispute at the centre of the discussion the discussion conducted to resolve it will also be of a greater or lesser complexity. As Barth and Krabbe have indicated (1982), disputes may be categorized according to their complexity. Argumentative discussions can be categorized in analogous manner. This means that in order to make an analysis of argumentative discussions possible we shall first have to answer the following question:

(1) *What standard types of argumentative discussion is it necessary to distinguish in connection with the resolution of disputes?*

The second difficulty is that the argumentation advanced in an argumentative discussion may have *a structure of greater or lesser complexity*. Argumentation is advanced in order to justify or refute an expressed opinion, but not every pro-argumentation or contra-argumentation stands entirely alone. One argumentative act complex may support or complement another, and it may be only together that they constitute a complete attempt at justification or refutation. This implies that a proper assessment of the argumentation put forward in an argumentative discussion is only possible after it has first been established how the various argumentative act complexes that are performed in the discussion are related.

Establishing the relationships between the argumentative act complexes that together form a complete attempt at justification or refutation amounts to explicitizing the structure of the argumentation put forward by the language user fulfilling the role of protagonist of the standpoint defended in the argumentation in respect of the expressed opinion. The argumentation advanced may be variously structured, so that in an analysis of an argumentative discussion it is necessary to give a characterization of the argumentation structures present in the discussion. This means that to make an analysis of argumentative discussions possible we shall have to answer the following question:

(2) *What argumentation structures is it necessary to distinguish in connection with the resolution of disputes?*

The *third* difficulty is that the discussion may include performances of *various kinds of speech act*, and not all these speech acts need necessarily contribute to the resolution of the dispute at the centre of the discussion. In the first instance one might suppose the prototype of an argumentative discussion to be a dialogue in which nothing but *argumentative* speech acts were performed, but this is not the case. Not only do such dialogues not occur, they would not lead to the resolution of disputes about expressed opinions even if they did.

To be able to bring disputes about expressed opinions to a resolution, non-argumentative speech acts have to be performed as well as argumentative ones. Not only are non-argumentative speech acts indispensable for the externalization of the dispute and the conclusion of the discussion, they are also necessary for eliciting argumentation and reacting to argumentation. In addition, the precizations of expressed opinions (and premisses) recommended by Naess (1966) can also be of vital help in resolving disputes. So non-argumentative speech acts certainly need not necessarily be intrusive or irrelevant in a discussion.

Of course it is not the case that all non-argumentative speech acts always contribute to the resolution of a dispute. Some may fulfil a constructive role and others not, and speech acts which are rational at one stage of the process of resolution need not necessarily be so at another stage. This means that to make an analysis of argumentative discussions possible we shall have to answer the following question:

(3) *What speech acts can contribute to the resolution of disputes about expressed opinions and at what stages of the discussion may they be performed?*

The *fourth* difficulty is that in discussions in colloquial language the illocutionary force of speech acts is often not indicated explicitly, and it is not always immediately obvious *what illocutionary force* must be attributed to a speech act. As we have already observed in chapter 2, the illocutionary force of the act complex *argumentation* is not expressed by a performative formula. Recognition of this speech act will have to depend on other pointers, e.g. the presence of illocutionary indicators such as 'so', 'because' and 'for' (none of which, however, can offer a watertight guarantee that the speech act actually is argumentation).

Similar problems of interpretation can in principle occur (to a greater or lesser extent) with other speech acts. Because the resolution of disputes about expressed opinions depends partly on the illocutionary force allotted to speech acts and the role in the discussion that these speech acts are regarded as having on that basis, it will be useful to indicate how these problems of interpretation may be solved. This means that to make an analysis of argumentative discussions possible we shall have to answer the following question:

(4) *How may problems of interpreting speech acts in argumentative discussions best be solved?*

These four questions will be tackled in chapters 4 and 5. In section 4.2 we identify four standard types of argumentative discussion and show that the starting point of an analysis of such discussions must be the *simple single discussion*. In section 4.3 we identify four *stages of discussion* in a simple single discussion and indicate which *argumentation structures* must be distinguished in the stage of the discussion that is most crucial to the resolution of a dispute. In sections 5.1-4 we show what *speech acts* may contribute to the resolution of a dispute and how they are *distributed* over the various stages of the discussion. In section 5.5 we discuss how *problems in interpreting* speech acts in rational discussions can be solved.

4.2. SIMPLE SINGLE DISCUSSIONS

4.2.1. *Standard types of disputes and argumentative discussions*

Disputes in which expressed opinions are externalized always involve at least two language users who have committed themselves in different ways to the expressed opinions under discussion. It is a characteristic of a dispute that at least one point of view is always advanced that is not shared by the parties to the dispute. However, it is also possible for a dispute to be appreciably more complicated than that, and the complexity of a dispute may be further characterized by establishing exactly what standpoints are adopted when the dispute arises. We shall clarify this with the help of an example.

Suppose three people hear someone on television propound the view that women have a logic of their own; suppose also that the three people, having heard this view propounded, embark upon a (serious) discussion of the question 'Have women a logic of their own?' One of them then says 'In my opinion it is true that women have a logic of their own', the seconds says 'In my opinion it is not true that women have a logic of their own', and the third says 'I do not know whether or not it is true that women have a logic of their own'.[26]
    The question of whether women have their own logic has now led to three explicit reactions, no two of which are the same. The first is an assertion in which the question is answered in the *affirmative*, the second is an assertion in which the question is answered in the *negative*, and the third is neither an assertion in which the question is answered affirmatively nor an assertion in which the question is answered negatively, and is in fact *not an answer* to the question at all.
    The three speech acts with which the language users in this example react to the question constitute three different reactions to the expressed opinion 'Women have a logic of their own'. In all three cases there are references to *women*, to which is attributed the predicate that *they have a logic of their own*. This means that these three speech acts have the same *propositional content*. The expressed opinion to which the three reactions relate is thus the *common* propositional content of the speech acts whereby these reactions are express-

ed. Different reactions to an expressed opinion functioning as a common propositional content may be regarded as different *points of view* in respect of that expressed opinion.

If we abbreviate the *expressed opinion* in respect of which language users adopt an attitude as O, it is then possible to identify three possible *attitudes to O*: a *positive* point of view, a *negative* point of view and a *zero* point of view. In our example the first language user takes a positive attitude to O, the second a negative and the third a zero attitude. We shall abbreviate the three possible attitudes as follows:

(a) *positive point of view:* $+/O$
(b) *negative point of view:* $-/O$
(c) *zero point of view:* $\emptyset/O$

If a language user advances a positive point of view in respect of O, then he is further *positively committed to O* and if he advances a negative point of view he is *negatively committed to O* (unless he revokes his positive or negative point of view). A language user adopting a zero attitude to O is *not committed to O either positively or negatively*.

Thus we can only speak of an externalized *dispute about an expressed opinion* if at least one language user has committed himself to that expressed opinion either positively or negatively by advancing a positive or negative point of view in respect of it and if at least one language user has explicitly made it known that he *does not subscribe* to that point of view or at least *has expressed doubt as to its acceptability*. We shall assume from now on that these conditions have been met.

This does not necessarily mean, it should be stressed here, that for a dispute about an expressed opinion to arise *two different points of view* concerning the expressed opinion must have been propounded. For a dispute about an expressed opinion it is sufficient (*and* necessary) for *one* point of view to be expressed and for this then to have doubts expressed about it (generally by a different language user). If none of the language users expresses doubt about the point of view expressed by another language user, this situation can never arise and there is no question of a dispute about an expressed opinion.

So a dispute only exists if a language user has propounded a view and *doubt is subsequently expressed* about the acceptability of that view. How strong this doubt is and exactly how it is expressed is immaterial to the initiation of the dispute. The possibilities vary from expressions of uncertainty such as 'I'm not quite so sure about that' or 'I don't think I quite agree with you on that' to uncompromising rejections such as 'What on earth makes you think that?' or 'That's absolute rubbish'.

In practise, however, a dispute will often involve the propounding of more than one *different* point of view. A language user who does not entirely subscribe to the positive attitude to the expressed opinion 'Women have a logic of their own' is easily tempted to oppose it with the negative attitude that it is not true that women have a logic of their own.

Reacting to the expressed views of others often goes hand in hand with propounding points of view relating to *other* expressed opinions, e.g. the view that women attach more importance to feelings. The situation is then as follows:

> *Point of view language user 1:* $+/O_1$
> *Point of view language user 2:* $-/O_1$; $+/O_2$

O_1 here is an abbreviation of the expressed opinion 'Women have a logic of their own' and O_2 of the expressed opinion 'Women attach more importance to feelings'. It will be clear that this does not exhaust the possibilities. For example, language user 1 may go on to adopt a positive attitude to the expressed opinion 'Women's logic is more natural than men's' (O_3). Even more complicated, but no less realistic, is a situation in which each language user sets the opposite point of view against every point of view advanced by the other. In our example it would look like this:

> *Point of view language user 1:* $+/O_1$; $-/O_2$; $+/O_3$
> *Point of view language user 2:* $-/O_1$; $+/O_2$; $-/O_3$

Disputes can vary in complexity in different ways, and because the complexity of a dispute has implications for the discussion to be conducted in order to resolve it, we believe a distinction has to be made between different types of dispute. We shall here identify four *standard types of dispute*.

In the first place, we believe, it is necessary to differentiate between *single* and *multiple* disputes. Single disputes have to do with *one and no more than one expressed opinion* and *multiple* disputes have to do with *more than one expressed opinion*. Multiple disputes can always be broken down into a number of different single disputes. For example, the multiple dispute in the last example about women and logic is composed of three single disputes, the first of which relates to O_1, the second to O_2 and the third to O_3.

Second, we believe it is necessary when analysing disputes to distinguish between *simple* and *compound* disputes. In simple disputes only *one (positive or negative) point of view* is advanced in respect of an expressed opinion and in compound disputes *two different points of view* (one positive and one negative) are propounded in respect of one and the same expressed opinion.

In the last example the three single disputes are all compound, so that we may refer to a *compound multiple dispute*. Besides compound multiple disputes it is also possible for *simple multiple disputes, compound single disputes* and *simple single disputes* to occur.

Simple single disputes, in which a single positive or negative point of view in respect of a single expressed opinion is advanced (and has doubt cast on it) represent the *basic form* of dispute. All the other standard types of dispute can be analysed as a *composite* of simple single disputes. If we indicate the expression of doubt with a question mark we can then characterize the two variants of the basic form of a dispute as follows:

(a)*Language user 1: +/O*
   Language user 2: (?)/(+/O)
(b)*Language user 1: –/O*
   Language user 2: (?)/(–/O)

It is important to realize that the doubt expressed by a language user in a dispute does not bear directly on the expressed opinion but on the *point of view or attitude* expressed by another language user *in respect of* the expressed opinion. Perhaps it is also important here to observe once more that expressing doubt, while it may *accompany* the adoption of the opposite attitude, *is not identical* to propounding the opposite point of view. In variant (a) of the basic form of dispute, for example, language user 2 does not *necessarily* have to take the view *–/O* and in variant (b) he does not *necessarily* have to adopt attitude *+/O*. *Automatically to attribute to him his own point of view in respect of O* would be to suppose erroneously that *disputes must always be compound.*

4.2.2. *The resolution of simple single disputes*

Language users who have externalized a difference of opinion and have embarked on a dispute about an expressed opinion could, of course, leave it at that, but very often they will undertake an attempt to *resolve* the dispute. Disputes are resolved when the language users who have expressed doubt about points of view have withdrawn these expressions of doubt or when the language users who have advanced points of view retract those points of view.

   If two language users wish to resolve a dispute by means of an argumentative discussion, one of them must challenge the other to defend his point of view by verbal means and the language user advancing the point of view concerned must accept the challenge. That is to say, the last language user in the discussion assumes the role of *protagonist* of the point of view concerned and his challenger assumes the role of *antagonist*. The dispute is then resolved when either the antagonist explicitly drops his doubts and accepts the protagonist's point of view, or the protagonist explicitly relinquishes his point of view.

To be able to establish exactly when this situation occurs (or ought to occur), it is necessary to make a number of distinctions in respect of the *discussion* being conducted by a protagonist and antagonist. These distinctions parallel those that we earlier made with regard to disputes. Thus *single* discussions may be distinguished from *multiple* ones, and *compound* discussions from *simple* ones. A single discussion is one designed to resolve a single dispute, and so on.

Discussions aimed at resolving disputes about expressed opinions can (analogously with the categories of disputes) be divided into four *standard types*: *simple single discussions, simple multiple discussions, compound single discussions* and *compound multiple discussions*. The basic form of discussion is a *simple single discussion*, in which *one and only one point of view in respect of one and only one expressed opinion is attacked and defended*. All other standard types of discussion can be broken down into a *composite* of simple single discussions.

In a simple single discussion a language user acting as a protagonist is the protagonist of *one point of view only*, and the same applies, *mutatis mutandis*, to a language user acting as antagonist, in respect of his *doubt* concerning this point of view. The protagonist's task is to *defend* this point of view (and no other) and the antagonist's job is to *attack* the same point of view (and no other). Since these attacks and defences are aimed at *solving* the dispute about the expressed opinion under discussion, the statements made by the protagonist and antagonist in an argumentative discussion must be designed to bring about agreement on the question of whether the expressed opinion concerned *is acceptable or not*.

This implies that the antagonist's attacks consist in principle of statements calculated to elicit argumentation in favour of the protagonist's point of view and that that argumentation is then (or may be) called into question. It also implies that the protagonist's defences consist in principle of statements advancing argumentation in favour of his point of view and in favour of the argumentation attacked. In a simple single discussion only the language user acting as protagonist advances a point of view, not the language user acting as antagonist. Only the protagonist advances argumentation.

Advancing argumentation for a point of view amounts to making statements in support of that point of view. Depending on whether the protagonist adopts a *positive* or a *negative* attitude, the statements that he advances in defence of his point of view will be either *pro-argumentation* or *contra-argumentation*. The antagonist elicits from the protagonist in a simple single discussion either pro- or contra-argumentation and may then in turn cast doubt on it. The antagonist himself puts forward *neither pro-argumentation nor contra-argumentation*.

In the case of pro-argumentation the protagonist tries to convince the antagonist of the *acceptability* of an expressed opinion by attempting to *justify* the expressed opinion by performing the illocutionary act complex of *argumentation*. In the case of contra-argumentation the protagonist tries to convince the antagonist of the *unacceptability* of an expressed opinion by attempting to *refute* the expressed opinion again by performing the illocutionary act complex of *argumentation* (cf. chapters 2 and 3).

We can now indicate more precisely when disputes about expressed opinions are *resolved*. For a *simple single dispute* this is the case when and only when the antagonist explicitly *accepts* the expressed opinion to which the protagonist takes a positive attitude or the protagonist *no longer accepts* the same expressed opinion, or if the antagonist explicitly *rejects* the expressed opinion to which the protagonist takes a negative attitude or the protagonist *no longer rejects* the same expressed opinion.

A dispute is resolved *in favour of the protagonist* if the antagonist decides to adopt the same attitude as that advanced by the protagonist at the start of the discussion. In the case of pro-argumentation this means that both the protagonist and the antagonist now have a *positive attitude* with regard to the expressed opinion, and in the case of contra-argumentation it means that they both have a *negative attitude*. In either case the perlocutionary effect that the protagonist was trying to achieve with his argumentation has been brought about.

A dispute is resolved *in favour of the antagonist* if the protagonist retracts the view that he propounded at the start of the discussion. In the case of pro-argumentation this means that the protagonist *no longer takes a positive attitude* in respect of the expressed opinion and in the case of contra-argumentation that he *no longer takes a negative attitude*. However, this does not necessarily mean that he now has a *negative* or *positive* point of view respectively: he may also have a *zero point of view* (cf. section 8.2). This last is the perlocutionary effect associated with a succesful attack by the antagonist.

All disputes can be broken down into one or more simple single disputes and all discussions can be broken down into one or more simple single discussions aimed at resolving such disputes. This means that in principle the distinctions we have drawn are part of the toolkit needed for the analysis of discussions. The toolkit is not yet sufficient to solve *all* the problems that may present themselves in the analysing of discussions, but it does already provide us with the means of reaching a satisfactory solution to the first of the problems that we identified in section 4.1. Figure 4.1 summarizes the distinctions we have made so far.

Using these distinctions we can now formulate the following guidelines for the analysis of discussions:

(1) *Establish what expressed opinions are the subject of dispute.*
(2) *Establish what simple single disputes constitute these disputes.*
(3) *Establish which simple single disputes are the point at issue in the discussion.*
(4) *Establish whether the points of view advanced and called into question in the discussion are positive or negative.*
(5) *Establish which language users in the discussion fulfil the roles of protagonist and antagonist in respect of these points of view.*
(6) *Establish to what extent the disputes are resolved in the discussion and whether they are settled in favour of the protagonist or the antagonist.*

EXPRESSED OPINION *O*

point of view	positive: +/*O*	negative: –/*O*	zero: ∅/*O*
dispute			
LANGUAGE USER 1	+/*O*	–/*O*	
LANGUAGE USER 2	(?)/(+/*O*)	(?)/(–/*O*)	
decision to embark on discussion			
LANGUAGE USER 1	PROTAGONIST P of view +/*O*	PROTAGONIST P of view –/*O*	
LANGUAGE USER 2	ANTAGONIST A of view +/*O*	ANTAGONIST A of view –/*O*	
discussion			
PROTAGONIST P	*defends* view +/*O* = attemps to *justify O* = advances *pro-argumentation* for *O* = attempts to *convince* A of *acceptability* of *O*	defends view –/*O* = attempts to *refute O* = advances *contra-argumentation* against *O* = attempts to *convince* A of *unacceptability* of *O*	
ANTAGONIST A	*attacks* view +/*O* = draws P into *pro-argumentation* for *O* (&) *attacks* pro-argumentation for *O*	*attacks* view –/*O* = draws P into *contra-argumentation* against *O* (&) *attacks* contra-argumentation against *O*	
resolution of the dispute			
in favour of P	successful *defence* of view +/*O* = Language user 1 *maintains* view +/*O* & Language user 2 *retracts doubt* about view +/*O* and *accepts O*	successful *defence* of view –/*O* = Language user 1 *maintains* view –/*O* & Language user 2 *retracts doubt* about view –/*O* and *rejects O*	
in favour of A	successful *attack* on view +/*O* = Language user 2 *maintains doubt* about view +/*O* & Language user 1 *retracts* view +/*O* and no longer calls *O* acceptable	successful *attack* on view –/*O* = Language user 2 *maintains doubt* about view –/*O* & Language user 1 *retracts* view –/*O* and no longer calls *O* acceptable	

Figure 4.1. Overview of a simple single discussion.

4.3. THE STRUCTURE OF SIMPLE SINGLE DISCUSSIONS

4.3.1. *The stages of the discussion*

As we observed at the end of the previous section, the toolkit we have developed so far is not sufficient to solve *all* the problems that may present themselves in the analysis of argumentative discussions. In a proper analysis of an argumentative discussion it is important not only to establish what simple single disputes are at the centre of the discussion and the extent to which these disputes are resolved, but also to establish how this is done. This means that a person analysing an argumentative discussion must have an insight into the *structure* of a simple single discussion.

The analysing tool required for laying down guidelines for the structural analysis of a simple single discussion will, we believe, address itself to the various stages that can be identified in the resolving of a dispute and the structure of the argumentation advanced to help resolve it. In section 4.3.1 we discuss which *stages of discussion* correspond to the stages in the resolving of the dispute and in section 4.3.2 which *argumentation structures* it is important to identify.[27]

The confrontation stage and opening stage

A dispute arises when a language user advances a point of view and a language user (probably a different one) casts doubt on that point of view. The language users can then see that they have a dispute about an expressed opinion and may simply leave it at *identifying the dispute* (*stage 1*).

However, they may also decide to undertake an attempt to resolve the dispute by means of a discussion. This implies that one of them must be prepared to attack the point of view that occasioned the dispute and the other must be prepared to defend it. The existence of a dispute is a necessary, but not sufficient, condition for the start of a discussion. It is also necessary for there to be a language user prepared to assume the role of *protagonist* and one prepared to take on the role of *antagonist* (*stage 2*).

In the case of simple single disputes the allocation of the roles is fairly straightforward: the language user advancing the point of view will normally act as protagonist and the language user who expresses doubt will then be the antagonist. The language user advancing the point of view makes an assertion about an expressed opinion. This entitles his collocutor to challenge him to support his assertion, and this in principle imposes on him an obligation to reply to the challenge.

One *preparatory condition* for making assertions, it will be recalled, is that the speaker has evidence or arguments for what he asserts (Searle 1970:66), and according to the *maxim of quality* for the conduct of dialogues the speaker may not say anything for which he knows he has no sufficient evidence (Grice 1975:46). This means that in principle the listener is entitled to assume that the speaker believes he can remove his doubt and that in principle the speaker must make an attempt to do so if encouraged.[28]

The argumentation stage

Once the language users have established what dispute is at the centre of the discussion and have assumed the positions of protagonist and antagonist, they can start resolving the dispute by *argumentation* (*stage 3*).

This implies that the protagonist of a positive point of view will try to defend that point of view by advancing pro-argumentation to justify the expressed opinion to which his attitude relates and the protagonist of a negative point of view will try to defend it by putting forward contra-argumentation to refute the expressed opinion to which it refers. The antagonist eliciting this argumentation *can cast doubt on the constellations of statements* constituting the protagonist's argumentation (or on parts of those constellations) or, in the case of pro-argumentation, on the *justificatory potential* of those constellations, or, in the case of contra-argumentation, on their *refutatory potential*. In this way he can continue to draw the protagonist into advancing new argumentation for as long as it takes for one of the parties to be forced to abandon the position he adopted at the start of the discussion, in which case the dispute is resolved.

The argumentation advanced in the resolving of a dispute can, even in a simple single discussion, have an extremely complex structure, which is in principle determined by the reactions advanced by the antagonist or anticipated by the protagonist. To reach a resolution of the dispute it is necessary that the discussants have insight into the structure of the argumentation, for otherwise they will be unable to establish exactly what the consequences will be of the success or failure of the various attacking and defending speech acts for their assessment of the acceptability or unacceptability of the expressed opinion being discussed and for any further discussion. So analysis of the structure of the argumentation will have to be a major part of an analysis of the discussion.

The concluding stage

A discussion designed to resolve a dispute will have to be concluded with an answer to the question of whether the dispute has been *resolved* (*stage 4*).

Naturally, not every discussion will automatically lead to the resolving of the dispute, and it sometimes happens that when the discussion is over the protagonist still takes the same attitude and the antagonist still has his doubts, without either of them being open to an accusation of irrationality. Be that as it may, a discussion is never complete unless the discussants have collectively established its outcome. If this is not done, it is unclear whether the discussion has had any point.

The conclusion of a discussion does not, of course, have to be final. A discussion that has been temporarily suspended may subsequently be reopened, for example because it becomes possible to adduce new argumentation. Following the termination of a discussion it is also possible for a new discussion to arise on account of some more or less severely modified dispute relating to a modified version of the expressed opinion. In that case all four of our stages of discussion have to be gone through again. Figure 4.2 is an overview of them.

4.3.2. *The structure of the argumentation*

The third stage in a simple single discussion, the *argumentation stage*, is crucial to the resolution of a dispute and is sometimes even regarded as 'the discussion proper'. In our observations on this stage of the discussion we noted that its complexity depended on the structure of the argumentation. This means that in any analysis of an argumentative discussion it is important to establish what argumentations are advanced at this stage of the discussion and how those argumentations are related. The antagonist's reactions play an important part in the formation of a particular structure in the protagonist's argumentation and therefore deserve a little more attention.

It is possible to identify several different sorts of reaction from the antagonist. Besides the possibilities already mentioned - acceptance by the antagonist of the protagonist's argumentation, the antagonist's casting doubt on the justification or refutation potential of the protagonist's argumentation, or his expressing doubt regarding particular argumentative statements - there is also a possibility that he *will himself try to demonstrate the wrongness of an argumentative statement by the protagonist*. As soon as that happens he is no longer only the antagonist with regard to the protagonist's point of view, but has also effectively become the protagonist of a view of his own. This standpoint consists of the negation of his collocutor's statement.

The consequence of this is that from that moment onwards the discussion *is no longer simple*, though the dispute that is the *issue* of the discussion remains simple, since it does not of course follow automatically from the fact that a language user acting as antagonist adopts his own attitude to a *statement by the protagonist* that he also adopts a particular attitude of his own to the *expressed opinion at the centre of the discussion*.

In practice this situation can arise very easily, which is why it is important to take proper account of the fact that a distinction has to be made between discussions in which the issue is a simple dispute and in which the antagonist has *no view of his own* concerning argumentative statements by the protagonist, on the one hand, and discussions in which the issue is a simple dispute but in which the antagonist *has a view of his own* regarding argumentative statements by the protagonist, on the other.

In the first of these two cases the interlocutors keep rigidly to the roles they assumed when the dispute arose, so that the discussion is *consistently simple*. In the second case the allocation of roles changes, so that the discussion is *not consistently simple*. Not consistently simple discussions must not be confused with discussions that *from the outset* are compound, i.e. *wholly compound discussions*. In wholly compound (simple) discussions *both pro-argumentation and contra-argumentation* are advanced in respect of the disputed

CONFRONTATION STAGE	The externalization of a dispute (*stage 1*)
1.1	Language user 1 advances a positive or negative point of view in respect of expressed opinion *O*
1.2	Language user 2 casts doubt on this view

OPENING STAGE	The decision to conduct an argumentative discussion (*stage 2*)
2.1	Language user 2 challenges language user 1 to defend his point of view in respect of *O*
2.2	Language user 1 accepts the challenge from language user 2
2.3	Language user 1 and language user 2 decide on an attempt to resolve the dispute by means of discussion
2.4	Language user 1 and language user 2 decide who is to take the role of protagonist and who the role of antagonist in the discussion
(2.5)	(Language user 1 and language user 2 agree the rules of discussion to be followed)
(2.6)	(Language user 1 and language user 2 agree when they will regard the discussion as concluded)

ARGUMENTATION STAGE	The advancing of argumentation and reaction to it (*stage 3*)
3.1	The proptagonist advances argumentation in defence of his view
3.2	The antagonist reacts to the protagonist's argumentation by casting doubt on the constellations (or on parts of the constellations) of statements that constitute the argumentation or on the justificatory or refutatory potential of those constellations, or by accepting the argumentation
(3.3)	(The protagonist advances new argumentation in defence of his standpoint)
(3.4)	(The antagonist reacts to the protagonist's new argumentation by casting doubt on the constellations (or on parts of the constellations) of statements that constitute the argumentation or on the justificatory or refutatory potential of those constellations, or by accepting the argumentation)
(3.5)	(etc.)

CONCLUDING STAGE	Determining how the discussion ends (*stage 4*)
(a)	The dispute is resolved in the protagonist's favour
(b)	The dispute is resolved in the antagonist's favour
(c)	The dispute is unresolved but the discussion is terminated (perhaps *pro tem.*)

Figure 4.2. Stages of discussion in a simple single discussion.

expressed opinion, while in a not consistently simple discussion the argumentation that is advanced is either *exclusively pro-argumentation* (where the protagonist defends a positive point of view in respect of the expressed opinion) or *exclusively contra-argumentation* (where the protagonist defends a negative point of view).

A not consistently simple discussion does contain *contra-argumentation*, but (assuming that the protagonist is defending a positive attitude) it relates to an expressed opinion which is the expression of the propositional content of one or more of the statements making up the protagonist's argumentation, and it comes from the antagonist. A distinction should be made between *two sorts* of contra-argumentation: (1) contra-argumentation originating from a *protagonist* (in a wholly compound dispute there are *two* such protagonists) of a negative attitude to an expressed opinion that is asserted and doubted in the dispute which is at the centre of the discussion and relates to the *initial expressed opinion*, and (2) contra-argumentation coming from an *antagonist* of an attitude to an expressed opinion that is asserted and doubted in the dispute which is at the centre of the discussion and relates to *a statement advanced by the protagonist in defence of his point of view.*

In a wholly compound discussion a succesfull contra-argumentation against an initial expressed opinion means that *the positive view of that expressed opinion is refuted.* In a not consistently simple discussion a successful contra-argumentation against an argumentative statement in defence of an initial expressed opinion does not mean that the positive point of view in respect of the initial expressed opinion is refuted, but that *a pro-argumentation (or part of one) for that initial expressed opinion has been rebutted.* This is a difference of principle which, in view of the issue under discussion, is of great practical importance (and which is concealed if a discussant claims to have won the discussion on the grounds that he has rebutted part of his opponent's argumentation).[29]

Besides advancing contra-argumentation against all or part of his opponent's argumentation, a discussant can also indicate that he does not accept all or part of it. This he does by casting doubt on the statement or statements concerned or by describing them as insufficient justification or refutation. In all these cases this means that strictly speaking a *new* dispute has arisen which in turn gives rise to a *new* discussion, the outcome of which may, however, be crucial to the resolution of the original dispute.

To avoid confusion it is necessary here to introduce some terminological distinctions which will enable us in our analysis to keep the various sorts of case apart. Among the terms we have already used is *initial* (or *original*) *dispute*, which serves to differentiate disputes on which the discussion turns from disputes arising *during a discussion occasioned by an initial dipute*; these we shall term *subdisputes.*

Analogous to this distinction is the distinction between the *principal discussion*, which has to do with the original dispute, and *subdiscussions* occasioned by subdisputes. Subdisputes - and sometimes also subdiscussions - arise when a statement by the protagonist in the principal discussion is called into question by the antagonist in the principal discussion, when insuffcient justificatory or refutatory potential is ascribed to the protagonist's argumentation or when all or part of the argumentation is bombarded with contra-argumentation. In the last of these cases there is then a *compound subdispute* which can give rise to a *compound subdiscussion*. In the other cases a *simple subdispute* arises, and possibly also a *simple subdiscussion*.

Analogously to these distinctions, it is also possible in a simple single discussion to differentiate between *initial expressed opinions* and *initial points of view* (or *views* or *attitudes* or *standpoints*) on the one hand and *subordinate expressed opinions* and *subordinate points of view* (etc.) on the other. Using this distinction, it is then possible to regard the argumentation relating directly to the initial expressed opinion as the *principal argumentation* and argumentation relating to a subordinate expressed opinion as *subargumentation*.

As regards the complexity of the argumentation advanced in the course of the discussion the following possibilities exist:

(1) the argumentation consists of *one (principal) argumentation*
(2) the argumentation consists of *two or more principal argumentations* each of which in the discussion *is individually sufficient* to justify or refute the initial expressed opinion, for which however *neither is individually necessary*
(3) the argumentation consists of *two or more principal argumentations*, *each of which is individually necessary* to justify or refute the original expressed opinion, for which however they are *sufficient only in combination*
(4) the argumentation consists of *one or more principal argumentations and one or more subargumentations*

Single argumentation

In case 1 the protagonist has advanced a single pro-argumentation or contra-argumentation for or against the initial expressed opinion and has presented this argumentation as necessary and sufficient to justify or refute that expressed opinion, and the antagonist has accepted the argumentation as necessary and sufficient (or at least has not reacted to it). Here is an example:

initial expressed opinion I0: 'Women have a logic of their own'
point of view +/I0: 'I think women have a logic of their own'
expression of doubt about point of view +/I0: (?)/(+/I0)
pro-argumentation PA for I0: 'Women solve puzzles quite differently from men'

In such cases we refer to *single* argumentation. The protagonist's argumentation then displays the *basic structure*. In all other cases there is a *composite of single argumentations*, when the argumentation displays a *complex structure*.

Multiple argumentation

In case 2 the argumentations constituting the argumentative composite are both individually sufficient, but neither is by itself necessary. In fact, then, this is a series of separate and independent single argumentations for or against the same initial expressed opinion. It is, of course, necessary that at least *one* of these argumentations actually be advanced, but in principle it does not matter *which* argumentation is chosen. In this case we refer to *multiple* argumentation. An example follows:

> $+/IO$: 'He was breaking the law'
> PA_1 : 'He was on the wrong side of the road'
> PA_2 : 'He had no lights'
> PA_3 : 'He went through a red light'

Co-ordinative compound argumentation

In case 3 the single argumentations constituting the argumentative composite, unlike those in case 2, are each individually necessary and only sufficient together. In such cases we refer to *compound* argumentation. Since the single argumentations making up these compound argumentations are all principal argumentations of equivalent status, we refer here to *co-ordinative compound argumentation*. The following is an example:

> $+/IO$: 'This book has no literary qualities'
> PA_1 : 'The style is defective'
> PA_2 : 'The dialogues sound artificial'
> PA_3 : 'The plot contains no surprises'
> PA_4 : 'Little is left to the imagination'

A crucial point of difference between *multiple* argumentation and *co-ordinative compound* argumentation is that the antagonist's calling into question of statements adduced has different consequences. In the example of the traffic offence it is not necessary for the protagonist to be able to furnish evidence for all the argumentative statements he makes. If he succeeds in removing the antagonist's doubts about only *one* of his arguments, that will be enough to resolve the dispute. In the case of the book that has to manage without literary qualities this is not so. The antagonist will only be convinced, we may suppose, when the protagonist succeeds in providing evidence to support *all* his argumentative statements to the antagonist's satisfaction; removing the doubts about only one of his statements will not be enough. Multiple argumentation consists of a *disjunction* of single argumentations, while co-ordinative compound argumentation consists of a *conjunction* of single argumentations.[30]

Subordinative compound argumentation

In case 4 an attempt is made to remove the antagonist's doubt about one or more principal argumentations for or against the initial expressed opinion by advancing new argumentation to support these principal argumentations themselves. This means that there is always a new dispute or subdispute giving rise to a new discussion or subdiscussion. Here again the argumentation is *compound*, but in contrast to co-ordinative compound argumentation this is a *composite of principal argumentation and subargumentation*. This is why in such cases we speak of *subordinative compound* argumentation. Let us look at an example:

> +/*IO* : 'Women have a logic of their own'
>   *PA* : 'Women solve puzzles quite differently from men'
>   =
>   *SO* : 'Women solve puzzles quite differently from men'
>   *PA* : 'Women start at several places at once, whereas men start in
>   one place'

In the above example, *SO* stands for Subordinate expressed Opinion. Every argumentation advanced by the protagonist can in principle be challenged by the antagonist and thus give rise to a new discussion or subdiscussion, from which yet other new subdiscussions may flow, and so on. The *initial expressed opinion* is thus an expressed opinion that occurs in *none* of the argumentations occurring in the discussion or discussions in progress. This is the difference between the initial expressed opinion (*IO*) and a subordinate expressed opinion (*SO*).

The consequence of the 'dropping out' of an argumentative statement that is part of a subordinative compound argumentation is in principle that the entire compound argumentation of which it is part loses its supporting function. One might say that a subordinative compound argumentation is a *chain* of single argumentations which stands or falls with the *weakest link* in the chain. [31]

Figure 4.3 is an overview of the distinctions we have made in respect of the argumentation structure.

We may now add to the guidelines for the analysis of simple single discussions, formulated at the end of section 4.2, some guidelines relating to the analysis of the *argumentation structure*, i.e. the way in which the argumentation advanced at the argumentation stage of the discussion is structured. The argumentation may have the basic structure, but it may also be complex. A complex structure of argumentation can be analysed as a multiple, co-ordi-

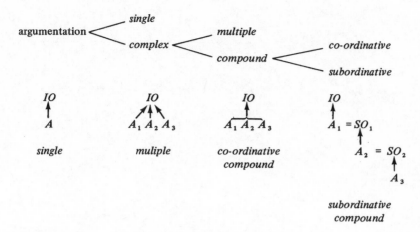

IO   = initial expressed opinion
SO   = subordinate expressed opinion
A   = single argumentation

Figure 4.3. Overview of argumentation structures.

native or subordinative compound composite of single argumentations. Using the distinctions we have made, we can now formulate the following guideliness for analysing the argumentation structure:

(7)   *Establish what single argumentations constitute the argumentation.*
(8)   *Establish what multiple argumentations are formed by the single argumentations.*
(9)   *Establish what co-ordinative compound argumentations are formed by the single argumentations.*
(10) *Establish what subordinative argumentations are formed by the single argumentations.*

Chapter 5

The distribution of speech acts in rational discussions

5.1. EXPRESSED OPINIONS, ARGUMENTATION AND ASSERTIVES

The argumentation advanced in discussions about expressed opinions in order to resolve disputes about those expressed opinions consists of elementary illocutionary acts which together constitute one or more argumentative act complexes. In chapter 2 we stated that these elementary illocutionary acts belong in principle to the category of the *assertives*. In the practice of argumentation, however, illocutionary acts are often performed which appear not to belong to that category. Furthermore, argumentative discussions often contain performances of illocutionary acts which are unquestionably *not* assertives, and which are not actually part of the argumentation, but which nevertheless contribute to the resolution of the dispute.[32]

This means that is is not always going to be immediately obvious exactly which speech acts may contribute to the resolution of the dispute and what role they play in doing so. We shall therefore have to answer the following two questions:

1. *Do the elementary illocutionary acts composing the illocutionary act complex argumentation always belong to the category of the assertives?*
2. *What other illocutionary acts can contribute to the resolution of disputes about expressed opinions?*

We shall answer question 1 in this section and question 2 in section 5.2.[33]

A speech act that is indispensable in an externalized dispute about an expressed opinion and which is not part of the illocutionary act complex *argumentation* but is an *assertive* is the speech act whereby the protagonist makes known his *attitude* or *point of view* in respect of the expressed opinion. If the utterance of a point of view boils down to the performance of an *assertive*, this means, according to a criterion introduced by Searle, that its propositional content *must always be capable of being characterized as true or false* (1979:12-13).

The propositional content of an *assertive* in which a point of view is propounded always consists (as we indicated earlier) of the *expressed opinion* to which an argumentation refers. This means that Searle's criterion appears to put us at odds with the premiss that expressed opinions need not necessarily be exclusively statements of a factual nature, but may also be ethical, aesthetic or other normative statements to which the *true/false* criterion does not easily apply.

We believe it is possible to adopt an *attitude* to all kinds of statements. Statements such as 'Carmiggelt is Holland's most entertaining writer', 'You had no right to put me on that list' and 'Even in academic circles people practise discrimination to their heart's content', none of which can be characterized simply as true or false, may all serve as expressed opinions. This means that attitudes or points of view need not refer exclusively to propositions that are either true or false but may also relate to other propositions whose *acceptability* (in the broader sense) may be a point of discussion.

If a language user states his attitude in respect of the acceptability of (the propositional content of) a particular statement or combination of statements, he thereby indicates that he regards that statement or those statements as an expressed opinion. By advancing a positive or negative point of view he has *committed himself positively or negatively* to that expressed opinion. In principle this implies that he must be prepared to defend his point of view in respect of the expressed opinion against attack from those to whom he has communicated it.

This means that every statement capable of having the specific consequence that it gives rise to a dispute in which the person making the statement has a conditional *obligation to defend* his statement, may be regarded as an *expressed opinion*. This obligation to defend (the result of a certain committedness) we consider to be a general feature of *assertives*, distinguishing them as a class from other illocutionary acts. According to this view, then, both the advancing of an expressed opinion and the propounding of a point of view may be regarded as the performance of an *assertive*.

This view is supported by Austin's definition of *verdictives*, a class of illocutionary acts which, in view of the *illocutionary point* which they serve, Searle says must be counted among the *assertives* (1979:13). Because this observation is not immediately obvious from what Austin and Searle have to say on the classification of illocutions, we shall elucidate our claim (at the same time extending Searle's ideas). We shall begin by pointing out a vagueness in Searle's conception of *assertives*.

Though Searle states that *assertives* are characterized by the fact that they can be said to be either *true* or *false*, it is unclear how far he actually believes that *only* statements with truth value belong to the class of *assertives*. It is possible that his chief concern was to formulate as clear a distinguishing criterion as possible and that it is not his intention to limit the *assertives* to statements with truth value.

This last surmise is founded on three considerations. In the first place Searle immediately adds to his proposed truth test the warning that it constitutes neither a necessary nor a sufficient condition (1979:13). In the second place he presents his taxonomy as an exhaustive classification of illocutionary acts, but the statements that cause problems for us cannot be accomodated in any of the categories identified by Searle besides *assertives* (*directives, commissives, expressives* and *declaratives*, which Searle calls *declarations*). In the third place the fact that Searle believes that the *expositives* and *verdictives* of Austin's original classification have the same illocutionary point as his own *assertives* can be satisfactorily explained only if the statements that cause difficulties for us are assigned to the *assertives*.

In his definition of the illocutionary point of the members of the class of *assertives*, Searle explicitly links them to the *truth* of the expressed proposition (it is strange, incidentally, that he leaves no space for such illocutions as *deny*, linked to the *falsity* of the proposition). Austin, however, does not make this exclusive link in his definition of the class of the *verdictives*. In his comparison of his own classification with that of Austin, Searle notes that his *assertives* correspond to Austin's *verdictives* (and *expositives*) but passes no comment on this whatever. Austin gives the following definition of *verdictives*:

> Verdictives consist in the delivering of a finding, official or unofficial, upon evidence or reasons as to value or fact, so far as these are distinguishable. ... Verdictives have obvious connexions with truth and falsity, soundness and unsoundness and fairness and unfairness (1976:153).

We believe that is is important to hold on to Searle's idea that the illocutionary point must be the prime factor when it comes to classifying illocutionary acts and hence that it must also be taken into account when classifying *assertives*. However, we also think that the fact that the expressing of a specific committedness is a purpose common to both statements with truth value and statements with a sort of 'acceptability value' allows us to align the category of the *assertives* more closely with the wider scope of Austin's *verdictives*. We regard it as the illocutionary point of the members of the class of *assertives* to *commit the speaker (to a greater of lesser degree) to the acceptability or unacceptability of the expressed proposition.*

If we start from this definition of *assertives*, then all the examples of expressed opinions that we gave earlier fall into the category of the *assertives*. At the same time this removes the suggestion that the elementary illocutionary acts that can act as expressed opinions *must be factual assertions*. For the time being, then, the proposition that a point of view can *always* be expressed by means of an *assertive* can be upheld, and the same applies, of course, to the *argumentation* adduced for or against all these different expressed opinions. In 'That is a magnificent painting, because the palette is perfectly balanced', for example, both the *expressed opinion* and the *argumentation* are expressed by means of an *assertive*.

A different problem appears to present itself in a case such as the following: 'Let's take an umbrella, or do you want to get wet?' Here we are clearly dealing with argumentation, but equally clearly the elementary illocutionary acts performed do not belong to the class of the *assertives*.

A satisfactory description of this example would seem to be that the speaker makes the listener a *proposal* which he tries to justify with a (rhetorical) *question*. Is this an *expressed opinion* in the form of a *proposal* and a (single) *argumentation* in the form of a *question*? If this were so, it would mean that it was not only members of the class of the *assertives* that were capable of expressing an expressed opinion and argumentation, but also members of *other classes* (in this case members of the class of the *directives*). This, however, is an erroneous conclusion.

The utterance 'Let's take an umbrella' should not be seen as the expressed opinion at the centre of the dispute that the speaker is trying to resolve with the aid of the utterance 'or do you want to get wet?' Rather it is a statement indicating that the speaker recognizes the possibility of a dispute arising about his proposal. This dispute might then be centred on the question of whether the proposal was a *good* one. The expressed opinion on which this particular dispute is centred is not formulated explicitly, but that is always possible. For example, the speaker might say: 'It is advisable to take an umbrella.' This statement is an elementary illocutionary act of the *assertive type*.[34]

In fully externalized discussions the expressed opinions and the argumentation must always in our view consist of elementary illocutions belonging to the class of the *assertives*. Expressed opinions and argumentations consisting superficially of illocutions of some other type must first be analysed in such a way that it is clear exactly what *assertives* are involved. If these expressed opinions and argumentations could not be construed as *assertives* a resolution of the dispute would be impossible, since it is only possible to resolve disputes thanks to the specific committedness associated with the performance of *assertives*. This answers the first of the two questions that we asked at the beginning of this section.[35]

5.2. ILLOCUTIONARY ACTS AND THE RESOLUTION OF DISPUTES

The question that now has to be answered is what other illocutionary acts or act complexes, besides the illocutionary act complex *argumentation, can contribute to the resolution of a dispute* in a discussion. This means that we must answer the question of what speech acts can occur in an argumentative discussion that is a *rational discussion*. In addressing ourselves to this question we shall confine ourselves to consistently *simple single discussions*.

Asking informative questions, requesting precization and *providing elucidation* are all examples of the illocutionary acts that may occur in discussions. To what extent can illocutionary acts like these contribute to resolving disputes? To answer this question we must first distinguish between speech acts that are linked to *one particular stage of the discussion* on the one hand and speech acts which can in principle occur at *any stage of the discussion* on the other.

Those speech acts that are linked to one particular stage of the discussion must be performed only at that stage. Assuming the discussion stages identified in section 4.3.1, they are the following speech acts (which we have *italicized*).

I *The confrontation stage*
1. language user 1 makes an *assertion* in which he expresses a point of view in respect of *O*
2. language user 2 *casts doubt on* language user 1's point of view
3. language user 1 *upholds his assertion*
4. language user 2 *upholds his doubt*

II *The opening stage*
5. language user 2 *challenges* language user 1 to defend his point of view
6. language user 1 *accepts the challenge*
7. language user 1 and language user 2 *decide* to discuss language user 1's point of view
8. language user 1 and language user 2 *agree* how the roles of P(rotagonist) and A(ntagonist) shall be distributed in the discussion
9. language user 1 and language user 2 *agree* the rules to govern the discussion
10. language user 1 and language user 2 *agree* how the discussion shall be terminated

III *The argumentation stage*
11. P performs an illocutionary act complex of *argumentation*
12. a A *accepts* the illocutionary act complex of *argumentation*
     b A *does not accept* the illocutionary act complex of *argumentation*, but *requests* P to perform a new illocutionary act complex of *argumentation*
(13.) (as 11.)
(14.) (as 12.)
(15.) (and so on)

IV *The concluding stage*
16. a language user 1 *upholds his assertion* (see 1)
     b language user 1 *retracts his assertion* (see 1)
17. a language user 2 *retracts his doubt* (see 2) (consequence of 12.a)
     b language user 2 *upholds his doubt* (see 2) (consequence of 12.b)
18. language user 1 and language user 2 *decide* to terminate the discussion
19. a language user 1 and language user 2 *observe* that the dispute is resolved in favour of language user 1 (consequence of 16.a and 17.a)

      b language user 1 and language user 2 *observe* that the dispute is resolved in favour of language user 2 (consequence of 16.b and 17.b)

      ç language user 1 and language user 2 *observe* that the dispute is unresolved (consequence of 16.a and 17.b)

      d language user 1 and language user 2 *observe* that the dispute no longer exists, yet has not been resolved in favour of either language user 1 or language user 2 (consequence of 16.b and 17.a)

(20.)   (language user 1 and language user 2 *decide* to embark on a new discussion with the same or a different dispute as the point at issue)

The speech acts which language users 1 and 2 (protagonist P and antagonist A respectively at the argumentation stage) perform at the various stages of the discussion may be summarized as follows. Language user 1 has made *assertions* (in I, III and IV), has *repeated* (upheld) and possibly *retracted* them, has advanced *argumentation* (in III), and has *accepted the challenge* issued by language user 2 (in II). Language user 2 has *cas doubt* on assertions by language user 1 (in I, III and IV), has *repeated* (upheld) and possibly *retracted* this doubt, and has *challenged* language user 1 to defend his point of view (in II). Language user 1 and language user 2 have (in II and IV) collectively *taken decisions, arrived at agreements* (in II), and *made observations* (in IV).

The speech acts of language user 1

The speech acts performed by language user 1 in the discussion belong to one or other of the two classes of illocutionary acts. The *assertions*, it goes without saying, belong to the class of the *assertives*, and the acceptance of the challenge issued by language user 2 is a form of *acceptance* and belongs to the class of the *commissives*. Language user 1's share in the discussion consists largely of performing illocutionary acts of the *assertive* class.

   In I an assertion by language user 1 precipitates the dispute, in IV this assertion is repeated or retracted, and in III assertions are used in the performance of the illocutionary act complex of *argumentation*. It is only in II that there are no *assertives*: at this stage language user 1 undertakes to enter into a discussion with language user 2 in which he will defend his point of view. This is *the only point* in the discussion at which language user 1 independently performs an illocutionary act from the category of the *commissives*. Illocutionary acts not belonging to either the *assertives* or the *commissives* (i.e. *directives, expressives* and *expositives*)[36] are performed by language user 1 *at no stage in the discussion*.

   The *repetition* (or *upholding*) of an assertion or the *retraction* of an assertion, which language user 1 can do in I and IV, does not constitute an independent illocutionary act and must therefore – like the pronouncement of an assertion – be accounted one of the category of the *assertives*. The reason for language user 1's repetition (and hence upholding) of an assertion is that he wishes to make it explicitly clear that despite language user 2's doubts he regards himself as still committed – positively or negatively, as the case may be – to the acceptability of the proposition, expressed in the assertion, that constitutes the expressed opinion. Upholding assertions does not constitute a separate class of illocutionary acts but it is set apart *within the class of the assertives* by a specific *contextual position* (cf. Searle 1979:6).

The *retraction of an assertion* involves an *illocutionary negation* of the assertive concerned. Searle introduced the concept of 'illocutionary negation' in *Speech Acts* in order to make clear the difference from *propositional negations*. In 'I promise not to come' there is a *propositional* negation and in 'I do not promise to come' there is an *illocutionary* negation. In the former a promise is given, albeit one with a negative propositional content; in the latter, no promise is given – on the contrary, it is rather a *refusal* to make a promise (1970:32).

In *Foundations of Illocutionary Logic* Searle and Vanderveken describe the role of illocutionary negation (or denegation) as follows:

> The illocutionary point of the performance of an act of illocutionary denegation ... is to put the speaker in a position of explicit non-commitment to the illocution ... (n.d.: III-35)

Searle and Vanderveken's characterization is perfectly applicable to the retraction of an assertion. By retracting an assertion the speaker (in this case language user 1) explicitly makes it clear that he no longer regards himself as committed to the propositional content expressed in the assertion. This means that he no longer holds a *positive* or *negative* point of view in respect of the expressed opinion, but a *zero* point of view or a *negative* or *positive* point of view respectively.

Language user 1 can retract an assertion at two stages of the discussion, viz. in I and in IV. If he does so in I, he makes an immediate end of the dispute (thereby precluding the initiation of a discussion at all). If he retracts his assertion at stage IV, then the dispute is resolved *by the discussion* that has taken place.

The speech acts of language user 2

Like those performed by language user 1, the speech acts performed by language user 2 during the discussion belong to one or other of the two classes of illocutionary acts, albeit not to the same one. Language user 2's part in the discussion consists chiefly of *casting doubt* on the assertions of language user 1 and *provoking* language user 1 into making more assertions. It is by the calling into question of language user 1's assertion at stage I that the dispute is precipitated, and it is by calling language user 1's assertions into question in III that language user 2 obliges him to advance new argumentations. The necessity of this last is reinforced when in III language user 2 follows every expression of doubt with a *request* that language user 1 advance new argumentation, thus encouraging him to make more assertions. At stage I language user 2 can also *retract his doubt* concerning language user 1's assertion, thereby putting an end to the dispute. In III he can *accept* language user 1's argumentation and must then after all in IV *retract his doubt* about the assertion, so that as a consequence of the discussion the dispute is resolved (in language user 1's favour).

Thus language user 2's part in the discussion consists first of *casting doubt, upholding doubt* and *retracting doubt* in respect of assertions by language user 1 and second of *eliciting assertions* from language user 1. To what categories of speech act do these activities belong? To start with the simplest cases: *encouraging* the making of assertions, *requesting* the making of assertions and *eliciting* assertions are all attempts on the part of language user 2 to make language user 1 perform a *speech act*. The verbal acts which language user 2 performs with this design in mind therefore belong to the category of the *directives*.

This *casting doubt, upholding doubt* and *retracting doubt* may be characterized, drawing on the concepts of 'illocutionary negation' and 'repetition', by starting from the illocutionary act *acceptance*. Casting doubt on an assertion can be defined as a *refusal to accept* it, i.e. as the *illocutionary negation* of *acceptance*. Upholding doubt about an assertion is then the *repetition* of the *illocutionary negation* of *acceptance*. Retracting doubt about an assertion, finally, can be regarded – by analogy with the retraction of an assertion – as the *illocutionary negation* of *casting doubt*, i.e. as the *illocutionary negation* of the *illocutionary negation* of *acceptance*, and hence as *acceptance*.

In the last case we are dealing with the acceptance of an assertive not previously accepted. Just as with the element of repetition, this has to do with the contextual position of the speech act of retracting doubt, and *this*, therefore, has no consequences for the category to which the speech act belongs. Since all three cases can be reduced to the illocutionary act of *acceptance* – they are successively cases of *non-acceptance, repeated non-acceptance* and *acceptance following non-acceptance* – and since *acceptance* belongs to the class of the *commissives*, it is also clear that language user 2's contributions, in so far as they are not *directives*, are *always members of the class of commissives*.

The speech acts of language user 1 and language user 2 collectively

For it to be possible to resolve a dispute, the discussion must also contain performances of speech acts which cannot be performed unilaterally by one of the interlocutors but require joint approval. These speech acts may therefore be termed *joint* speech acts by language user 1 and language user 2. This does not, of course, mean that the two language users have to perform particular speech acts in chorus.

The speech acts performed jointly by language users 1 and 2 occur exclusively at stage I or stage IV. Language users 1 and 2 jointly open the discussion at the beginning of II by *deciding* to conduct a discussion to resolve the dispute and they terminate the discussion at the end of stage IV by *deciding* to do so. In II, moreover, the interlocutors must arrive at a number of *agreements* concerning the apportionment of roles in the discussion, the rules for the discussion and how the discussion should be terminated. In IV, finally, they must *establish* the result of the discussion: whether or not the dispute has been resolved and, if so, in whose favour. To what category do the speech acts performed by language users 1 and 2 in all this belong?

This is not a particularly easy question to answer because the speech acts concerned are performed *by more than one language user at the same time*. Searle's theory takes no account of this possibility, so that it may be legitimately questioned whether indeed one may speak of (elementary) *illocutionary acts* at all in such cases. But although there are serious theoretical problems attaching to this question, it is in fact possible to use Searle's classification of illocutionary acts to produce a satisfactory characterization of the joint speech act activities of the two language users in the discussion.

Let us begin by looking at the joint linguistic activity of language user 1 and language user 2 which entails that at the end of the discussion they *establish* what result the discussion has had. Since what we are dealing with is a factual *observation* or *ascertainment*, it is clear that the illocutionary acts involved will belong to the class of the *assertives*. The role played in the discussion by *decisions* and *agreement* is similarly clear. The language users commit themselves explicitly to conducting themselves in a particular manner throughout the discussion.

By reason of these decisions and agreements language user 1 and language user 2 *oblige* themselves and each other to perform *certain* illocutionary acts. It will be plain enough that the illocutionary acts that they perform when arriving at agreements and taking decisions belong to the class of the *commissives*. The committing effect of the decisions and agreements will be, for example, that they cannot simply withdraw from the discussion whenever they please, that they must adhere consistently to their roles as P or A respectively, and that they must adhere to the rules governing the discussion.

These joint decisions and agreements constitute a necessary (but naturally not a sufficient) condition for achieving a resolution of a dispute and accentuate the *co-operative nature* of discussions. Although as parties to a dispute language user 1 and language user 2 are *on opposite sides*, by their joint decision to start discussing they express their intention of attempting to resolve the dispute *in joint consultation* and in accordance with *common rules of discussion*.

In all, then, there are three categories of illocutionary acts that are eligible for performance in discussions: *assertives* and *commissives* by language user 1, *commissives* and *directives* by language user 2, and *commissives* and *assertives* by language users 1 and 2 jointly. The operations that may be applied to these are *illocutionary negation* and *repetition*. The distributions of these classes of illocutionary acts over the various stages of the discussion, and their roles in them, are summarized in fig. 5.1.

5.3. THE ROLE OF SPEECH ACTS AT DIFFERENT STAGES IN THE DISCUSSION

As figure 5.1 shows, the speech acts performed jointly by language user 1 and language user 2 occur exclusively at discussion stages II and IV. This is hardly surprising, since it is at stage II that they jointly decide to start discussing and come to agreements about the way the discussion should be conducted and the way in which it is to be terminated, and it is at stage IV that they jointly decide to terminate the discussion and establish what result it has produced. Since at stage I there is only a dispute, the discussion not yet having opened, it is equally unsurprising that that stage contains no *directives*: all that is necessary is that it become plain that one of the interlocutors holds a point of view that is called into question by the other. For this, only *assertives* and illocutionary negations of *commissives* are needed. Something of the kind also applies to stage IV, which also contains no *directives*. Here all that happens is that the result of the discussion is established and that a decision is taken to terminate the discussion (and possibly to start a new one). For this, only *assertives* or *commissives* are needed.

No *assertives* occur at discussion stage II. This is understandable considering that this is the 'negotiation' stage, when the interlocutors use *commissives* to commit themselves to their intention of making a joint attempt to resolve their dispute by discussing the disputed point of view according to commonly agreed rules. Discussion stage III, finally, contains *directives, commissives* and *assertives*, and this is the only stage at which these all occur: it is at this crucial argumentation stage that *assertives* are used to advance argumentations, that *commissives* (or illocutinary negations of *commissives*) are used to cast doubt, or not cast doubt, on those argumentations, and that *directives* are used to elicit new argumentations.

All the *assertives* appearing in the discussion relate directly or indirectly to the original expressed opinion, except for the joint assertion of language users 1 and 2 at the end of the discussion concerning its result. The other *assertives*, all of which come from language user 1 (P), are *reactions* to *directives*, all of which come from language user 2 (A), except for the first *assertive*, which constitutes the immediate cause of the dispute. Conversely the *directives* of language user 2 (A) are always calculated to make language user 1 (P) perform *assertives* entailing the performance of the illocutionary act complex *argumentation*, except for the *directives* by means of which language user 2 challenges language user 1. The *commissive* with which language user 1 accepts this challenge is the only *commissive* performed by him only on his own account in the whole of the discussion.

The fact that the chief element of the contributions made to the discussion by language user 1 (P) is *assertives* and that language user 1 performs no *directives* can be explained by the role that P plays in a consistently simple

		Language user 1 (P)	Language user 2 (A)	Language users 1 + 2
I	1.	*assertive*: POV		
	2.		ILL NEG of *commissive*: non-acceptance of POV (= casting doubt on POV)	
	3.	REP of *assertive*: upholding of POV		
	4.		REP of ILL NEG of *commissive*: non-acceptance of POV (= upholding of doubt about POV)	
II	5.		*directive*: challenge to language user 1	
	6.	*commissive*: acceptance of challenge from language user 2		
	7.			*commissive*: decision to discuss
	8.			*commissive*: agreements re apportionment of roles
	9.			*commissive*: agreements re rules for discussion
	10.			*commissive*: agreements re termination of discussion
III	11.	*assertive*: IAC ARG		
	12.a.		*commissive*: acceptance of IAC ARG	
	b.		ILL NEG of *commissive*: non-acceptance of IAC ARG & *directive*: request to language user 1 for IAC ARG	
	13-15.	(idem)	(idem)	
IV	16.a.	REP of *assertive*: upholding of POV		
	b.	ILL NEG of *assertive*: retraction of POV		
	17.a.		*commissive*: acceptance of POV (= retraction of doubt about POV)	
	b.		REP of ILL NEG of *commissive*: non-acceptance of POV (= upholding of doubt about POV)	
	18.			*commissive*: decision to terminate discussion
	19.			*assertive*: establishing result of discussion

POV = point of view   ILL NEG = illocutionary negation
REP = repetition   IAC ARG = illocutionary act complex *argumentation*

Figure 5.1. Distribution of speech acts in rational discussions.

single discussion. His chief task is to *defend* his stated point of view in respect of the expressed opinion, and this he does by performing *assertives*. P himself has no attacking role to play, so that there is no point in his trying to elecit *assertives* from A. And since P cannot perform even a single *directive*, he has, moreover, no way whatsoever of hindering A in the execution of his attacking role. Thus P is unable, for example, to give A *orders*, nor can he *forbid* him anything. Because P is prohibited from the performance of even a single *directive*, A can perform his critical task unhindered.

The role fulfilled by A in a consistently simple single discussion also makes clear why he, for his part, performs no *assertives*. His only task is to attack P's point of view and argumentation; he himself has nothing to defend. He can therefore concentrate fully on his attacking task. Thus the way in which illocutionary acts are distributed between P and A in rational discussions offers A the best possible opportunity of acquitting himself of his critical task.

Expressives

Rational discussions contain no illocutionary acts belonging to the classes of the *expressives* or *declaratives* (with the exception of one specific subclass of the *declaratives* which we shall be discussing later). This can be explained as follows. The illocutionary point of *expressives*, according to Searle, is to give expression to the state of mind, specified in the sincerity condition, with regard to a state of affairs specified in the propositional content (1979:15). To this Searle adds that the *truth* of the proposition expressed is *presupposed* (1979:15-16). In rational discussions truth (or acceptability in the wider sense) is not presupposed: on the contrary, it is the very subject of discussion.

Declaratives

In his exposition of *declaratives* Searle says that with two exceptions they always require an *extralinguistic institution* (the church, the law, private ownership, etc.) in which speaker and listener occupy a *specific position* (1979:18). The two exceptions are *supernatural declaratives* (God: 'Let there be light') and *declaratives relating to language usage* (*defining, naming, labelling* etc.). In all other cases, then, some sort of *authority* or *power* is required for the performance of a *declarative*.

It will be clear that in discussions whose purpose is to resolve disputes through argumentation there can be no place for authority or power. Moreover such discussions are not confined to particular specific institutions. On the contrary, in some (totalitarian) institutions they are impossible or prohibited. In any event, *declaratives* can have no part to play in rational discussions. Thus a language user cannot, for example, off his own bat *declare the discussion closed*. The exclusion of *declaratives* from discussions constitutes a *guarantee for both parties* that they will be able to perform their defending and attacking roles without hindrance.

Commissives and directives

We have now given a limitative statement of the *sorts* of speech act that may occur in rational discussions: *assertives, commissives* and *directives*. However, it will be clear that *not all members* of the classes of the *assertives, commissives* and *directives* in a discussion will automatically make a contribution to the resolution of the dispute. In the case of *commissives* and *directives* they very often will not, and of the *commissives* only *accept* (and its illocutionary negations and repetitions) is possible, and only then in so far as in the discussion it relates to *agreements* and *decisions* in respect of the conduct of the discussion or serves to indicate that *points of view* or *argumentations* are or are not accepted. The members of the class of the *directives* remain limited to *challenging* (challenging language user 1 to defend his point of view) and *requesting* (requesting language user 1 to come forward with new argumentations). Only those *commissives* and *directives* that fulfil this well-defined role may be performed in rational discussions.

Assertives

Do such limitations also apply to the *assertives*? If we start from the definition that we gave in section 5.1 of the role of *assertives*, then it seems to us that all members of the class are eligible to occur in a rational discussion (if, at least, we ignore *boast* and *complain*, which Searle (1979:13) erroneously regards as *assertives*). This means that there are no special conditions applying to the *propositional content* expressed in an *assertive*, nor to the *force* by which the illocutionary point is made (cf. Searle 1979:5). Thus an *assertive* occurring in a rational discussion may refer to anything and the degree of *certainty* can vary from *extremely high* to *extremely low*.

As long as a language user commits himself, to even the slightest degree, to the acceptability of the propositional content, there is an *assertive* capable of becoming the precipitator of a dispute. The *assertives* occurring in a rational discussion can thus vary from *state* (hypothetically or otherwise), *suppose* and (cautiously) *propose*, through *assert, posit, postulate* and claim, to *assert confidently, state with certainty* and *guarantee*. The point at issue in a discussion is not the *strength* of the *belief* expressed by language user 1 in an *assertive*, but the fact that by performing an *assertive* he has expressed a (cautious or firm) *view* with regard to an expressed opinion and that this is a view *to which he can be held* or which can be *called into question* by language user 2.

This is the case in every illocutionary act whose illocutionary point is the same as the illocutionary point of the *assertives* as a class. Language user 1's committedness can only be removed by his *retraction* of an *assertive*, and that can only be done by means of an *illocutionary negation* of the *assertive* concerned. For example, by saying 'I no longer claim that women have a logic of their own' language user 1 can retract the assertion 'Women have a logic of their own' and thus abandon his standpoint that women have a logic of their own. Since the illocutionary negation of this *assertive* removes language user 1's committedness, there is nothing left for language user 2 to call into question and the dispute has been resolved.

What we have said in the foregoing applies to *assertives* in which a point of view in respect of the *initial expressed opinion* is expressed, to *assertives* referring to a *subordinate expressed opinion* and also to *assertives* used in the performance of an illocutionary act complex of *argumentation* (which may relate either to the initial expressed opinion or to a subordinate expressed opinion). Of course, there may be an association between the force with which an opinion is expressed in an *assertive* and the force with which a particular argumentation in respect of the expressed opinion is expressed by means of *assertives*. If the expressed opinion in an *assertive* is expressed more forcefully, then the argumentation will generally also be presented with greater force. Indeed, Searle and Vanderveken believe this to be a *sine qua non*:

> ... one is required to have stronger grounds for what one swears to than for what one merely advances as a hypothesis. (n.d.: III-12)

The force with which the illocutionary point of an *assertive* is made should not, incidentally, be confused with the *scope of the propositional content* expressed in the *assertive*. The illocutionary force of an *assertive* has to do with the illocutionary act as a whole, whereas the scope of the propositional content naturally extends only to the propositional content. In example i the illocutionary force varies and the propositional scope remains the same, while in ii the illocutionary force remains the same and it is the propositional scope that varies:[37]

(i)   a   It is absolutely certain that women have a logic of their own (*definite assertion*)
      b   It is probable that women have a logic of their own (*cautious assertion*)
(ii) a   I think it is true that all women have a logic of their own (*universal statement*)
      b   I think it is true that certain women have a logic of their own (*particular statement*)

The illocutionary acts that may occur in rational discussions (precisely determined members of the classes of the *commissives* and *directives*, with a precisely determined role in the discussion, and all members of the class of the *assertives*) may all have a contribution to make to the resolution of disputes. It should not be concluded from this, however, that all these illocutionary acts always, by definition, actually make such a contribution, and it is therefore more accurate to say that these members of these classes can *in principle* contribute to the resolution of disputes. In this respect they differ from the other members of their classes and from all members of the classes of the *expressives* and *declaratives*.

5.4. THE ROLE OF USAGE DECLARATIVES

Besides the illocutionary acts that may occur at particular stages in a rational discussion there are also speech acts that are *not linked to particular stages of the discussion* but which may nevertheless contribute to the resolution of a dispute. They may be divided into two groups: (1) speech acts capable of contributing to the achievement of the *illocutionary effect* of illocutionary acts and (2) speech acts in which the performance of one or more of the speech acts referred to under 1 is *requested*.

The purpose of these speech acts is to ensure mutual *comprehension* of the interlocutors' speech acts. As we observed earlier, in rational discussions it is a condition of the achievement of (inherent and consecutive) perlocutionary effects that the illocutionary effect must occur that the listener *understands* the speaker's speech act. The speech acts that may help this illocutionary effect to be achieved are: *definition, precization, amplification, explication* and *explicitization*. To what category of illocutionary acts can these speech acts be regarded as belonging?

Just as in argumentation, we are not dealing here with *elementary* illocutionary acts but with illocutionary *act complexes* (cf. section 2.3). An *explication*, for example, is always an explication of another speech act (for the benefit to another language user) and almost always consists of *two or more elementary illocutionary acts* which are in principle *assertives*. Here the situation is comparable to that of argumentation. An explication is an explication only at a *higher textual level* and it is only at this higher textual level that the illocutionary act complex of *explication* maintains a relation with the speech act by which the explication is provided.

Definition is probably a case apart. This illocutionary act complex belongs to a subclass of the *declaratives*, for which no extralinguistic institution is required in which speaker and listener occupy a specific position. Searle regards this subclass as containing *abbreviate, name, call* and *dub* as well as *define* (1979:18). We call the members of this subclass *usage declaratives*. They are the *only exception* to the rule that *declaratives* cannot occur in rational discussions.

The other illocutionary act complexes furthering the comprehension of illocutionary acts are difficult to accommodate in Searle's taxonomy. Searle himself would probably say that they were part of a subclass of the *assertives*, with the extra feature that in speech acts belonging to that subclass a certain *relation to the context* is expressed. However, even then we should not describe what we were looking at as *elementary assertives*. The most natural solution would seem to be to place them in the class referred to by Austin as *expositives*, which he defines as follows:

> Expositives ... make plain how our utterances fit into the course of an argument or conversation, how we are using words, or, in general, are expository. (1976:152)

> Expositives are used in acts of exposition involving the expoundig of views, the
> conducting of arguments, and *the clarifying of usages and of references.*
> (1976:161; our italics)

Examples given by Austin include *define, interpret* and *explain*. We shall
count all these examples as *usage declaratives*.

Usage declaratives can occur at any stage of the discussion, since at any stage
of the discussion it is possible for the interlocutors to fail to understand one
another to a greater or lesser extent, so that they have a need of amplification,
explication, precization, and so on. It is therefore necessary not merely that
these speech acts are permitted in a rational discussion but also, in principle,
that it is permitted to *request* them at any stage in the discussion. The second
group of speech acts not associated with any particular discussion stage is
therefore composed of *directives* in which one language user *requests* another
to perform an illocutionary act complex belonging to the subclass of the
usage declaratives.[38]

The role that a *directive* can play in a rational discussion is thus not limited
to *requesting argumentation* and *challenging* a language user to defend his
point of view, but also embraces *requesting* the performance of a *usage
declarative* designed to guarantee the illocutionary effect of performed
illocutionary acts. Here again it should be remembered that both the
performance of and a request for a *usage declarative* can *in principle* contribute to the resolution of a dispute. This does not mean, of course, that *every*
performance of a *usage declarative* and every *request for a usage declarative*
will *automatically* make a constructive contribution to the resolution of the
dispute at *any* arbitrary point in the discussion. A language user who
constantly asks for precization or definitions of the terms used holds the
discussion up and is a positive hindrance to the resolution of the dispute.

Figure 5.2 summarizes the illocutionary acts and act complexes that are
capable of contributing to the resolution of disputes and which may therefore occur in rational discussions.[39]

To the guidelines for the analysis of simple single discussions that we
formulated at the end of sections 4.2.2 and 4.3.2 we can now add some
guidelines relating to the speech acts that can be performed in rational
discussions. The speech acts that may contribute to the resolution of the
dispute at the centre of the discussion may be identified in the following
manner:

(11)   *Establish what performances of* assertives *in the discussion serve to
       express* opinions (initial or subordinate) *and* argumentations.
(12)   *Establish which performances of* other illocutionary acts *must be
       interpreted as* assertives *serving to express* opinions (initial or subor-
       dinate) *and* argumentations.

illocutionary acts	discussion stage	language user(s)	role
ASSERTIVES (ILL NEG, REP)	I	language user 1	expression of a point of view (POV) in respect of *O*
	II	language user 1 (P)	performance of IAC ARG
	IV	language user 1	maintaining (REP) or retraction (ILL NEG) of POV
	IV	language user 1 + 2	establishing result of discussion
COMMISSIVES (ILL NEG, REP) *-accept* *-decide* *-agree*	I	language user 2	acceptance, non-acceptance (ILL NEG), maintaining of non-acceptance (REP, ILL NEG) of POV
	II	language user 1	acceptance of challenge from language user 2 to defend POV
	II	language user 1 + 2	decision to start discussion, agreement of role allocation and rules for discussion
	III	language user 2 (A)	acceptance, non-acceptance (ILL NEG) IAC ARG
	IV	language user 2	acceptance, non-acceptance (ILL NEG), maintaining of non-acceptance (REP, ILL NEG) of POV
	IV	language user 1 + 2	decision to terminate discussion
DIRECTIVES *-challenge* *-request*	II	language user 2	challenging of language user 1 to defend POV
	III	language user 2 (A)	request to language user 1 for performance of IAC ARG
	I-IV	language user 1, 2	request by language user 1, 2 for performance of UD (usage declarative)
USAGE DECLA-TIVES (IAC)	I-IV	language user 1, 2	performance of a UD (definition, precization, amplifi-tion, explication, explicitization)

POV	= point of view	IAC ARG	= illocutionary act complex
ILL NEG	= illocutionary negation		argumentation
REP	= repetition	UD	= usage declarative
P	= protagonist		
A	= antagonist		

Figure 5.2. Illocutionary acts and act complexes in rational discussions.

(13) *Establish which performances, illocutionary negations and repetitions
      of the illocutionary act* accept *occurring in the discussion relate to an*
      assertive *or to the illocutionary act complex* argumentation.

(14) *Establish which performances of the illocutionary act* accept *occurr-
      ing in the discussion relate to joint* agreements *or* decisions *regarding
      the conduct of the discussion.*

(15) *Establish which performances of the illocutionary act* challenge *oc-
      curring in the discussion relate to the* defence *of the point of view by
      the protagonist.*

(16) *Establish which performances of the illocutionary act* request *occurr-
      ing in the discussion relate to the advancing of* new argumentation *by
      the protagonist.*

(17) *Establish which* usage declaratives *occurring in the discussion further
      the achievement of the* illocutionary effect *intended by one or more
      illocutionary acts performed in the discussion.*

(18) *Establish which performances of the illocutionary act* request *occurr-
      ing in the discussion relate to the performance of one or more* usage
      declaratives.

5.5. THE INTERPRETATION OF SPEECH ACTS

The analysis of speech acts in rational discussions is only possible if it is first
possible to establish the *illocutionary force* of the speech acts performed in
the discussion. Since the illocutionary force of speech acts is not always
expressed explicitly in discussions, and since it is not always possible to infer
their illocutionary force from the context, the interpretation of the illocutionary force can sometimes present certain difficulties. It is therefore necessary
to add to the guidelines that we have already given, with guidelines for the
interpretation of the force of illocutions.

   In chapter 2 we observed that a speaker wishing to present a complex of
speech acts as *argumentation* will have to ensure, for the sake of comprehensibility, that the listener is able to identify the illocutionary force. This naturally applies in like manner to the other speech acts performed in the discussion
for the purpose of resolving the dispute, such as *usage declaratives* containing
a definition, precization, amplification, or explication. In this section we
shall pay some attention to the problems that may occur in argumentative
discussions when it comes to the labelling and recognition of illocutionary
forces.

Even where the illocutionary force of a speech act is not indicated explicitly,
this need not necessarily lead to uncertainty or misunderstanding concerning
the correct interpretation. The (verbal and non-verbal) *context*, for example,
will in many cases make the illocutionary force clear (cf. Searle 1970:68). Of
course, in principle the risk of obscurity is greater in such cases, and this fact
is important to us because it means that the listener cannot be sure of *what
exactly he can hold the speaker to.*

For example, if it is unclear whether an assertion by language user 1 is to be treated as the expression of a particular *point of view* in respect of an expressed opinion, then neither will it be clear whether or not language user 2 is entitled to challenge language user 1 to defend that point of view or whether language user 1 would be obliged to take up such a challenge. And if during the concluding stage of the discussion language user 2 has failed to make clear whether or not he accepts the *initial expressed opinion*, then it is unclear whether the dispute has been resolved or not. Clarity in respect of the illocutionary force of the illocutionary acts and act complexes in a discussion is important for the avoidance of vaguenesses and possible misunderstandings regarding the *committedness* of the language users to speech acts and the *consequences* thereof for the further course of the discussion.

According to Searle (1970:68) the *principle of expressibility* guarantees that the illocutionary force of an illocutionary act not expressed explicitly *can always be made explicit*. It has already been observed in chapter 2 that this presents problems in the case of the illocutionary act complex of *argumentation*. Unlike the illocutionary force of e.g. *promises, requests* and *orders*, the illocutionary force of *argumentation* cannot in principle be expressed by means of an *explicit performative formula* of the 'I hereby ... you that/to ...' type. For example, 'I hereby promise you to return the book tomorrow' is possible but 'I hereby argue you that women have a logic of their own' is not.

The possibility in such cases of indicating the illocutionary force by means of *illocutionary indicators* such as 'for', 'because', 'since', 'so', 'hence' and 'therefore' is equally inadequate to produce a completely reliable rule, since indicators of this kind are not used exclusively in an argumentative sense, and that means that an appeal still has to be made to the context during interpretation.

Many writers approaching the analysis of argumentation with practical pretensions have ascribed an important function to these 'argumentation-indicating' words, but they seldom point out their ambiguity. Generally it is found sufficient to give lists of examples of such 'illative particles' (Lambert & Ulrich 1980:49) or 'warranting connectives' (Fogelin 1978:35). Finocchiaro, who refers to 'reasoning indicators' is one of the few to sound a note of caution:

> Reasoning indicator words, however, are only hints, since it is possible to express reasoning without them and since it is possible for them to have other meanings which do not indicate reasoning; but we will not consider such complications at the moment (1980:311-12).

Wunderlich differentiates not only between explicit performative formulas and illocutionary indicators but also between these and *explicit performative formulas in the wider sense* (1972:17). These, he says, provide a sort of *comment* in which the illocutionary force of an utterance is made clear. As an example he quotes: 'I shall come tomorrow. That is a promise', in which the second sentence provides the necessary explication of the first. We believe that the notion of explicit performative formulas in the wider sense offers starting points for solving the problem of how illocutionary forces that cannot be expressed by means of 'ordinary' explicit performative formulas can nevertheless be indicated unambiguously. In our view this might be done by establishing *standard paraphrases*.

Standard paraphrases offer language user 1 the possibility of making his argumentation recognizable as *argumentation* without vagueness and with no chance of misunderstanding, and offer language user 2 the possibility, in the event of any uncertainty, of *requesting* an explicitizing standard paraphrase (or of himself submitting to language user 1 such a standard paraphrase by way of hypothesis). Let us look at some examples:

(a) Assertives by means of which a point of view is advanced in respect of an expressed opinion

In the case of *assertives* there is an existing explicit performative formula, but it cannot be used to indicate that an assertive is one in which a *point of view* is being advanced in respect of a particular expressed opinion. For example, a person wishing to advance the point of view that women have a logic of their own may say 'Women have a logic of their own' or (in full) 'I assert that women have a logic of their own'. In discussions, however, it is preferable to indicate explicitly exactly which expressed opinion is involved and exactly what attitude is being adopted towards it. The illocutionary force of an *assertive* by means of which a point of view is being advanced in respect of an expressed opinion *O* might be indicated in a standard paraphrase as follows:

'My point of view in respect of *O* is that *O* is/is not the case.'

For example, if language user 1 wishes to stress that his attitude is not positive but negative, the standard paraphrase might be extended as follows: 'My point of view in respect of *O* is not that *O* is the case but that *O* is not the case.' Should language user 1 wish to adopt no attitude (i.e. a zero attitude), he could do so like this: 'My point of view is not that *O* is the case, nor that *O* is not the case, for I have no view (yet).'

(b) Assertives by means of which an illocutionary act complex of argumentation is performed

As already observed, there is no suitable explicit performative formula for assertives having this function. The following standard paraphrase might be usable here:

'My argumentation for/against *O* is: ...'

The illocutionary act complex of *argumentation* may consist either of a *single argumentation* or of a (co-ordinative or subordinative) *compound argumentation*. In the formulation of the standard paraphrase account has been taken of the fact that it is possible to defend either a *positive* point of view in respect of *O* (in which case the argumentation is *pro-argumentation*) or a *negative* point of view (in which case it is *contra-argumentation*).

(c) Usage declaratives by means of which terms are defined, made more precise, amplified, explicated or explicitized

As with the illocutionary act complex of *argumentation*, there is here no explicit performative formula available to us. The following standard paraphrase may be regarded as the general form of the *usage declarative*:

'. . . is a *[usage declarative]* of *[term]*.'

Here a definition, precization, amplification, explication or explicitization would replace the '. . .', '*term*' would be the term to be defined, made more precise, and so on. This standard paraphrase can be used by either language user at any stage of the discussion.

For all *commissives* and *directives* that may occur in a rational discussion there is an explicit performative formula that can serve as a standard paraphrase, except for the *usage declaratives* and (in part) the *assertives*. When retracting and maintaining a point of view it is enough to use a simple explicit performative formula, as it is also when establishing the result of the discussion. For expressing the point of view that is being maintained or retracted, to which the result of the discussion relates, it is however necessary to have an explicit performative formula in the wider sense. The same applies to the performance of the illocutionary act complex *argumentation* and the illocutionary act complexes of *definition, precization, amplification, explication* and *explicitization*.

As we remarked when introducing the notion of the standard paraphrase, the standard paraphrases of the illocutionary acts and act complexes performed in a discussion are means of avoiding vaguenesses and misunderstandings in the discussion by explicitizing the illocutionary force of speech acts, where necessary, and their relation to other illocutionary acts and act complexes, so that it becomes possible to establish exactly to what the discussants have committed themselves in the course of the discussion. However, in discussions in colloquial speech there is no need to make use of the relevant standard paraphrase on the performance of *every* illocutionary act or *every* illocutionary act complex, since often the context will make it sufficiently clear what the correct interpretation is. In such circumstances it would be merely disruptive to use standard paraphrases. Moreover, ordinary idiom provides discussants with a number of expressions that can sometimes be used instead of the standard paraphrases formulated above. Here are some examples.

Instead of (a)
- 'I think women have a logic of their own'
- 'I am of the opinion that women have a logic of their own'
- 'In my view women have a logic of their own'

Instead of (b)
- '..., for they solve problems by a totally different method than men'
- '..., because they solve problems by a totally different method than men'
- '...: they solve problems by a totally different method than men'

Instead of (c)
- 'Of course I don't mean all women – there are always some exceptions – but most'
- 'By a logic of their own I mean ...'
- 'Of course, I'm talking now about women in present-day western societies – things were quite different in the past'

Expressions such as these are by no means always unambiguous. Sometimes, however, the verbal media of which language users avail themselves in a discussion may be considerably 'more implicit'. There are two important reasons why a language user must try to clarify an illocutionary act or act complex in a discussion by explicitizing the illocutionary force and the role played by the speech act at a particular stage of the discussion: (1) a language user fulfilling the communicative role of listener when the speech act was performed has requested it, and (2) the language user performing the speech act in the communicative role of speaker fears, or even expects, that misunderstandings will arise. In either case the standard paraphrase can fulfil a useful function.

The danger of misunderstandings appears to be greatest when *assertives* are performed, because they can have a variety of roles in the discussion. They may serve to advance, maintain or retract a point of view concerning the expressed opinion at the centre of the discussion, they may perform the illocutionary act complex of *argumentation* and they may establish the result of the discussion.

A further complicating factor is that *assertives* can also be used in the performance of usage declaratives. A language user who at a given moment in the discussion fulfils the role of listener will sometimes have to decide whether an *assertive* that has been advanced is to be interpreted as the *argumentation* for a particular point of view or as an *amplification* of it. If the force and role of the speech act concerned have not been indicated unambiguously this can easily lead to problems.

The importance of distinguishing between an *argumentation* and an *amplification* is clear. An amplification is designed to increase the listener's comprehension, and will have to be judged accordingly. An argumentation has to be judged on its justificatory or refutatory potential in respect of the disputed expressed opinion and on the acceptability of the statements which constitute the argumentation. Each of these two illocutionary act complexes has its own consequences for the further course of the discussion. An amplification regarded as unsound will in principle be followed by a request for further *amplification*, whereas argumentation regarded as unsound will in principle have to be followed by a request for further *argumentation*.

In a discussion in which the language users involved in the dispute are themselves physically present, all this need not present any insuperable difficulty. In cases of doubt the listener can ask the speaker for clarification or can immediately submit his own interpretation to the speaker, while as soon as it becomes necessary the speaker can indicate of his own accord what role is played by one of his speech acts by tacking onto it a standard paraphrase or a suitable variant of it from everyday idiom. Should it become apparent as the discussion progresses that the listener has misinterpreted the speaker's utterances, it is thus still possible for the speaker to correct the misapprehension.

Where the discussion is in writing the situation is generally rather different. The language users are then forced to rely solely on their own interpretation of other language users' speech acts, and in such cases it is wisest to be as explicit as possible. The problem remains, however, what line of action should be taken in interpreting doubtful cases.

Since the purpose of argumentative discussions is to resolve disputes through argumentation, it is the failure to recognize argumentation as argumentation, in particular, than can easily result in an unsatisfactory conclusion to the discussion. For example, the protagonist may erroneously adhere to his point of view, or the antagonist may mistakenly continue to have his doubts. In cases in which the interpretation of an *assertive* presents problems (because *assertives* can be part of either an argumentation or a declaration or explication) it is wisest, therefore, *always to choose an argumentative interpretation*, since this ensures that no part of the argumentation that might be crucial to the resolution of the dispute can escape the listener's attention.

Recommending this strategy of the *maximum argumentative interpretation of assertives* offers advantages for the resolution of disputes. It can be justified by referring to the *purpose* of the discussion and the obligation on the speakers in rational discussions to make the illocutionary force of their statements *recognizable*. It is important to note that adopting the strategy of the maximum argumentative interpretation of *assertives* shifts the *burden of proof* from the *listener* (or reader) to the *speaker* (or writer).

As in sections 4.2.2, 4.3.2 and 5.4, we shall close this section by formulating some guidelines, whose purpose in this case is to further the satisfactory interpretation of the illocutionary force of speech acts and the role that they fulfil in resolving the dispute.

(19)   *Establish for which speech acts the illocutionary force is not indicated explicitly and find out whether it can be established from indications provided by the verbal and non-verbal context.*

(20)   *Establish for which speech acts the illocutionary force remains unclear and find out what role these speech acts may play at the stage of the discussion concerned.*

(21)   *Establish what the illocutionary force of the problematical speech acts might be, considering the role they may have at a particular stage in the discussion, and give a standard paraphrase of the speech acts concerned.*

(22)   *Establish which of the problematical speech acts performed at the argumentation stage are assertives and allocate to those speech acts a maximum argumentative interpretation.*

Chapter 6

Unexpressed premisses in rational discussions

6.1. UNEXPRESSED PREMISSES AND THE CO-OPERATIVE PRINCIPLE

In the guidelines for the analysis of argumentative discussions formulated in sections 5.4 and 5.5 no account is taken of the fact that when the illocutionary act complex of *argumentation* is performed some parts of the argumentation may remain *implicit*. These implicit components of the argumentation may be important (perhaps even crucial) for the resolution of the dispute, and for a satisfactory analysis of an argumentative discussion it is therefore necessary for them to be *explicitized*. Explicitization is sometimes a serious problem, and we have made it our purpose to draw up guidelines for the explicitization of implicit argumentative components (*aim 4*).

Elements of the argumentation that the speaker does not explicitly put into words may still be part of the attempt at justification or refutation that takes place in the argumentation. By long-standing terminological convention, such components of the argumentation, which have not been formulated explicitly but which are nevertheless regarded as part of the argumentation, are called *suppressed* or *tacit premisses*. Language users often employ suppressed or tacit premisses without any intention of misleading other interlocutors and without their argumentation being defective. It is for this reason that we prefer to use the term *unexpressed premisses*. In this chapter we shall be concerned with the question of how to establish the *presence* of an unexpressed premiss in an argumentation and how to *identify the statement* that may be regarded as an unexpressed premiss in that particular argumentation.[40]

Many authors rightly observe that in practice there is nothing unusual about all sorts of elements in argumentation remaining implicit.[41] But this does not mean that language users are constantly trying to lead one another up the garden path by presenting defective argumentation. Very often it is completely unnecessary (and thus even disruptive) to explicitize exactly what one means. A general explanation for this, we believe, can be offered by starting from the theoretical insights of Grice in respect of the conduct of conversations.

According to Grice the conduct of conversations is based on a *co-operative principle* (CP) which he formulates as follows:

> *Make your conversational contribution such as is required, at the stage at which it occurs, by the accepted purpose or direction of the talk exchange in which you are engaged* (1975:45).

According to Grice there are four kinds of maxim that enable language users to conform to this principle: the maxims of *quantity, quality, relation* and *manner*.[42] Generally speaking every language user will adhere to these maxims and, so long as there are no indications to the contrary, assume that his collocutor is also adhering to them. Cases in which the speaker leaves certain elements implicit, yet the listener still understands what he means over and above what he 'literally' says, can then be explained by assuming that, in combination with the co-operative principle, these maxims enable the interlocutors to convey *conversational implicatures*.

If a speaker is both able and in a position to adhere to a particular maxim, yet deliberately and openly violates it, even though there is no reason to suppose that he has completely abandoned the co-operative principle, then according to Grice it is possible for a conversational implicature to arise (1975:49). The maxim concerned is then *exploited* by the speaker in order (by way of the conversational implicature) to convey more than he says explicitly. It depends partly on the listener whether the desired transfer is actually completed, since the implicature is not (by definition) offered to him explicitly and he therefore has to 'infer' it with the tools available to him (which include the 'literal' utterance and the maxims).

The steps in the train of reasoning that the listener must go through in order to achieve this follow roughly the following pattern:

(a) the speaker has said p;
(b) there is no reason to suppose that he is not observing the maxims, or at least the co-operative principle;
(c) he cannot say p and still observe the co-operative principle, unless he thinks q;
(d) he knows (and knows that I know that he knows) that I am capable of seeing that it is necessary to assume that he thinks q;
(e) he has done nothing to prevent me from thinking q;
(f) it is his intention that I should think q, or at least he has no objection to my thinking q;
(g) therefore he has implicated q.

It is of course unlikely that in practice the listener will consciously go through all the steps of this analytical reconstruction (in Grice's well-known example of B telling A that C is still not in prison, it may be so, for example, that A does not even know how he has deduced that B ascribes potential dishonesty to C). But that is not actually necessary for the conveyance of a conversational implicature. On the other hand Grice does say that the presence of a conversational implicature must be capable of being worked out in the way described:

> for even if it can in fact be intuitively grasped, unless the intuition is replaceable by an argument, the implicature (if present at all) will not count as a *conversational* implicature; it will be a *conventional* implicature (1975:50).

The co-operative principle only applies in conversations in which in principle the participants have a *common goal*, the *contributions to the conversation* have a bearing on one another in such a way that *they are mutually interdependent* and there is a sort of (often tacit) *agreement* about the moment at which the conversation can be regarded as *completed*. Following on from this, Grice takes the view that observing the co-operative principle and the maxims can be characterized as *rational* in roughly the following way:

> any one who cares about the goals that are central to conversation/communication (e.g., giving and receiving information, influencing and being influenced by others) must be expected to have an interest, given suitable circumstances, in participation in talk exchanges that will be profitable only on the assumption that they are conducted in general accordance with the CP and the maxims (1975:49).

In rational discussions, the purpose of which is to resolve disputes about expressed opinions, these conditions are amply fulfilled. Although the fact that the two parties may undertake every kind of attempt to have the rightness of their standpoint confirmed may at first sight give the impression that they have opposing goals, they are nevertheless also aiming for a *common goal*. And although the roles they take upon themselves in the discussion mean that they have to make more or less opposite argumentative moves, are *mutually interdependent*.

Furthermore, their verbal acting is subject to *jointly agreed regimentation* which determines how the discussion is to be conducted and how it may be terminated. This means, we believe, that the co-operative principle may be assumed to apply to all discussions about expressed opinions, in the sense in which we refer to them, and that language users wishing to conduct themselves as rational discussants will in principle have to observe the conversational maxims.

Broadly speaking this view coincides with that expressed by Holdcroft in 'Speech Act and Conversation' (1979). Holdcroft debates whether Grice's co-operative principle really applies both to conservations in which the communicative roles of speaker and listener keep changing sides and the interlocutors have conflicting interests, such as quarrels and negotiations, and to argumentations and debates.

Here the application of the co-operative principle appears at first sight to come up against the conflicting interests of the interlocutors, but on closer inspection Holdcroft thinks this is a mistaken interpretation, since in principle the interlocuters have *equal rights* and, moreover, a *common interest* in co-operation:

> It is worth their while to participate in a verbal exchange in order to find some
> resolution of the conflict of interests which is acceptable to all parties. Cooper-
> ation for a limited purpose against a background of conflict and general suspi-
> cion is surely intelligible (1979:133).

The assumption that language users wishing to resolve a dispute about an
expressed opinion by means of a discussion will in principle observe the
co-operative principle enables us to explain why it is possible for language
users to omit elements of their argumentation without immediately being
guilty of misleading or manipulating their listeners and without their argumentation automatically being unsound or defective. The same assumption
also enables us to explain why listeners try to explicitize unexpressed premisses in the argumentation, as well as helping us to indicate what aids are
available to assist them in that endeavour and how they may go about the
task. In section 6.3 we shall go into these problems of explicitization in some
detail.

Although in practice the unexpressed parts of the argumentation often
present no difficulties whatever, many argumentation theorists nevertheless
regard the explicitization of unexpressed premisses as one of the hardest
tasks facing language users engaged in a discussion.[43] This is understandable,
since it is a necessary condition of a proper assessment of argumentation that
the unexpressed premisses should be adequately explicitized and the fact that
in practice language users have no trouble with unexpressed premisses does
not automatically guarantee that they also explicitize them adequately. On
the contrary, it often emerges that in their evaluation of argumentation they
either overlook certain unexpressed elements or fill in the gaps with quite
arbitrary (and often highly dissimilar) substitutes.

Considering the importance attached to the proper explicitization of unexpressed premisses by many authors, one would be justified in supposing that
they pay a great deal of attention to developing methods and establishing
procedures to be followed by language users wishing to conduct themselves,
in this respect, as rational discussants. Such, however, is not the case. In the
published work on the analysis of argumentation unexpressed premisses
constitute a rather neglected subject - a circumstance that has not gone
unremarked by others.[44]

The rare givers of practical advice to have tried in recent years to formulate
well-founded guidelines for the explicitization of unexpressed premisses all
emphasize, not without a certain pride, that they are providing the reader
with something quite new. Thus Scriven introduces his textbook *Reasoning*
with the observation 'as far as I know, there has never been an even moder-
ately successful attempt to analyze the concept of an assumption' (1976:xvi).
Lambert and Ulrich, in *The Nature of Argument*, announce that 'we introduce
(for the first time, as far as we know) a step-by-step procedure for identifying
an argument in everyday discourse', at the same time stressing the importance of explicitizing 'suppressed premisses' (1980:x). Curiously it is of all
people Fogelin, who has repeatedly pointed out how important it is to

explicitize unexpressed premises, who in his practical textbook *Understanding Arguments* seems to regard it as sufficient to observe that 'our everyday discourse leaves much unstated' and 'these things that are simply understood must be *made explicit*. This is often illuminating and sometimes boring' (1978:182).

Despite the fact that these authors - and they are not alone in this - regard unexpressed premises as central and fundamental links in an argumentation, crucial to its evaluation, it still has to be said that they fail to establish satisfactorily what conditions must be fulfilled by an adequate explicitization of unexpressed premises, and that they also fail to provide properly grounded instructions for the way language users should approach the task of making unexpressed premises explicit. In sections 6.4 and 6.5 we shall therefore examine this problem more closely and attempt to provide a better alternative.

It seems to us that the main cause of the lack of properly grounded instructions for explicitizing unexpressed premises is the failure to locate the problem in a *theoretical framework* suitable for an approach to the individual problems involved. Often, indeed, the necessity of a theoretical approach is simply quietly ignored.

In this connection an interesting illustration is provided by Fogelin's ironic remark that logicians who concern themselves with argumentation are rather sparing when it comes to providing information on the tricky question of the unexpressed premises (1967:107). Though it dates from 1967 Fogelin's remark has lost none of its topicality, for in this respect little has changed for the better since then.

And as long as logical insights are not combined with theoretical insights into the conduct of conversations we believe it is unlikely to. The problem of unexpressed premises is not a purely *logical* one, but rather a *conversational* one. Approaches to unexpressed premises that ignore this starting point will therefore be bound to be defective. To introduce our own approach, we shall begin by indicating some important shortcomings in current approaches to unexpressed premises.

6.2. SHORTCOMINGS IN CURRENT THEORETICAL APPROACHES

6.2.1. *The Standard Logical Approach*

The essential questions to be answered by a theory of unexpressed premises are (a) how can a listener know *that* something is unexpressed in the argumentation and (b) how can he establish *what* it is that is unexpressed. These questions can be clarified by reference to a Gricean example:

   (1) John is English; he is, therefore, brave

If we treat (1) as an argument in which a premiss has been omitted, it is then plausible that the complete argument looks like this:[45]

(2) John is English
(3) all Englishmen are brave
therefore
(4) John is brave

In this reconstruction of the complete argument premiss (3) has been added to the premiss of the original argument (1). This means that in this reconstruction premiss (3) is treated as the *unexpressed premiss* of argument (1). If our analysis is correct, then, (3) may therefore be regarded as an example of what we call an *unexpressed premiss*. Translating our problem into the language of logic, we can now establish that the following questions have to be answered:

(a) *How does the listener know that a premiss has been omitted from (1)?*
(b) *How can the listener establish what the omitted premiss is?*

Various logicians have attempted to answer both these questions. In doing so they have elected for a similar approach in which the treatment of unexpressed premisses is brought under the heading of syllogistic logic. Since this approach follows what is broadly speaking always the same pattern, we shall refer to it as the *standard logical approach*. In our outline of this standard approach our starting point is the representative textbooks on logic by Copi (1972), Kahane (1973) and Rescher (1964).

In the standard logical approach it is pointed out that it is perfectly usual in arguments in ordinary discourse for premisses to be left out or for conclusions to be missing. The explanation for these omissions from the argumentation is that in practice it is *not necessary* for everything to be formulated explicitly,[46] since speaker and listener have access to *common knowledge*, which enables the speaker to rely on the listener himself supplying the premisses or drawing the conclusions omitted.

Besides efficiency it looks as if the *rhetorical persuasive power* of arguments also plays a part. The speaker can increase the effect of his argumentation on the listener by not going into too much detail and by presenting premisses or conclusions as a matter of course by not mentioning them explicitly.

An argument in which a premiss or conclusion is lacking is called in syllogistic logic an *enthymeme*. Rescher gives the following definition:

> An *enthyme* is an argument that can become a categorical syllogism with the addition of one or more statement (as premiss or conclusion). Alternatively, it may be thought of as a categorical syllogism one of whose three constituent statements has been omitted or left unstated (1964:161).

Unstated premisses are thereby accommodated in the theory of *categorial syllogisms*. These, we shall observe for the sake of clarity, are arguments consisting of three categorical statements (two premisses and a conclusion), such as the classic example: (1) All men are mortal, (2) All Greeks are men, *therefore*: (3) All Greeks are mortal.

For the listener the omission of a premiss means that he is faced with an argument which, in the form in which it is presented, is *invalid*. What attitude should he adopt in the face of such an argument?

Naturally he can content himself with the observation that the argument is invalid, and then go on to reject the conclusion, but this is unsatisfactory if only because it all too easily dismisses a phenomenon that in argumentation in colloquial language is the rule rather than the exception and which could never be eliminated altogether anyway. However, he may also adopt a rather more co-operative attitude and assume that the speaker means more than he has stated explicitly. In principle, according to the standard logical approach, a rational listener will choose the latter attitude.

Kahane gives the following argumentation for this:

> Obviously, there is no point in declaring an argument in everyday life invalid when the addition of premises accepted by all concerned will render the argument valid. Life is short and we have neither the time nor the inclination to be precise and complete about everything(1973:224)

Ignoring the fact that Kahane appears to regard 'precision' as an absolute concept here, we can observe that the consequence of this view is that the listener himself must try to obtain the necessary degree of precision and completeness. And this implies, according to the standard logical approach, that he must try to augment the enthymeme in order to turn it into a valid categorical syllogism.

Rescher opines that in justification of this approach an appeal can be made to the 'Principle of Charity':

> The governing rule in the reconstruction of enthymematic arguments is the principle of charity - one should, insofar as possible, try to *make the argument valid and its premisses true* (1964:162).

The reason for Rescher's reservation ('insofar as possible') is that it is *not* always possible to make a valid categorical syllogism out of an enthymeme, and that sometimes it can only be done by using a premiss that is patently untrue.

Examples of enthymemes in which the latter situation arises are (1) 'Some Englishmen are not brave, therefore all Englishmen have red hair', and (2) 'All Englishmen are brave, therefore all Scotsmen are brave'. In (1) there is a violation of the rule that invalid categorical syllogisms it is impossible for one of the premisses to be negative and the conclusion positive and the rule that a term distributed in the conclusion ('Englishmen') must also be distributed in the premisses. Argument (2) can only be made valid by adding the patently untrue premiss 'All Scotsmen are Englishmen'.

The appeal that Rescher makes to the 'Principal of Charity' in respect of enthymemes also occurs, in this general sense, in the work of other writers.[47] Even if we simply assume that the listener is going to let himself be guided by Rescher's Principle of Charity, however, the question still arises of whether it really is all that simple to add to an incomplete argument in order to make it valid, even assuming that this is possible in principle. This is a question that the standard logical approach does not ask, though there is a suggestion that the answer to it would be affirmative.

Only Copi has anything concrete to say on the subject:

> In most cases there is no difficulty in supplying the tacit premiss that the speaker intended but did not express (1972:224).

Such optimism, however, is justified only if unexpressed premises are linked exclusively with categorical syllogisms, as they are in the standard logical approach.

A listener who knows that a syllogism by definition contains two premisses, and who is faced with an argument in which there is only one premiss, can easily deduce from this that one premiss has been omitted, and by assuming the complete argument to be a valid syllogism he can also quite easily reconstruct the entire argument, since the way is pointed, as it were, by the rules for valid categorical syllogisms. Indeed Purtill, who gives detailed instructions for supplementing a valid enthymeme, believes that the procedure is a 'mechanical' one (1979:196), though he does also think that in 'real-life arguments' it is by nó means always possible for this mechanical procedure to be put into practice (1979:9).

If one knows the rules for valid categorical syllogisms one knows that the following enthymeme can only be made valid by adding the premiss 'All B is C': 'All A is B, therefore all A is C'. Problems only arise if the restriction to categorical syllogisms is lifted, in which case the listener no longer has the security afforded him by syllogistic logic. For example, he can no longer assume that every valid argument will have two and no more nor less than two premisses. Neither can he take refuge in syllogistic system of unambiguous criteria for determining the validity of arguments. Consequently he is no longer able to establish with certainty whether or not the argument is valid and whether a premiss has been omitted.

Examples of arguments whose validity or invalidity in the form in which they are presented is not obvious abound in everyday usage. We regard the arguments (1) 'John is taller than Peter, Peter is taller than Charles, *therefore* John is taller than Charles', and (2) 'Wage increases lead to higher inflation, higher inflation is undesirable, *therefore* wage increases are undesirable', as intuitively valid, but their validity cannot be demonstrated in any of the known logical systems as long as the arguments take this form.

Argument (1), borrowed from Kahane (1973:223) must first be supplemented with a premiss formulating the *transitive* relation in 'X is taller than Y' before the argument becomes valid in predicate logic. Something similar applies in the case of argument (2), though here the premiss to be added would have to be slightly more complicated.

The standard logical approach ignores these problems, with Copi taking what must be regarded as an extremely soft option:

> Any kind of argument can be expressed enthymematically, but the kinds of enthymemes that have been most extensively studied are incompletely expressed syllogistic arguments (1972:225).

If it were possible to treat every argument as a categorical syllogism, of course, all problems would be swept aside, but that is not the case. It is easy to find examples of arguments that cannot be treated as categorical syllogisms: (1) John is English and John is brave, *therefore* John is brave, (2) If John is English, then John is brave; John is English, *therefore* John is brave, (3) All English people are brave people, *therefore* all heads of English people are heads of brave people, (4) All English people are brave people, some nice English people are not brave people, *therefore* no English people are nice English people, (5) All English people are brave-or-not-brave, all English people are cowardly-or-not-cowardly, *therefore* some brave-or-not-brave people are cowardly-or-not-cowardly.

The validity of (1) and (2) depends solely on the relations between the statements and can be demonstrated quite easily in *propositional logic*: in the case of argument (1) by applying the *simplification* rule and in the case of argument (2) by applying the *modus ponens* rule. The validity of (1) and (2) cannot be demonstrated in syllogistic logic, since that logic deals with statements in which *relations between classes* are expressed and determines which combinations of classes and relations make valid deductions possible. In (1) and (2), however, there are no categorical statements, nor is it easy to see how the first premiss of (1) and the first premiss of (2) might be formulated as categorical statements.

The validity of arguments (3), (4) and (5) can be demonstrated in *predicate logic* but not in syllogistic logic. In the case of (3) the trouble with a syllogistic treatment is that the classes named in the premiss ('English people' and 'brave people') are not the same as those referred to in the conclusion ('heads of English people' and 'heads of brave people'). Furthermore, (3) has only one premiss, not the two required of a valid categorical syllogism.

Argument (4) is invalid as a syllogism because a term distributed in the conclusion ('nice English people') is not distributed in the second premiss. This argument is, however, valid in predicate logic, since the two premisses constitute a *contradiction*. In syllogistic terms argument (5) is invalid because its conclusion is a *particular* statement, whereas the premisses are *universal* statements. Here again, however, the validity of the argument can be demonstrated in predicate logic, this time because the conclusion is *logically true* (cf. Kahane 1973:227-9).

But these examples are constructed ones, and one is therefore justified in wondering whether they will ever actually occur in discussions in colloquial speech. This consideration (which is, however, seldom expressed explicitly) might explain why logicians place the treatment of unexpressed premisses in the framework of syllogistic logic, since for the analysis of arguments used in argumentation in colloquial speech 'complicated' logical systems such as predicate logic might well prove to be unnecessary.

But this has never been demonstrated and Purtill is one of the few people to assert openly that syllogistic logic offers advantage compared with predicate logic because it is more attuned to the patterns of reasoning used in argumentation in colloquial speech (1979:158). His conclusion entirely accords with this starting point:

> For all their very limited and artificial form syllogistic arguments are surprisingly flexible and useful (1979:233).

Yet it is still risky simply to *presume* that syllogistic logic affords an adequate framework for treating unexpressed premisses. That would be to ignore the compelling reasons which originally made it necessary for logicians to develop more advanced logical systems (and which relate, among other things, to the limited scope of syllogistic logic). It would also be to ignore the fact that it is easy to give many examples of arguments not susceptible of analysis by means of syllogistic logic, which have not only not been shown to be unimportant for the practice of argumentation but which (in view of their more 'complicated' nature) may be supposed to be precisely the sort of arguments that might easily pose difficulties.

In any event, we believe that it is important not to deny out of hand that in the explicitization of unexpressed premisses the listener may be forced to take refuge in logics which do not conform to the theory of categorical syllogisms. This means that in principle the listener is faced with a problem of *choice*, since a number of logical systems have been developed which to some extent each have a different scope (and each of which may be associated with different methods of systematization and different criteria of validity).[48] In terms of scope, for example, there are differences between propositional logic, predicate logic and modal logic.

The choice of one logic or another may have consequences for the *supplementation* of incomplete arguments. Thus we have already made the argument 'John is English, therefore he is brave' valid by adding to it the premiss 'All Englishmen are brave'. The argument thus reconstructed - 'John is English; All Englishmen are brave, *therefore* John is brave' - is demonstrably valid in predicate logic and (with a slight modification) according to the theory of categorical syllogisms, but to be able to prove its validity in propositional logic we should have to add (for example) the premiss 'If John is English, then John is brave'. Where the argument is one which appears intuitively to be valid but whose validity cannot be demonstrated in any of the available logics, it may indeed be exceedingly difficult to decide what sort of addition needs to be made.

As soon as a listener who is trying to make an argument valid loses the security of syllogistic logic (in itself fragile enough, since he does not always know for certain whether or not that logic is applicable) he finds himself facing problems that are simply ignored in the standard logical approach to unexpressed premisses. Where these problems arise, therefore, the standard logical approach is always deficient.

Since it has not been demonstrated that these problems are of subordinate importance, the optimism associated with this approach in respect of the possibilities for the listener to explicitize unexpressed premisses is misplaced (which is not to say, of course, that those possibilities do not exist). In any event it is necessary to allow for the possibility that critics of the syllogistic preoccupations of proponents of the standard logical approach have right on their side. Indeed, Scriven has no doubts on this point at all, merely stating bluntly:

> The enthymeme approach is not even moderately successful as a pragmatic device (1976:xvi).

But even more important, to our way of thinking, than the neglect of the 'technical' problems facing the listener that is associated with the adoption of the standard logical approach to unexpressed premisses, is the neglect of the *conversational context*. This neglect is reflected by the fact that it is simply assumed that the listener is prepared to undertake the attempt to supplement an incomplete argument in order to make it valid.

The important and obvious question of what *reason* the listener might have for undertaking such an attempt is bypassed with a reference to the Principle of Charity. This interesting principle may indeed apply here, but it does not in itself explain why the listener should adopt so charitable (not to say 'merciful') an attitude towards the speaker's argument. It seems to us that an explanation for this can only be found by starting from the conversational context and by drawing into one's approach to unexpressed premisses the purpose of the discussion. At the same time, as we shall show in section 6.3, this opens up possibilities of a more refined analysis of the listener's conduct.

6.2.2. *The Presuppositional Approach*

We shall now turn to a consideration of an alternative to the standard logical approach to unexpressed premisses which we term the *presuppositional approach*, because it treats unexpressed premisses as presuppositions. Proponents of the presuppositional approach include Rescher (1961), Öhlschläger (1977) and Nuchelmans (1978). In the first instance it appears to offer new possibilities, but falters on certain basic notions. Our treatment of it will therefore be brief.

In 'On the Logic of Presupposition' Rescher distinguishes three different sorts of presupposition, the third of which is the most interesting from our point of view:

A third fundamental sense of the term relates to the 'presuppositions' of inference. The validity of an inference can require the satisfaction of some appropriate precondition or prerequisite. An illustration is: To infer 'X is an A' from
'X is a B' presupposes that 'All B's are A's' (1961:525).

Öhlschläger (1977) borrows Rescher's term *inferential presupposition*
(Schluss-Präsupposition), which he then uses to analyse the following argument:

(5) Fritz is a member of the union
(6) and hence a socialist

The argument '(5), hence (6)' can be regarded, according to Öhlschläger, as
an incomplete argument that can be made valid by adding a premiss. He
gives two possible additions:

(7) All union members are socialists
(8) Whenever someone is a member of the union, he is a socialist

Additions (7) and (8) are called *inferential presuppositions* for the following
reason:

> In order that (6) may validly be inferred from (5), it is a necessary condition that
> either (7) or (8) be true (trans. fr. 1977:12).

True, Öhlschläger is here guilty of confusing logical *validity* and *soundness*,
but it is still clear that, following Rescher, he wishes to treat unexpressed
premisses as presuppositions. This is confirmed when he later (without
incidentally advancing any particularly remarkable points of view) expounds
his approach in greater detail (1979:88-99).

Echoes of a similar approach to unexpressed premisses occur in Nuchelmans's introduction to the philosophy of language (1978), where he reviews
the subjects that he regards as falling within the scope of *pragmatics* and
includes among them *presuppositions*. His definition of a 'pragmatic presupposition' is based on the first definition of the term given by Stalnaker:[49]

> A speaker pragmatically presupposes that B at a given moment in a conversation
> just in case he is disposed to act, in his linguistic behaviour, as if he takes the truth
> of B for granted, and if he assumes that his audience recognizes that he is doing so
> (1973:448).

According to Nuchelmans a speaker presupposes that *p* is the case if in his
linguistic conduct he shows signs that he assumes the truth of *p* and assumes
that his audience understands this. The connection between unexpressed
premisses and pragmatic presuppositions is made by Nuchelmans in the
following way:

> A classic example [of a pragmatic presupposition] is an enthymeme or argument with a suppressed premiss: the person who presents such an argument as valid evidently takes the truth of the omitted premiss for granted and assumes that the listener will realize that he is doing so. Clearly, ordinary discourse is full of such presuppositions: what is explicitly stated in a linguistic utterance is as a rule embedded in a matrix of unformulated knowledge shared by speaker and listener (trans. fr. 1978:55).

Nuchelmans believes it to be characteristic of ordinary linguistic usage that many elements remain *implicit*. Thus argumentation in colloquial speech often contains unexpressed premisses that have to be explicitized in any logical reconstruction because they belong to the premisses of the argument.

The embedding of the treatment of unexpressed premisses in a *pragmatic theory of linguistic usage*, which is what in principle happens in the presuppositional approach, seems to us to place unexpressed premisses in a more adequate theoretical perspective than that offered by the standard logical approach, since it is founded expressly on the *functional* and *social* character of argumentation and thus provides better opportunities of explaning the use of unexpressed premisses by speakers and listeners.

Despite this, the presuppositional approach gets bogged down in its starting points and is not carried through consistently, so that the possibilities it offers have so far not been exploited. In view of the general and introductory nature of the work in which he propounds his ideas it would be a mistake to expect more than this from Nuchelmans's contribution, but Öhlschläger is undoubtedly something of a disappointment in this respect. Certainly it cannot be maintained that the presuppositional approach to unexpressed premisses, at the stage of development it has reached today, is a viable alternative to the standard logical approach.

Rescher's and Öhlschläger's actual contribution consists of no more than the recognition that unexpressed premisses can be treated as *presuppositions*, and Nuchelmans adds to this the observation that generally speaking a speaker *assumes what the listener is assumed to know* and therefore omits things that he assumes the listener will be able to supply himself, while at the same time *the listener is aware* that the speaker is doing this. According to Nuchelmans the use of unexpressed premisses can be explained by assuming the obviousness of the omitted statements and (by association) by assuming the existence of knowledge shared by speaker and listener.

Both of these elements can of course have some relevance for explaining the use of unexpressed premisses, but in this elementary form they also occur in published work in which no connection is made between unexpressed premisses and presuppositions. In suggesting reasons that a speaker may have for leaving certain steps in his argumentation implicit concepts such as 'taken for granted' (Hamblin 1970:237), 'common knowlegde' (Quasthoff 1978:16) and 'common agreement' (Fogelin 1978:182) are regularly resorted to. Even in the standard logical approach these elements are not unrepresented. There is of course no objection, *per se*, to regarding unexpressed premisses as pragmatic presuppositions, but the advantages of doing so can only become clear when the theory has been worked out more thoroughly.

We regard it as a major shortcoming of the presuppositional approach that it does not make clear, any more than the standard logical approach, what *reason* the listener can possibly have for taking so kindly an attitude to the speaker's arguments as to supply the omitted premisses himself.

The presuppositional approach focuses exclusively on the motives (conscious or otherwise) of the *speaker*, and the omission to which this gives rise constitutes, in our opinion, the crux of the difficulties involved in finding a satisfactory explanation of the use of unexpressed premisses (and this perhaps explains why the presuppositional approach gets no further than basic ideas).

6.3. UNEXPRESSED PREMISSES AS CONVERSATIONAL IMPLICATURES

In our view the best way of explaining the manner in which language users employ unexpressed premisses in practice is to treat the problem of unexpressed premisses as a *conversational* problem requiring analysis at the *pragmatic* level. In this analysis we make use of theoretical explicatory insights into the conduct of conversations which have been put forward by Grice in 'Logic and Conversation' (1975). In so doing we shall assume, as we explained in 6.1, that language users wishing to resolve a dispute about an expressed opinion by means of a discussion will conduct themselves as rational discussants at least to the extent that they will observe the *co-operative principle*.

We believe that the chief reason why listeners try to explicitize unexpressed premisses (like the reason why speakers advance argumentation) is that their purpose is to *resolve* a dispute. This means that they must be *co-operative* at least to the extent that they observe the co-operative principle and draw the conclusions attaching to the observance of that principle. This does not explain, however, exactly *how* listeners go about explicitizing unexpressed premisses. The explanation of that, we believe, can be found by treating unexpressed premisses as *conversational implicatures*.

We shall again avail ourselves of argument (1): John is English, therefore he is brave. As in section 6.2.1, we start from the assumption that the complete argument can be reconstructed as follows:

(2) John is English
(3) All Englishmen are brave
therefore
(4) John is brave

Grice uses (1) as an example of a *conventional implicature*, but it is also an example of an argument in which *a premiss has been omitted*. We assume that

(3) is the unexpressed premiss of (1), just as Grice does, incidentally, in *Some Aspects of Reason* (the text of his unpublished *Kant Lectures*), in which he calls (3) a 'suppressed premiss' (1977).

In 'Logic and Conversation' Grice says that the conclusion in (1), namely that John's braveness follows from his being English, is a *conventional implicature*. In this case it is based on the non-truth-functional meaning of the word 'therefore'. According to Grice, the speaker uttering (1) has *said* that the person referred to in 'he' is English, and also that that person is brave, and by virtue of the *meaning* of his words he has also accepts liability for the fact that the assertion that the person concerned is brave 'follows' from the fact that he is English.

This last is an *implicatum* of what he has said. Because this implicatum can be inferred from the conventional meaning of the words uttered by the speaker (in particular, 'therefore'), Grice refers in this case to a *conventional* implicature. The (not especially clear-cut) difference between this and a *conversational* implicature, he says, is that no conversational maxims are involved in the creation of a conventional implicature.

We believe that (1) can also produce a *conversational implicature* and that (3) can be regarded as a *conversational implicatum* of (1), since in his efforts to reconstruct (3) on the basis of (1) the listener's train of reasoning may be as follows:

> The speaker has *said* 'John is English, therefore he is brave'. The speaker has obviously *put forward an argumentation*, i.e. he advances 'John is English' (2) in support of (justification of) the expressed opinion 'John is brave' (4). In this form, however, the argument 'John is English, therefore he is brave' is invalid, so his argumentation is *unsound*. Thus the speaker has obviously violated the *maxim of relation* (since on the face of it (2) has nothing to do with (4)). But I have no reason to suppose that he is ignoring the *co-operative principle*. The argument can be made *valid* by *adding* 'All Englishmen are brave' (3). The *speaker* knows this, and *obviously assumes* that I do too. The speaker has made no effort to *prevent* his argument being interpreted in this obvious manner. He therefore *intends* me to add 'All Englishmen are brave' to the premiss of his argument. The statement 'All Englishmen are brave' is therefore the *unexpressed premiss* of his argumentation.

This analytical reconstruction of the listener's train of thought not only utilizes Gricean insights into the conduct of conversations, here applied from the listener's angle, it also has, in that the logical criterion of 'validity' has been brought into the reconstruction, an extra guideline that is specifically applicable to conversational implicatures in genres of text in which an argument is propounded and that is lacking from other genres of text.[50] Moreover one of the starting points of the reconstruction is the essential condition for (*pro-*)*argumentation* that we formulated in section 2.5 and which decrees that argumentation is an attempt on the part of the speaker to use certain statements to justify a particular expressed opinion to the satisfaction of the listener.

The reconstruction can be further refined by more explicitly involving our analysis of the illocutionary act complex of *pro-argumentation* (see 2.5) in the inference plan (the illocutionary act complex of *contra-argumentation* is ignored here because of the nature of the example taken as the starting point, but in principle the same would apply). In particular, this means that more emphasis can be placed on the fact that the recognition of a constellation of statements as a *pro-argumentation* implies that the listener knows that the speaker is trying *to convince him of the acceptability of a particular expressed opinion* (the essential condition) and that assuming that the correctness conditions for the performance of that act complex have been satisfied entails, *inter alia*, the listener assuming that the speaker *regards the constellation of statements advanced by him as a justification of the expressed opinion that will be acceptable to the listener* (third preparatory condition).

The inference plan for unexpressed premisses

Against this background Grice's general inference plan for conversational implicatures can be augmented and made more specific in such a way that it becomes applicable to the explicitization of unexpressed premisses. This means that it is now possible to make an analytic reconstruction of the inference of unexpressed premisses (the ordering in steps being to some extent arbitrary). We believe that the way a listener goes about the task of inferring unexpressed premisses in the case of *pro-argumentation* can be reconstructed as follows:

(a) *The speaker has said "p, therefore q".*

(b) *The speaker has evidently put forward an argument, witness certain illocutionary indicators; that is to say, he is trying to convince me of the acceptability of q by trying to justify q by means of p.*

(c) *q can only be justified by means of a valid argument (and the speaker knows that and knows that I know that), but "p, therefore q" is not a valid argument.*

(d) *The speaker has thus offended against the maxim of relation, but there is no reason to suppose that the speaker is not (or no longer) adhering to the co-operative principle.*[51]

(e) *The speaker believes that I shall regard his argumentation as a justification of the expressed opinion and he knows that he can be held to his argumentation; therefore I must assume that he assumes that I shall see how his argument can be validated.*

(f) *The argument can be validated by adding premiss r to premiss p and the speaker assumes (and assumes that I assume that he assumes) that I have enough logical insight to validate the argument "p, therefore q" by the addition of r.*

(g) *The speaker has done nothing to prevent me making the addition of r, so that I may assume that it is his intention to allow me to make that addition or at least that he will raise no objection to it.*

(h) *Thus r may be regarded as the unexpressed premiss in the speaker's argumentation.*

With this analytical reconstruction we hope we have demonstrated satisfactorily how certain important problems of explication in respect of unexpressed premisses in pro-argumentation can be answered in principle. (A similar reconstruction is easily made for contra-argumentation.) This has been achieved by assuming an adherence to the co-operative principle and Grice's maxims and treating unexpressed premisses as conversational implicatures.

What this approach amounts to is that the explicitization of an unexpressed premiss is treated as an activity on the part of the listener that is directed towards remedying an apparent violation of a maxim in the speaker's argumentation by augmenting the argumentation in such a way that it conforms to the co-operative principle. The reason for the listener's willingness to do this is that the purpose of the discussion of which the argumentation is a component is to resolve a dispute about an expressed opinion. A listener wishing to observe the co-operative principle therefore assumes that the speaker is also observing it, even though on the face of it this appears not to be the case.

Among the aids available to the listener for explicitizing unexpressed premisses are his familiarity with the *conditions for the performance of speech acts* and with the *co-operative principle* and the *maxims for the conduct of conversations*. He will also, of course, make use of his knowledge of what the speaker has literally said, shared knowledge of the purpose of the conversation, other shared background knowledge, and the verbal and non-verbal context (to which we shall return later).

The fact that the listener avails himself of the conditions for speech acts and the conversational maxims does not, of course, mean that he can be regarded as having a developed theory of speech acts and conversational conduct at his disposal. What it *does* mean is that as a mature language speaker he must be deemed capable of more or less intuitively bringing the conditions for the performance of speech acts into his interpretation of them and more or less intuitively applying the co-operative principle and the maxims.

In Grice's general inference plan for conversational implicatures there is no speech act aspect (as there is in our steps (b) and (e)), even though (with the necessary modifications) it could also be involved in the inference of other conversational implicatures besides unexpressed premisses.[52]

But the most important difference between our plan and Grice's general one is that our listener (in steps (c), (e) and (f)) is offered extra security by involving the aspect of the validity of arguments in the process of inference. The guideline for the listener trying to identify unexpressed premisses that is provided by the logical criterion of validity is naturally not going to be available in a *general* plan for the inference of conversational implicatures.

A listener whose purpose is to resolve a dispute about an expressed opinion and who therefore observes the co-operative principle and assumes that the speaker is doing likewise will assume, if an *invalid argument* occurs in the speaker's argumentation, that *a premiss is missing* from that argument, and he will try to *make the argument valid by the addition of a premiss*. His preparedness to do so, which is a product of the co-operative principle, is also appealed to in the Principle of Charity. The listener need not necessarily, of course, have a theory about the validity of arguments: here again he will depend largely on his intuition.

Empirical investigation will have to determine the extent to which the *agreement on criteria of validity* that is required before invalid arguments can be made valid in particular instances actually exists in practice between interlocutors,[53] though in fact even agreement of this kind is no guarantee that these common criteria will always be *applied* by language users evaluating argumentation, nor is it true that this empirical research would render *normative* investigations superfluous, since it does not follow from the empirical fact that certain language users apply (or think they ought to apply) corresponding criteria when assessing particular argumentations, that those criteria are therefore always going to be the ones best suited to the assessment of that argumentation.

The listener can put into practice his willingness to add an extra premiss to, and thus make valid, an argument advanced by the speaker that is invalid by virtue of its incompleteness (on the basis of rules for the validity of argument forms) by reconstructing it in such a way that there is no longer any violation of a conversational maxim. If this is how the listener approaches his task, he is in principle contributing to the resolution of the dispute to which the argumentation relates, and is thus conducting himself in a co-operative manner.

This approach also explains why the listener tries to validate an invalid argument put forward by the speaker by adding to it a *true* premiss, since if he were to add a *false* premiss this would mean that he was simply assuming that the speaker, without having any clear purpose in doing so, was violating the first maxim of *quality*.

This assumption would be against the co-operative principle, wheras the listener's attempt to make the argument valid implies precisely the opposite, i.e. that he assumes the co-operative principle to be operating. The demand that is made on the listener in the Principle of Charity is, *stricktly speaking*, too onerous. It cannot possibly be required of the listener that *he* guarantee the truth of a premiss that is part of the *speaker's* argument. The most that can be asked of him is that he should not unnecessarily augment the argument with a premiss that he knows to be false.[54] We shall return to this point in the following sections.

6.4. THE CONDITIONS FOR EXPLICITIZED UNEXPRESSED PREMISSES

In his inference plan Grice simply *says* that in cases in which his analysis shows a conversational implicature to be involved, a speaker who is observing the co-operative principle not only says *p* but also thinks the implicatum *q*. However, he says nothing about *how the listener arrives at q, rather than something else, from p*. Why, for example, does he not end up at *r, s* or *t*? The question of how the listener, with the tools available to him, arrives at one particular statement, and not at one of the other statements which constitute the theoretical alternatives, is not adequately answered, as Grice himself admits.[55]

Numerous author's, among them Bach and Harnish (1979), have rightly stressed that Grice's theory of conversations provides more possibilities of explaining pragmatic usage phenomena than any other approach so far propounded, and indeed it is difficult to see how these usage phenomena could be explained without recourse to the kind of categories distinguished by him. Even so, there is a grave defect in the theory. Its explanatory force is too great: too many different solutions (*q, r, s, t*) to the same problem can be covered by a single explanation.

It is certainly an important bonus that we can now give an explanation of the use of unexpressed premisses that is better than all the theories proposed hitherto. And in fact it may be impossible and even unnecessary to find an explanation good enough to enable us to draw up a watertight and universally applicable procedure for the explicitization of unexpressed premisses. This does not detract from the fact that it will only be possible to draw up usable and useful guidelines for explicitizing unexpressed premisses that are difficult to trace when the difficulty that is encountered has, as far as possible, been resolved.

A number of writers attribute the difficulty in some degree to an excessive vagueness of the maxims formulated by Grice, and try to improve the theory by proposing *precizations*.[56] We agree that improvements are necessary, but at the same time we believe that the theory as it stands is in principle good enough for our purposes. As regards the explicitization of unexpressed premisses the chief improvement that we believe can and must be made is that the theory be extended to indicate *what conditions must be fulfilled by an explicitized unexpressed premiss*.

It is necessary to have an indication of this because otherwise it is unclear by what principles a listener must allow himself to be guided when choosing from the various possible conversational implicata that might serve as supplementation of an incomplete argument. In any event, as already observed, an unexpressed premiss must at the very least have the quality of being able to make the speaker's argument *valid* if added to it as a premiss (otherwise the maxim of *relation* is not observed).

However, this immediately raises the question of whether *every* addition that makes the argument valid can be regarded as an unexpressed premiss.

Our answer to this question is , of course, negative; but that brings us straight away to the question of how *selection* from the candidate statements is to take place.

In the rare practical publications about arguing and discussing that pay any attention at all to unexpressed premises, the importance of detecting them is generally stressed at some length, but there is usually a complete absence of concrete instructions that the reader may follow. With the occasional favourable exception, these publications do not, therefore, provide points of contact for the solution of the difficulties associated with explicitizing unexpressed premises.

Black's *Critical Thinking* is a good example of this. Black regards explicitizing unexpressed premises as the chief task to be performed when evaluating argumentation (1952:27-8). 'Make certain that all unexpressed premises have been included' is his advice, therefore, when he gives his procedure for analysing argumentation (1952:69). As to the manner in which he might be able to comply with this exhortation, however, the listener is left in the dark.

Recent publications which *do* go into the problems that may occur in the explicitization of unexpressed premises include Scriven (1976), Schellens & Verhoeven (1979) and Lambert & Ulrich (1980). They all turn out to be of our opinion, i.e. that not every addition that makes an argument valid can be regarded as an unexpressed premiss of the argumentation of which the argument is a part, but they do not provide a satisfactory alternative.

Lambert and Ulrich are the most unequivocal in their judgement that not every premiss that makes the argument valid can be considered to be an unexpressed premiss. *Every* invalid argument, they say, can be made valid by the addition of an *if...then...* sentence:

> One can, after all, always find such a premise for any argument simply by joining the original premises by the appropriate number of conjunctions '... and —' and then prefixing the complex sentence so produced by 'if...' and the conclusion of the original by 'then —' (1980:60).

Scriven is rather less clear on this point. He distinguishes between *minimal assumptions*, which from the logical angle are necessary to make the argument valid, and *optimal assumptions*, which from the logical point of view are equally adequate but are 'stronger' than minimal assumptions and are, moreover, 'independently well-supported' (1976:43). Although Scriven does not elaborate on this and gives no general rule for choosing between minimal assumptions and optimal assumptions in concrete instances, he gives the impression of preferring the latter. At least, this is a possible inference from a remark that he makes about the *purpose* of explicitizing unexpressed premisses, when referring to an example:

> We look for the kind of factual claim that is likely to have evidential support, as
> well as being logically adequate for the argument. This usually means that we go
> a little stronger than the minimal assumption that would do the job, and thus
> finish up with what was earlier called the 'optimal assumption' (1976:86).

Schellens and Verhoeven, too, differentiate between a *minimal assumption*, which they call the *logical minimum*, and more comprehensive possibilities. Although they do not reject the logical minimum as a possible addition, they prefer one 'based on knowledge of the world', one which, 'viewed pragmatically ... comes more naturally to mind in the context concerned' (trans. fr. 1979:8).

What they mean by a 'logical minimum' becomes clear from their examples: an *if ..., then ...* sentence in which the premiss formulated explicitly is filled in for the *antecedent* and the conclusion comes in the place of the *consequence*. But exactly how one is supposed to establish what more comprehensive addition comes more naturally to mind is something they omit to say.

All these authors pronounce themselves (more or less clearly and more or less forcefully) in favour of an explicitization of unexpressed premisses that goes further than what would logically speaking be necessary to validate the argument. In other words they agree with us that having traced the logical minimum is not a sufficient condition to be able to say that the unexpressed premiss has been explicitized. However, what other conditions still have to be met is still unclear. Is the listener supposed, perhaps, to set himself the difficult task of finding out what the speaker 'had in mind' when he advanced his argumentation? Or must he establish what the speaker himself wishes to regard as the unexpressed premiss?

On this point it is again Lambert and Ulrich who are clearest. To them, there is no question but that what the speaker himself regards as the (unexpressed) premiss of his argument constitutes the norm. According to them, an added premiss only counts as an unexpressed premiss if it not only makes the speaker's argument valid but is also *self-evident* in the speaker's eyes (the 'criterion of obviousness') and, moreover, if it is also clear that the speaker *believes* it and expects the listener to believe him (the 'criterion of belief') (1980:58-9).

However, they do add the rider that the criteria of obviousness and belief do not constitute *carte blanche* to treat any statement regarded by the speaker as obvious and credible as an unexpressed premiss in the argumentation concerned. Candidates for such treatment are only those additions to the argument that the speaker actually supposes to be *premisses* (1980:60).

Scriven takes more or less the same attitude as Lambert and Ulrich. This is immediately apparent from the fact that besides the 'minimal assumptions' and 'optimal assumptions' already mentioned he also distinguishes 'arguer's assumptions', which are what the speaker 'consciously assumed or would accept as an assumption if asked' (1976:43). It is not surprising, then, that Scriven should give the listener the following advice: 'try to relate the assumptions as you formulate them to what the arguer would be likely to know or would believe to be true' (1976:85).

There appears, however, to be something of a contradiction of this in the observation with which Scriven immediately follows it, namely that the explicitization of unexpressed premisses should *not* be primarily intended to assist in the reconstruction of the 'state of mind or body of beliefs' of the speaker. But he then goes on to qualify this remark again by adding that it can sometimes still be relevant to take account of these points.

Unlike Scriven and Lambert and Ulrich, Schellens and Verhoeven say nothing, when they come to set out a procedure for detecting what they refer to as implicit premisses, about establishing premisses that the speaker may have in mind but has not formulated explicitly. Although they express themselves in somewhat cautious terms, they appear to take the point of view that the listener must establish which statement the speaker is (also) *obliged to defend* (1979:7).

However, they omit to indicate the basis of the speaker's obligation to defend his argument, or how the listener can find out which statements the speaker is under an obligation to defend. On the other hand they do introduce a new and interesting element into the discussion about the explicitization of premisses, linking *externalization* of argumentation with *socialization* in the way we advocate.

Fortunately Grice's theory of conversation enables us to say more about the speaker's obligation to defend his argumentation and about how the listener can establish which statements the speaker is obliged to defend. A speaker who observes the co-operative principle must also observe the conversational maxims, and in the context of unexpressed premisses this means that he can be held to a statement that not only makes his argument valid (so that it accords with the maxim of *relation*), but also accords to the maxims of *quantity* and *quality*. It is up to the listener to find out to which statements this may apply, and in doing so he is guided by the maxims.

In the following section we shall indicate more precisely what this means for the explicitization of premisses, but we shall begin by explaining the consequences of the maxims for the conditions that an explicitized premiss has to fulfil. The maxim of *relation* dictates that the added statement must be a sentence which, if incorporated into the argument, will render it *valid*. The maxim of *quantity* decrees that the statement must be *informative* and the maxim of *quality* says that the statement must be an element of the speaker's *committedness*. Before we move on to section 6.5., in which we shall be examining how the listener can exploit these maxims for the explicitization of unexpressed premisses, here is a brief amplification of these conditions.

If a statement is added to the argumentation such that the argument expressed in the argumentation is rendered valid, then the maxim of *relation* is fulfilled. This does not mean, however, that it is sufficient simply to use the logical minimum (which can always be obtained by recasting the argument in the *modus ponens* mould), because the additional statement will not then automatically be so informative as to accord with the maxim of *quantity*. On the other hand there is also a danger that a statement will be added which, though it goes further than the logical minimum, conflicts with the maxim of *quality*, so that the listener becomes guilty of a fallacy of the straw man variety.

It follows from the listener's willingness that he himself should observe the co-operative principle when explicitizing unexpressed premisses in the speaker's argumentation, that he cannot attribute to the speaker any premiss that he does not believe the speaker believes to be true. This brings us back to the question of whether, when explicitizing unexpressed premisses, he must therefore make it one of his aims to establish what the speaker himself thinks or believes.

Quite apart from the practical difficulties that this may raise (particularly in the case of written communication), we believe the question must be answered in the negative on the grounds that to do otherwise would be to take an approach that is fundamentally wrong. It is our view that the correct application of the maxim of *quality* implies that the listener (or reader) must, on the basis of what the speaker (or writer) has said and with the assistance provided by rules for valid argument forms and the conditions applying to the speech act of argumentation, try to establish to what the speaker is *committed*. The speaker can also be held to statements to which he has committed himself *implicitly*, so that in principle he is also *obliged to defend* such statements. Whether these statements coincide with what the speaker 'actually' thought or subsequently comes to believe is irrelevant.

The conditions which, in our opinion, an explicitized unexpressed premiss must fulfil can be summarized as follows:

(a) *The explicitized premiss must be a statement which, if added to the speaker's argument as a premiss, would make the argument valid (and thereby prevent a violation of the maxim of relation).*
(b) *The explicitized premiss must be an informative statement (thereby preventing a violation of the maxim of quantity).*
(c) *The explicitized premiss must be a statement that is an element of the speaker's committedness (thereby preventing a violation of the maxim of quality).*

6.5. THE EXPLICITIZATION OF UNEXPRESSED PREMISSES

The question of exactly how listeners should go about the business of explicitizing unexpressed premisses is answered satisfactorily by none of the writers who concern themselves with unexpressed premisses. In this respect Lambert and Ulrich are probably the worst offenders. From the way they formulate their criterion of *belief* it becomes clear that in their opinion the listener must at all times start from what the speaker has literally said, but how, in that case, the unexpressed premiss is to be inferred they fail to mention , though they do later observe, unnecessarily, that the explicitization of unexpressed premisses is not a matter of mechanics but that the listener must keep a close watch on what is going on in a given *context* (1980:60).

For Schellens and Verhoeven, too, the context occupies a key position. The third step in their procedure is as follows:

> Add to the argument *the most natural premiss in the context* that validates the argument without rendering superfluous the premiss or premisses already given (trans. fr. 1979:8).

The crucial question that has to be answered in a procedure for explicitizing unexpressed premisses is, of course, assuming that one attributes such a central role to the context, how the listener is to find out what is most natural in a particular context. That he has to draw on his knowledge of the world, as Schellens and Verhoeven observe, would appear to be fairly obvious, but the essential question is again, of course, *how*, and on that point Schellens and Verhoeven offer him not even a clue.

With Scriven the listener is allotted the task of formulating the 'optimal assumptions' in the speaker's argument. Since these - if all is well - coincide with the 'arguer's assumptions', it would seem natural to *ask* the speaker direct what he *himself* regards as the premiss that is suppressed in his argumentation. But Scriven has little faith in such an approach, since in his view it is perfectly possible that the speaker himself will not know precisely what the answer to that question would be (it may even be a matter of 'unconscious assumptions'), and, moreover, there is a danger that he will supply more than is strictly necessary for the validation of his argument (1976:86).

So with Scriven too the listener is left to solve the problem himself, but at least - in contrast to the situation with Lambert & Ulrich and Schellens & Verhoeven - he is offered some sort of guidance: the listener must take account of the fact that the added statement (1) must be 'strong' enough to make the argument valid, and (2) must not be 'stronger' than necessary.

As an example of an addition that is 'too weak' Sriven mentions the simple observation that according to the speaker there is some kind of connection between the premiss and the conclusion or that this conclusion follows from this premiss (1976:163). Additions of this kind he calls 'entirely unhelpful', and his most serious objection to them is: 'You're not doing argument *analysis* by mentioning this, you're only repeating the argument' (1976:163).

Scriven expresses the opinion, though without further elaboration, that the added statement must be *new*, *relevant* and *convincing* (1976:173), albeit that the listener must not go too far or he will run the risk of being guilty of a straw man fallacy (1976:85). This would also cause him to violate the Principle of Charity, which decrees that he must try to find the 'best possible' rather than the 'worst possible' interpretation of the speaker's words

(1976:71). Attributing 'too strong' a statement to the speaker saddles him with a greater responsibility than is either necessary or admissible.

All in all, then, even the most concrete of the hints given in the practically oriented literature on unexpressed premisses are pretty vague. The examples so liberally given (especially by Scriven) and the explanatory material provided may, perhaps, help the listener a little further on his way, but in the end he is still forced to rely chiefly on his own imagination. Such a situation is naturally unsatisfactory from whichever angle one looks at it - whether from the viewpoint of the theory of argumentation or from the practical angle. We shall therefore try to formulate more adequate guidelines for the listener, starting from the conditions we have formulated which have to be fulfilled by explicitized unexpressed premisses, and with the help of Grice's theory of conversation.

Our starting point, we believe, must be that an argumentation in a discussion in ordinary discourse in which a premiss is suppressed must not automatically be regarded as an 'unfinished' or 'defective' argumentation from which something has been *lost* or *wrongly omitted*. Otherwise we should automatically regard some argumentation that in practice is perfectly normal and need present no difficulty at all, as imperfect or inadequate, and that appears to us undesirable and unnecessary.

In our opinion it is necessary when analysing the use of unexpressed premisses to distinguish between two different levels: the *pragmatic conversational level* of the discourse and the *logical semantic level* of a (valid) deduction. In the case of analysis on the first level attention is focused on the illocutionary act complex of *argumentation* and the way it is interpreted, and in the case of analysis on the second level the analysis concentrates on an *argument* expressed in that illocutionary act complex, and the way in which that argument must be judged.

In the case of a pragmatic conversational analysis it has to be assumed that nothing need be wrong with the argumentation just because the speaker suppressed a premiss, whereas in a logical semantic analysis it is necessary to carry out a reconstruction of the argument in which all its components are formulated explicitly. Both levels of analysis must eventually be linked, but they must not become confused or biased in any particular direction (as happens, we believe, in current approaches to unexpressed premisses).

The necessity of a logical reconstruction of the argument, constructed on the lines of a logical ideal, that can be regarded as underlying the argumentation, does not arise until the pragmatic conversational level of interpretation is left and one moves on to the logical semantic level of assessment. It is then necessary to construct a hypothesis concerning the premiss that has been left unexpressed and which has to added to the argument in order to make it valid. In the heuristic of drafting this hypothesis, however, indicators at the pragmatic conversational level may fulfil a guiding function.

Let us clarify our ideas by reference to our earlier example:
    (1) John is English; he is, therefore, brave
    (2) John is English
    (3) All Englishmen are brave
       (3')If John is English, then John is brave
       (3") All island-dwellers are brave
therefore
    (4) John is brave

We agree with Grice that in cases like (1) there is in fact a 'double' argument or, to put it another way, there are two *levels*. In the first place there is the argumentation as actually formulated by the speaker and in the second place there is an 'ideal' argument constituting an analytical reconstruction of the argumentation actually put forward (cf. Grice 1977:I-10). Explicitizing the unexpressed premiss is a logical semantic activity relating to the reconstruction of the idealized argument, not to the correction of the argumentation actually uttered.

At first Grice appears to be saying that he regards the listener's task as being to establish what the speaker was thinking but did not put into so many words, and that that is sufficient. However, closer inspection shows this to be erroneous, as he says that when it comes to finding out the exact wording of an unexpressed premiss he is not so much interested in a 'reportive' answer, representing the *psychological* dimension, as in a 'constructive' answer:

> We are in general much more interested in whether an inferential step is a good
> one to make than we are in what a particular person had in mind at the actual
> moment at which he made the step (1977:I-15).

We believe that what we ought to be interested in is establishing precisely what the speaker is *committed to* if the argument that he advances in his argumentation is explicitized so as to make it a valid argument. This implies that the listener must try to find out *what he can hold the speaker to* in view of the co-operative attitude that the speaker has adopted in the discussion in respect of the argument. Doubtless it will be no mere coincidence if this corresponds to what the speaker 'had in mind', but such a correspondence is neither necessary nor all-important.

A speaker who is observing the co-operative principle is committed not only to those speech acts that he has performed explicitly but also to what he has *implicitly made known* in his usage. This applies not only to his usage during discussions but also to his usage in the majority of other speech events. In their *Foundations of Illocutionary Logic* (to be published) Searle and Vanderveken give a clear example of this:

> For example if he (the speaker) asserts that all men are mortal and that Socrates is a man,
> he is committed to the assertion that Socrates is mortal even though he has not explicitly
> expressed the proposition that Socrates is mortal (n.d.:I-26).

What Searle and Vanderveken have to say here on the subject of an unexpressed *conclusion* applies equally to unexpressed *premisses*. If the speaker advances an argumentation in which an argument is expressed that is only valid when a premiss has been added to it, he is *committed by* what he *has* advanced explicitly to the premiss that needs to be added to his argument for it to be valid, and in principle he has an *obligation to defend* the statement in which that premiss is put in to words. Explicitizing unexpressed premisses thus amounts to formulating statements which put into words premisses that validate the speaker's argument and to which he is committed in the same way as to those statements that he *has* put forward explicitly.

A problem referred to earlier which is directly related to this - and here we return to the question of how far it is sufficient to formulate a *logical minimum* when explicitizing unexpressed premisses - is how the listener can *establish* what the speaker is committed to on the basis of what he has said. A simple answer would be: 'The speaker is committed to a statement with which his argument can be made *valid*'. After all, there seems to be unanimity on this requirement of validity among the authors concerned in the controversy about unexpressed premisses. But writers with more of an eye for accuracy immediately add to this that not *every* addition that validates the argument can therefore automatically be regarded as an (let alone *the*) unexpressed premiss. Such an answer is not merely simple: it is too simple.

The validity of the reconstructed argument is a *necessary*, but not a *sufficient*, condition for being able to say that an unexpressed premiss has been explicitized. For example, the addition of (3') to our example (1) unquestionably makes the argument valid, as may easily be demonstrated with the aid of the *modus ponens* rule of propositional logic. This is not enough, however, to be able to call (3') the unexpressed premiss of (1).

As we observed in section 6.4, *every* 'incomplete' argument can be made valid by filling in the given premiss as the antecedent in an 'if ... then ...' statement and treating the conclusion as the consequence. Our objection to this was that it did not provide an *analysis*, merely a *description*.

Of course the speaker assumes that (4) follows from (2), otherwise he would not have advanced (1). In fact, what happens here is simply that the argumentation is *repeated* in a different wording. The observation that according to the speaker (4) follows from (2) is a *conventional* implicature of (1), arising out of the non-truth-functional meaning of the particle 'therefore'.

A listener who fails to see that according to the speaker (4) follows from (2) has *failed to understand* that the speaker, in (1), has *argued*. This means that he has also failed to recognize the illocutionary force of (1) (cf. section 2.5). *Recognition of the illocutionary force of argumentation is a preliminary condition for the identification of unexpressed premisses.*

As we argued earlier, an unexpressed premiss must be regarded as a *conversational implicature*. From a Gricean point of view it would be to violate the maxim of *quantity* (and would perhaps even mean the complete abandonment of the co-operative principle) if 'If (2), then (4)' were to be called the conversational implicature of (1), since that statement provides *insufficient information.*

The same would apply to what Fogelin calls 'pure warrant statements' (1967:25). And this is to say nothing of the misapprehension that *inference rules* are regarded as unexpressed premisses, a false impression easily gained from Toulmin's model.[57]

In our opinion (3) must be regarded both as a conversational implicatum and as an unexpressed premiss of (1), since it is a statement which does, after all, provide an adequate and informative answer to the question 'What has (2) to do with (4)?' and therefore complies with the maxims of *relation* and *quantity.* The validity of the argument '(2) and (3), therefore (4)' is easily demonstrated in predicate logic (using *universal instantiation* and the *modus ponens* rule from propositional logic).

There is no question but that a speaker who advances (1) can also be held to (3). A speaker who said 'John is English, therefore he is brave, but I do not believe for one moment that Englishmen are brave' might not, perhaps, be guilty of a logical contradiction, but pragmatically speaking his utterance is no more correct than the statement 'The cat is on the mat, but I don't believe it is', which Austin gives as an example of *pragmatic inconsistency.*

Against this view, which accords with the conditions that have to be satisfied by explicitized premisses (and which we formulated at the end of 6.4), it might be argued that the conversational implicatum that we call, in our example, the unexpressed premiss of (1), may be the *conversational minimum* to which the speaker can be held, but that in a specific context there might be other possibilities too, which might be preferable. For example, it might be argued that in a particular context it would be better to regard (3"), rather than (3), as the unexpressed premiss of (1).

This does not appear to us as a particularly valid objection. In the first place it means that it is difficult to avoid the danger (which Scriven warns against) that the listener will create a straw man, in which case (without it being necessary for the validation of the argument) the listener would be violating the maxim of *quality,* since he would then be attributing to the speaker a statement of which he himself believed that the speaker believed that it was untenable.

In the second place, even if (3") in itself *were* tenable it would be difficult to defend the view that (3") could be described as an unexpressed premiss *of (1).* In that case, we believe, it would be more correct to assume that one was dealing with a *compound argumentation,* which might be constructed as follows:

(3")   All island dwellers are brave
(9)   All Englishmen are island dwellers
therefore
(3)   All Englishmen are brave

(2)   John is English
therefore
(4)   John is brave

This compound argumentation consists of *two (subordinatively ordered) single argumentations: (3") and (9), therefore (3)* and *(3) and (2), therefore (4)*. In this compound argumentation (3") is a premiss of the first single argumentation and (3) is a premiss of the second. A speaker wishing to defend (4) on the basis of the second single argumentation is in principle also obliged to defend (3) and (2). If the listener attacks (3), the speaker is forced to begin a *new* argumentation in which (3) occurs as an *expressed opinion* and (3") and (9) act as *premisses*. The statement (3") can therefore at most act as an unexpressed premiss in the argumentation for 'All Englishmen are brave', and not in the argumentation for 'John is brave' that is conducted in (1).

The advantage of this approach is that it becomes possible, in cases involving arguments like (1), to use Grice's co-operative principle and conversational maxims, together with certain logical rules (for example from predicate logic) for the validity of argument forms, to determine *precisely what statement must be regarded as the unexpressed premiss*.

Of course, the speaker is always free to take responsibility for more than what he is obliged to defend because of the argumentation he has advanced. This can become clear in the rest of the dialogue with the listener, and may lead to another new argumentation. However, the listener cannot simply assume that statements like (3") are unexpressed premisses of argumentations like (1). He must begin by treating argumentations like (1) as *single* argumentations, and must try to explicitize the unexpressed premisses of *these*.

The approach we suggest has the advantage that in the explicitization of unexpressed premisses the role ascribed to the *verbal and non-verbal context* can be established more clearly than is done in all the other approaches known to us. It is often the context (verbal and non-verbal) that is in practice responsible for the fact that when explicitizing premisses listeners frequently arrive at different (sometimes even widely divergent) results.

Among the reasons for this are that language users frequently have more or less *different* contexts in mind and that contexts are often *polyinterpretable*. Naturally it is impossible, and undesirable, to eliminate the role of the context completely (it would also go against our view that unexpressed premisses may best be approached as conversational implicatures). However, what we *can* do in order to improve the chance of achieving intersubjective agreement regarding unexpressed premisses is to start by limiting the role of the context so that the listener has enough to go on to draft an *initial hypothesis* of the statement to be regarded as the unexpressed premiss in such a way that the hypothesis has the firmest possible general basis and can later, if the need arises, be adjusted in dialogue with the speaker. It seems to us important that when taking his first steps the listener should have as much 'firm ground beneath his feet' as possible, but this does not, of course, have to mean that his first step also has to be his last.

Our recommendation to the listener that he regard an argumentation as in (1) as a *single argumentation* implies that (unless there is an unmistakable contra-indication) the listener should adopt the position that the context is *indeterminate.*[58] That is to say, to begin with he must assume as it were a 'neutral' context (actually an impossiblility), abstracting from his own interpretation of the context. Especially in situations in which the originator of the argumentation is not present, so that it is not possible at once to elicit confirming or denying reactions (situations which occur more frequently in written discussions than in oral ones), this starting point provides an opportunity of guaranteeing the greatest possible intersubjective agreement between the language users regarding the content of the argumentation and of avoiding unnecessary verbal misunderstanding.

In our example our recommendation means that the listener is advised to regard (3) and not (3") as the unexpressed premiss of (1). In a properly defined context, on the other hand, it is conceivable that the speaker will be willing (and even obliged) to assume responsibility for (3") too and defend it against any attack.

Even then, however, (3") may not, in our view, be regarded, *instead of* (3), as the unexpressed premiss *of* (1). It would then be greatly preferable to regard both (3) *and* (3") as unexpressed premisses of the subordinatively compounded argumentation. In order to make a terminological distinction between (3) and (3") one might call (3) a *general* unexpressed premiss and (3") a *particular* unexpressed premiss. This ties up with the distinction made by Grice between 'generalized' and 'particularized' conversational implicatures (1975:56). Of course, unexpressed premisses may occur not only in *single* and *subordinative* compound argumentation, but also in *co-ordinative* compound argumentation. However, this makes no difference to the principle of analysis.

It will be clear from the foregoing that we do not regard it as possible to draw up a procedure for the explicitization of unexpressed premisses which will automatically lead to the correct and only possible formulation of *the* unexpressed premiss in every concrete instance. To be able to arrive at a definitive filling in of unexpressed premisses which exceed the *conversational minimum* it will be necessary to include other factors in the analysis, in particular the (determined) verbal and non-verbal context.

The view that unexpressed premisses in an *indeterminate context* must first be approached as *conversational implicatures in a single argumentation* does, however, provide the listener with a systematic and useful 'search strategy' or *heuristic.*[59] This heuristic indicates how he can formulate an *hypothesis* regarding the premiss left unexpressed by the speaker, so that *preselection* can take place from the large number of potential unexpressed premisses and so that the problem of choice is reduced to *manageable proportions*.

We can now, to add to the guidelines that we gave in sections 5.4 and 5.5 for the analysis of rational discussions, formulate, by way of summary, some guidelines for the explicitization of unexpressed premisses which may be regarded as the (conversational) minimum that the speaker is obliged to defend. We propose that in the explicitization of unexpressed premisses in rational discussions the following guidelines be adhered to :

(23) *Establish, starting from an indeterminate context, the single argumentation of which the unexpressed premiss to be explicitized is a part.*

(24) *Establish which statements would validate the argument if they were added to the premiss or premisses of the argument expressed in this argumentation.*

(25) *Establish which of these statements is the most informative and regard it as the premiss that is unexpressed in the argumentation.*

Chapter 7

A code of conduct for rational discussants

7.1. A GENERAL RULE FOR SPEECH ACTS IN RATIONAL DISCUSSIONS

An acknowledged problem in the resolution of disputes about expressed opinions is the classical fallacies. Fallacies are speech acts intended by the speaker to make a contribution to the resolution of the dispute but often in fact obstructing the way to a resolution. It is therefore important to prevent speakers performing such speech acts and listeners accepting their performance. Fallacies can be avoided if the interlocutors adhere to a particular code of conduct when performing speech acts in discussions. We have therefore made it out purpose to draw up a code of conduct for rational discussants (*aim 5*).

The practical value of the rules to be proposed depends on the degree to which they further the *resolution of disputes*. We shall regard the extent to which they are capable of *preventing fallacies* as a criterion for this. In this chapter we formulate rules for a code of conduct for rational discussants and in chapter 8 we shall show that fallacies may be regarded as violations of these rules.

The rules formulated in this chapter are designed to further the resolution of disputes about expressed opinions by means of argumentative discussions. In other words, they are intended to enable language users to conduct themselves as rational discussants, and they are also calculated to prevent anything that might hinder or obstruct the resolution of a dispute.[60]

At the same time, however, they cannot of course provide a guarantee that language users observing them will always be able to resolve their disputes. We believe that every one of them is a necessary condition for the resolution of disputes, but that does not necessarily mean that they are a sufficient condition.

The resolution of a dispute can be made more difficult if certain *preliminary conditions* for rational discussions are not satisfied. In formulating dialectical rules for language users wishing to conduct themselves as rational discussants we shall in principle assume that these preliminary conditions have indeed been satisfied, but we shall nevertheless incorporate conditions which have to do with matters of principle and whose fulfilment depends on a free decision on the part of the discussants.

This means that we assume the discussants to be ordinary language users in ordinary circumstances, acting of their own volition and seriously, saying what they mean and regarding themselves as committed to what they say, understanding what is said and basing their judgement on it, permitted to adopt any point of view that they may wish to adopt, and to advance any information that they may consider relevant, saying nothing that they do not consider relevant, permitted to attack any statement that they consider worth criticizing, and prepared to defend any statement of their own that may be criticized by other discussants (cf. Van Eemeren, Grootendorst & Kruiger 1983: ch. 1.3).[61]

The rules that we formulate here have to do with the conduct of language users who wish to resolve a dispute about an expressed opinion by means of an argumentative discussion. Because they together constitute a dialectical system which enables language users to conduct themselves in a manner conducive to the resolution of disputes, they may together be regarded as a dialectical *code of conduct for rational discussants.*

Since the behaviour to which the rules relate is deliberate conduct for which the discussants bear a certain responsibility, the code relates to the *acts* performed by language users in discussions about expressed opinions. In the externalized discussions which concern us here, these acts consist of *speech acts.* This means that the code of conduct we are about to draw up is a code *for the performance of speech acts in discussions.*

In chapter 5 we looked at which speech acts can occur at the successive stages of a rational discussion. They all belong to the categories of the *assertives, commissives, directives* and *usage declaratives.* In a rational discussion, in other words, there are no *expressives* and no *declaratives* other than *usage declaratives.* Two operations may be performed on the permissible *assertives* and *commissives*: *illocutionary negation* and *repetition.*

In a code of conduct for rational discussants it is necessary to take account of the distinction between those speech acts which can in principle contribute to the resolution of disputes and those that cannot. As in chapter 5, our starting point is consistently *simple single discussions*, in which one and only one point of view in respect of one and only one initial expressed opinion is defended.

In the rule limiting the permitted speech acts to specific categories it is also necessary to specify the role of the speech acts permitted and the party by whom and the discussion stage at which they may be performed. We therefore propose the following rule:

Rule 1
The participants in a discussion may perform only speech acts of the categories of the assertives, commissives, directives and usage declaratives.

Rule 1.1.
Assertives and illocutionary negations or repetitions of assertives may be performed exclusively

a. *by language user 1 at the confrontation stage and at the concluding stage in order to express, maintain or retract his point of view in respect of the initial expressed opinion, and at the argumentation stage in order to perform the illocutionary act complex of argumentation;*
b. *by language users 1 and 2 together at the concluding stage in order to establish the result of the discussion.*

Rule 1.2.
Commissives and illocutionary negations or repetitions of commissives may be performed exclusively
a. *by language user 2 at the confrontation and concluding stages in order to cast doubt on language user 1's initial point of view or to uphold or retract that doubt, and at the argumentation stage in order to accept or refuse an illocutionary act complex of argumentation performed by language user 1;*
b. *by language user 1 at the opening stage to accept language user 2's challenge to defend his point of view;*
c. *by language users 1 and 2 together at the opening stage to decide to start discussing and to agree on the division of roles and the rules for the discussion and its termination, and at the concluding stage to take the decision to terminate the discussion.*

Rule 1.3.
Directives may be performed exclusively
a. *by language user 2 at the opening stage in order to challenge language user 1 to defend his point of view and at the argumentation stage to request language user 1 to perform an illocutionary act complex of argumentation;*
b. *by language user 1 or language user 2 at all stages of the discussion to request the other to perform a usage declarative.*

Rule 1.4.
Usage declaratives may be performed at any stage in the discussion by both language user 1 and language user 2 (whether or not requested to do so by the other) in order by means of definitions, precization, amplification, explication or explicitization to further the achievement of the illocutionary effect that the performer's own speech acts are understood.

As long as the conditions formulated in rules 1.1-4 have been satisfied, all the speech acts named in rule 1 can in principle contribute to the resolution of a dispute. No other speech acts may occur in a rational discussion, but this, as already observed, does not necessarily mean that every performance of a speech act that satisfies these requirements also automatically contributes to the resolution of the dispute.

In the rules that follow we must therefore specify in what circumstances the performance of a speech act actually does make such a contribution. This implies that we shall have to indicate for each stage of the discussion when the parties are *entitled* to perform a particular speech act or, indeed, when they are *obliged* to do so.

7.2. RULES FOR THE CONFRONTATION STAGE

At the *confrontation stage* of the discussion a point of view in respect of the initial expressed opinion is externalized (by language user 1) and doubt about this point of view is also externalized (by language user 2). If there is no dispute (whether externalized or not), then there is nothing to be resolved and an argumentative discussion is superfluous.

A dispute that is only partially or not at all externalized, while not rendering the conduct of a discussion superfluous, does make it difficult. In any event, a dialectically regimented discussion is then impossible, since rules for rational discussions have to do with the speech acts performed by the interlocutors concerned and the committednesses arising out of them.

So the importance of externalizing disputes is plain, and it therefore follows that one of the most important tasks to be achieved in formulating rules for rational discussion is the furtherance of an optimal externalization of disputes. This means that the discussants must be able to advance every point of view and must be able to cast doubt on every point of view.

The guarantee that this will be possible can be obtained by expressly granting each language user the *unconditional right* to advance or cast doubt on any point of view in respect of any expressed opinion in the face of any other language user. Permitting any point of view to be advanced excludes the possibility of *taboos* in rational discussions, and permitting any point of view to be called into question excludes the *immunization* of points of view against criticism. Moreover, granting this right unreservedly to both language users also guarantees that nobody is excluded from the discussion by, for example, being blackballed.

The performance of assertives and commissives

As we argued in 5.1, points of view are always expressed by means of *assertives*. The possibility in principle to advance or cast doubt on any point of view therefore means that there are no spceial conditions governing the *propositional content* of *assertives*. The same applies to the propositional content of the *commissive* by which a point of view is questioned or not questioned.

Calling a point of view into question implies the *illocutionary negation* of the *acceptance of the propositional content* of the *assertive* by means of which the point of view is expressed and the retraction of doubt implies the *acceptance of that propositional content*. The propositional content of the *commissive accept* is equal to the propositional content of the *assertive* to which that *commissive* relates. In respect of both the *assertives* concerned and the *commissives* concerned, it may therefore be said that the propositional content need not satisfy any special conditions.

The unconditional right of language users to advance and cast doubt on points of view means that in the performance of *assertives* and *commissives* in a discussion there are no special *preparatory conditions* applying to the *status* or *position* of speaker and listener in an *extralinguistic institution*.

While explaining the absence of *declaratives* from rational discussions we point out in 5.3 that the extralinguistic institutions necessary for declaratives may constitute an obstacle to the defending and attacking roles of the language users. The same applies to exploiting differences in status or position that are not the consequence of an extralinguistic institution. In a rational discussion it is not a question of might is right, but of the quality of the argumentation and the criticism.

That disputes may refer to any point of view and that all language users have the unconditional right to advance or call into question any point of view is the principle expressed in the following rule:

Rule 2
a. *No special conditions apply to the propositional content of the assertives by means of which a point of view in respect of an expressed opinion is expressed or to the propositional content of the commissive (or its illocutionary negation) by means of which a point of view is accepted or called into question;*
b. *in the performance of these assertives and commissives no special conditions apply to the position or status of speaker and listener.*

Consequences of rule 2

Rule 2 applies to all language users taking part in a discussion. By virtue of this rule, language users not only have the right to advance or call into question any point of view; they are also prohibited from in any way whatsoever preventing other language users from doing the same. The person who nevertheless attempts to prevent others doing the same denies them the right which all language users may claim on the strength of rule 2.[62]

Perhaps unnecessarily, we would also point out here that while rule 2 bestows on language users an *unconditional right*, it does not impose an *obligation* on them. A person who holds a point of view may at any time advance it, and a person who has doubts about a point of view may at any time express those doubts. Neither is *obliged* to do so.

In general, however, it is *advisable* to avail oneself of the rights bestowed by rule 2. If one is interested in *resolving* a dispute one will have to co-operate in its *externalization*. This means that one is *obliged* to make use of one's rights, and in this sense the unconditional rights bestowed on language users by rule 2 may be regarded as *conditional obligations*.

One consequence of the *unconditional* rights bestowed on language users by rule 2, for example, is that a language user who has just lost a discussion in which he defended a particular point of view against another language user retains the right again to advance *the same* point of view for the consideration of *the same* language user. This even applies to a language user who has already successfully defended a particular point of view but who subsequently himself begins to have doubts about it, or begins to defend the opposite point of view in respect of the same expressed opinion.[63]

Naturally in such a case the question then arises as to whether the other language user is going to be willing to embark on a new discussion with so deliberately obstructive or capricious a language user, and, indeed, whether this can reasonably be expected of him. We shall return to this latter question in our discussion of the rules of the opening stage.

The performance of usage declaratives

It is extremely important, right from the start of the confrontation stage of a rational discussion, that the interlocutors understand one another's speech acts as well as possible. If a speaker formulates his point of view or his doubts about a point of view unclearly, or if the listener fails to place the correct interpretation on what is said, there is a good chance that they will be at cross purposes. Indeed, it is quite conceivable that in precisely those circumstances no discussion will ensue at all, due to the listener seeing nothing in the formulation of what the speaker has said that causes him to call it into question.

The rules for rational discussions, therefore, must not merely be conducive to the externalization of disputes but must also, and more importantly, ensure that they are externalized *in the best possible way*. For this to be the case, speakers must *formulate* optimally and listeners must *interpret* optimally. However, it is no easy matter to say exactly when a formulation or interpretation is optimal. Moreover it is impossible to increase the productive and receptive linguistic skill of language users *during* a discussion. There is therefore no point in including a rule about it.

In any event it will be clear that in a rational discussion the formulations and interpretations must not stand in the way of the resolution of the dispute. The implication of this is that the speaker must choose formulations that are comprehensible *to the listener*, and that the listener must place on the speaker's formulations interpretations that he assumes to be in agreement with *the speaker's intention*. Furthermore, should it become necessary, speakers and listeners must be prepared to *replace* their formulations and interpretations *by better ones*.

As long as language users observe Grice's *co-operative principle*, it is more or less certain that they will seek the best possible formulations and interpretations. A particularly important role is played here by the maxim of *manner* ('Be perspicuous'), since associated with it are the submaxims: 'Avoid obscurity of expression' and 'Avoid ambiguity' (Grice 1975:46).

Since we are concerned here with discussions designed to resolve disputes, we may assume that the *co-operative principle* and its associated *maxims* apply. This constitutes additional grounds for not including a separate rule for formulating and interpreting in the rules that make up the code of conduct for rational discussants.

The desire for optimal formulations and interpretations does not automatically mean, unfortunately, that they are always achieved. A speaker who doubts the clarity of his formulation is therefore well advised for safety's sake to substitute for it a formulation that he himself regards as clearer, and a listener who doubts his interpretation of what has been said is well advised for safety's sake to put his doubts to the speaker or ask for amplification or precization.

Providing amplification and precization requires (as we pointed out in 5.4) the performance of a *usage declarative*. It is thus conducive to the resolution of disputes if it is possible for language users to perform *usage declaratives*, either on their own intitiative or at the request of others. This possibility is created in rules 1.3 and 1.4, in which all language users are granted the right to perform *usage declaratives* themselves (rule 1.4) and to request the other party to perform *usage declaratives* (rule 1.3). The question now is whether this right is to be interpreted as *unconditional* or *conditional*, or whether in some cases we must even regard it as an *obligation*.

The argument against interpreting it as an *unconditional* right is that language users might *abuse* it by constantly asking other language users for amplification and precization ('What exactly do you mean by that?') or by themselves continually giving definitions and explicitizations and thus causing the discussion to get bogged down. This objection might be met by linking the right with the condition that the language users *must really need* precization (for example) or that they *must genuinely believe* that the other language user has need of precization.

However, it seems to us that it is necessary to include such a condition in the rules for rational discussions. Our observations regarding clear formulations and correct interpretations seem to us to apply equally to the requesting and performing of *usage declaratives*. As long as Grice's *co-operative principle* is being observed (and that is the supposition underlying the rules as a whole), *improper* recourse to this right is excluded. In the rules this right is therefore treated as *unconditional*.

So, if they regard it as desirable, language users taking part in a discussion can always perform a *usage declarative* and they can always request another language user to perform one. However, this latter right would be an empty one if the other language users were able simply to ignore or refuse the request. A person who requests the performance of a *usage declarative*, we may assume on the basis of the *co-operative principle*, *needs* amplification, precization or whatever.

If the request produces no response, understanding between the language users is not as good as it might be, and this stands in the way of a resolution of the dispute. Thus the *right* of the one language user to ask the other language user to perform a *usage declarative* will have to be coupled with an *obligation* on the second language user actually to perform the *usage declarative* requested. Since this obligation does not exist until a request has been made, it is a *conditional obligation*.

The rights and obligations of language users in respect of *usage declaratives* are summarized in rule 3:

Rule 3
a. *At all stages of the discussion the interlocutors have the right to ask one another to perform a usage declarative, or to perform a usage declarative themselves;*
b. *a language user requested by the other interlocutor to perform a usage declarative has an obligation to perform the usage declarative requested.*

Usage declaratives may relate to the *illocutionary force* of the speech act and to the *propositional content* of the speech act. The question is how, in either case, the clarity that is demanded can be achieved. The illocutionary force of a speech act and its role at a particular stage in the discussion can be explicitized through the use of *standard paraphrases*, as we indicate in 5.5. There are no such standardized paraphrases, however, for the clarification, precization or amplification of the propositional content. Apart from the pioneering work done in this direction by Naess (1966), we know of no attempt to arrive at concrete guidelines in this area.

7.3. RULES FOR THE OPENING STAGE

At the *opening stage* of the discussion the language users decide to start discussing and make arrangements about the division of roles, the rules governing the discussion and the manner of its termination. Rules for rational discussions must indicate when language user 2 is entitled to challenge language user 1, when language user 1 is obliged to accept this challenge, who is to assume the role of protagonist and antagonist respectively, what rules apply at the *argumentation stage* and how the discussion must be concluded at the *concluding stage*. We shall address these questions in this order below.

The right to challenge

We propose to accord the right to challenge a language user to defend his point of view *unconditionally* to *every* language user who has called that point of view into question at the confrontation stage of the discussion. Since according to the terms of rule 2 every language user also has the unconditional right to cast doubt on any point of view of any other language user, this means that in principle there is no restriction whatsoever on the challenging of any language user in respect of any point of view by any language user. This unconditional right is encapsulated in rule 4:

Rule 4
A language user who has cast doubt on the other language user's point of view at the confrontation stage of the discussion is at all times entitled to challenge that language user to defend his point of view.

The right that is encapsulated in rule 4, while it may be an *unconditional right* of a language user who has called a particular point of view into question, is *never an obligation*, since challenging the other language user to defend his point of view must be regarded as an *invitation* to conduct a discussion of that point of view, and if the other language user accepts this invitation the challenger is committed to it. However, it is possible to conceive of circumstances in which a language user might have good reasons for not embarking on a discussion with this other language user, even though he does not accept the point of view. One might for example think of the obstructive and capricious language user to whom we referred in our discussion of rule 2. Nor do we see why casting doubt on a point of view should give rise to an *unconditional obligation* to challenge the proponent of this point of view. In rule 4, therefore, we think it is sufficient to grant language users an *unconditional right* which they may or may not take up.

The obligation to defend

As we observed in chapter 5, one of the implications of the *preparatory conditions* for the *assertive* by means of which a language user expresses his point of view in respect of an expressed opinion is the *obligation*, if asked to do so, to advance *argumentation* for that point of view. This, incidentally, is also a consequence of observing Grice's co-operative principle, particularly the maxim of *quality*. However, it should be said at once that it depends whether this obligation applies *under all circumstances, in all situations and in respect of every challenger*.

A challenged language user is as a rule *always* obliged to defend his point of view and he is acquitted of this obligation only by a *successful defence* of that point of view. A language user who has successfully defended his point of view is then no longer obliged to defend *the same point of view according to the same rules of discussion and with the same starting points and in the face of the same language user*, since that would merely result in a *repetition* of the discussion already conducted. It seems reasonable to us to apply to discussions the principle of *non bis in idem* that applies in a court of law.

This principle does not apply when there is *another* challenger or when the challenger is the same but the starting points or rules of discussion are *different*. In that case the language user who is challenged *is* obliged to defend the same point of view again. Unlike a dispute in law, an argumentative dispute is in principle never dealt with once and for all. The discussion can always be reopened. After all, it is perfectly possible (and in practice quite normal) for new light to be shed on the matter on the basis of new starting points. The rules for rational discussions must not exclude this possibility: on the contrary, they should encourage it.

It should be noted here that removing the obligation to defend by means of a successful defence in no way implies a diminution of the unconditional right, encapsulated in rule 4, to challenge a language user. Anybody who has advanced a point of view can be challenged to defend it, even if he has already successfully done so before. The *obligation* resting on the challenged language user *to accept the challenge* is, however, removed by a successful defence against the same challenger with the same starting points and the same discussion rules. It is not reasonable to constantly challenge someone, but nor is it unreasonable not always to accept every challenge.

As long as a language user has not yet successfully defended his point of view (to the satisfaction of whatever language user), his obligation to defend it continues unabated (assuming that he has not in the meantime retracted his point of view). There is only one exception to this rule. A rational discussion is impossible without certain *commonly shared starting points* and without *commonly shared rules of discussion*. Language users who are unable to reach agreement about the starting points and the discussion rules are also incapable of resolving the dispute and would therefore do better not to embark on a discussion. A challenged language user cannot be obliged to defend his point of view against a language user who refuses to tie himself down to particular starting points and discussion rules.

The general defence obligation and the exception are set out in rule 5:

Rule 5
The language user challenged by the other language user to defend the point of view that he has advanced at the confrontation stage of the discussion is always obliged to accept the challenge, unless the other language user is not prepared to tie himself down to certain commonly shared starting points and rules of discussion; the language user retains this defence obligation as long as he does not retract his point of view and as long as he has not successfully defended it against the other language user on the basis of the starting points and discussion rules agreed.

The obligation to defend that is referred to in rule 5 is a defence obligation (subject to certain limitations) that is a *matter of principle*. This means that (if the stipulated conditions have been met) the obligation to defend always applies, but there may be reasons why in practice it is not always immediately possible to fulfil the obligation.

One reason might be that the language user under a defence obligation may have *no time* to carry it out and conduct a discussion with his challenger. Perhaps, on reflection, he is not quite as sure of his case as he had thought, and he first wishes to assemble more thorough documentation or otherwise prepare himself. This, however, can mean at most a *postponement* of the discussion: the defence obligation is *not removed*, but remains undiminishedly in force until the language user has fulfilled his obligation or retracted his point of view.

By acknowledging the defence obligation encapsulated in rule 5 and accepting the other language user's challenge, the language user who has advanced a point of view indicates his *willingness to discuss*. The language user who has challenged him can in turn indicate his own willingness to enter into a discussion by committing himself to certain common starting points and discussion rules. Rule 5 is thus aimed at the *externalization* of the willingness to discuss that may be demanded of language users involved in a dispute.

Apportioning the burden of proof

Rule 5 also regulates the apportionment of the *burden of proof* in respect of a point of view. A person who advances a point of view and does not subsequently retract it carries the burden of proof for that point of view as soon as (in accordance with the conditions specified in rule 5) he is challenged to defend it. In other words the burden of proof in a discussion rests on the language user who by the terms of rule 5 has an obligation to defend a point of view.

In the case of *simple* disputes, which are our starting point here, the problem of apportioning the burden of proof is thus, in our opinion, solved by rule 5. With *compound* disputes, which in practice occur more often, the situation is more complex. Both parties may then have called each other's point of view into question and challenged each other. However, even then the question of who bears the burden of proof presents no problem in principle, since the answer is that according to rule 5 *both* language users have an obligation to defend their own points of view, so that *each* bears the burden of proof for his own point of view. The question is therefore not on whom 'the' burden of proof rests, but which language user is the first to *begin* defending his point of view. In a compound dispute, then, there is no question of *a* burden of proof that must be identified as resting on *one* of the two language users, but of a *dual* burden of proof. The problem of the apportionment of the burden of proof in a compound discussion is therefore not one of *choice* but of *order*.

The language users involved in a compound dispute must arrive at some agreement as to who is to open the defence of his point of view first. If they fail to agree on this, the discussion will probably be aborted, but the defence obligation in respect of both points of view remains in force. In the traditional view of the apportionment of the burden of proof, in a dilemma such as this a decision is *forced* by the ruling that the interlocutor who attacks an *established* point of view or an *existing* state of affairs must open with his defence (assuming, that is, that he is not in any case the *only* one on whom a burden of proof rests).[64]

Various authors have pointed to the *conservative* nature of this view. Moreover, it seems to us that it must often be difficult to determine which is the 'established' point of view.

Then again, a person wishing to observe the co-operative principle is not so likely (and certainly not without a good reason) to advance a generally accepted point of view. One reason why one might nevertheless wish to do so might be that another language user has advanced a point of view that conflicts with the generally accepted point of view. In that case, however, it would be sufficient to cast doubt on the dissenting point of view and to challenge the language user advancing it, on whom the burden of proof for that point of view would then rest, not because he had advanced a point of view that went against the prevailing view but because according to rule 5 he has a conditional obligation to defend al points of view that he advances.

Apportioning roles

The first arrangement that the language users must make before they can embark upon the *argumentation stage* of the discussion has to do with the *division of roles* in the discussion. The question is who will assume the role of *protagonist* and who the role of *antagonist*. The answer to this question would appear to be fairly obvious: the language user who, at the confrontation stage, advanced a point of view must assume the role of *protagonist* and the language user who has called that point of view into question must be the *antagonist*. In practice this will generally be what happens, but not necessarily. It is quite possible for the roles to be *reversed*.[65]

In practice the language users will often tacitly pass over the matter of the division of roles, and the language user who has advanced a point of view will almost automatically act as *protagonist* and the language user who has cast doubt on it will act as *antagonist*.

We propose to start from the commonest division of roles and leave it to the language users themselves to do things differently if they wish. One condition is that *both* language users agree to the apportionment of roles and that they adhere to their agreed roles *throughout*.

Rule 6
The language user who at the opening stage of the discussion has accepted the other language user's challenge to defend his point of view will at the argumentation stage fulfil the role of protagonist and the other language user will fulfil the role of antagonist, unless they agree otherwise; the division of roles will apply until the end of the discussion.

7.4. RULES FOR THE ARGUMENTATION STAGE

At the *argumentation stage* of the discussion the language user who has assumed the role of protagonist will try to defend the initial point of view against the language user who has assumed the role of antagonist. The question is *how* the protagonist can defend the point of view and *how* the antagonist can attack it. Moreover it is also the question when these attempts at defence and attack are *successful*, i.e. when the protagonist *has successfully defended* the initial point of view and when the antagonist *has successfully attacked* it.

Agreeing the rules of discussion

In a rational discussion, attacking and defending a point of view takes place in accordance with *commonly shared rules of discussion*. We shall discuss a number of these discussion rules for the argumentation stage of the discussion. As observed earlier, they must be regarded as *proposals* that only *come into force* when they have been *accepted* by the language users who fulfil the roles of protagonist and antagonist. This implies that the language users concerned *have declared themselves willing to conduct the discussion in accordance with these commonly shared rules*.

If the language users taking part in the discussion have done this, then the rules acquire the status of *conventions* to which the parties are *committed* throughout the discussion and to which they can hold each other. In fully externalized discussions this is done explicitly, but in practice it is again common for the language users to assume tacitly that they accept more or less the same rules for the discussion.

The difference between explicit conventions and non-explicit conventions need not necessarily have serious consequences for the course of the discussion. Indeed, if both parties are consistent in adhering to the rules, there is no difference at all. It is only where there is a disagreement over the *validity* of a rule applied by one of the parties or about the correctness of the *application* of a rule, that the advantage of explicitly agreed rules becomes apparent. Because they have been explicitly *formulated*, it is easier then to reach a ruling on the disputed validity or application of the rule.

One implication of explicitly agreeing the rules of discussion that we have already mentioned is that the language users are *committed* to those rules (at least for the duration of the discussion). This means that *during* the discussion the rules governing the discussion cannot be made the subject of the discussion. The rules apply for as long as *this* discussion between *these* language users lasts. The only question relating to the rules that may be raised *during* the discussion is whether they are being applied properly.

Of course, this does not mean that the rules cannot be discussed *after* the discussion, or *before* a new discussion begins. And it certainly does not mean that there are rules that can *never again* be discussed. *All* rules, without exception, may be called into question by any language user who perceives a reason for questioning them. The disputed rule then acquires the status of an *expressed opinion*, about which various points of view may be adopted (cf. rule 2). Any discussion arising over a rule is a *meta-discussion*.

Rule 7
Before the start of the argumentation stage of the discussion the language users who during the argumentation stage are to assume the roles of protagonist and antagonist agree what rules are to govern the protagonist's defence of his initial point of view and the antagonist's attack on that point of view, what rules determine whether a protagonist has successfully defended his point of view and what rules determine whether the antagonist has successfully attacked it; these

rules apply throughout the discussion and may not be questioned by either party during the discussion itself.

The attacking and defending of points of view

At the argumentation stage of the discussion, as we argued in chapter 5, three categories of speech act are performed: *assertives, commissives* and *directives*. The protagonist uses *assertives* to perform the illocutionary act complex *argumentation*, and only that act complex, and the antagonist either accepts or rejects the argumentation by performing either the *commissive accept* or *its illocutionary negation*.

The antagonist can then elicit a new illocutionary act complex *argumentation* from the protagonist by performing the *commissive request*. The protagonist can thus defend his point of view by performing one or more illocutionary act complexes of *argumentation* and the antagonist can attack that point of view by performing the *illocutionary negation* of *accept*.

In a rational discussion these are the *only permissible ways* of defending and attacking points of view. They represent a right of the protagonist and antagonist that is in principle *unlimited. Every* illocutionary act complex of *argumentation* performed by the protagonist may be attacked by the antagonist in this way (and in no other) and *every* illocutionary act complex of *argumentation* that is called into question may be defended in this way (and in no other).

As we indicated in 3.5, the *acceptance* of an illocutionary act complex of *argumentation* implies that the propositions expressed in the argumentation are accepted and that the constellation formed by the argumentative statements is regarded as a justification (pro-argumentation) or refutation (contra-argumentation) of the expressed opinion. An antagonist who *does not accept* the illocutionary act complex *argumentation* performed by the protagonist can therefore call into question not only (all or part of) its *propositional content* but also its *justificatory* or *refutatory potential*.

By casting doubt on the propositional content of an illocutionary act complex *argumentation*, the antagonist creates a *new dispute* in which this propositional content (whether in whole or in part) has the function of an *expressed opinion*. Since the protagonist has performed the illocutionary act complex *in support of* his point of view, he will adopt a *positive point of view* in respect of this expressed opinion, and this (according to rules 5 and 6) he will again be obliged to defend. Alongside the *initial dispute*, which has to do with the protagonist's *initial point of view*, there now arises a *subdispute* relating to this positive point of view. In this way it is possible for a whole *chain* of *subdisputes, subsubdisputes* and so on to arise. The protagonist's argumentation is then (as we indicated in 4.3.2) *subordinatively compound.*

The performance of an illocutionary act complex *argumentation* in defence of a point of view is always a *provisional* defence. Not until the antagonist has accepted the propositional content of the illocutionary act complex *argumen-*

tation performed by the protagonist can the point of view be regarded as having been defended *definitively*. If the point at issue is a *subordinate point of view*, this also means that the *initial point of view* has also been defended definitively (given, of course, that the argumentation advanced also has the requisite *justificatory or refutatory potential*).

Rule 8
a. *The protagonist may always defend the point of view that he has adopted, in respect of an expressed opinion, in the initial dispute or in a subdispute, by performing an illocutionary act complex of argumentation which then counts as a provisional defence of that point of view;*
b. *the antagonist may always attack a point of view by calling into question the propositional content or the justificatory or refutatory potential of the argumentation;*
c. *the protagonist and the antagonist may not defend or attack points of view in any other way.*

The protagonist has only *sufficiently* defended a point of view when he has successfully defended *both* the propositional content of the illocutionary act complex *argumentation and* its justificatory or refutatory potential. The discussion rules for the argumentation stage must include an explicit statement of when the protagonist's defence may be regarded as successful in both these regards. The rules must indicate when the antagonist is *obliged* to accept the propositional content and the justificatory or refutatory potential of the illocutionary act complex *argumentation* performed by the protagonist. If, and only if, the protagonist has defended a point of view in accordance with these rules and the antagonist is obliged, according to these rules, to accept the defence, it is then possible to say that the protagonist *has sufficiently defended* his point of view. If the protagonist *fails* in this, then the antagonist *has sufficiently attacked* the point of view (given, of course, that he has observed the other rules of the discussion).

When is the antagonist *obliged* to accept the propositional content of an illocutionary act complex *argumentation*? This is a question that can only be answered if the language users who are to take the roles of protagonist and antagonist agree, at the opening stage of the discussion, how they will decide on the acceptability of the propositional content of the illocutionary act complexes performed by the protagonist. To do this they must establish *explicitly* (1) *what propositions they jointly accept without further argument*, and (2) *how they will jointly decide on the acceptability of other propositions*.

The intersubjective identification procedure

The propositions that are *jointly accepted* may have to do with facts, truths, norms, values and value hierarchies. The language users are completely free in compiling their list of jointly accepted propositions. All propositions that they both accept can be included. One restriction, however, is that the list must be *consistent* in the sense that it must not contain propositions that are mutually contradictory. Otherwise it would be possible *always successfully to defend any pont of view against any attacker.*[66] That, of course, would make the *resolution of a dispute* completely impossible.

That a proposition appears on the list of accepted propositions means only that the language users are agreed that during the discussion they will *not cast doubt on* the proposition concerned. The list lays down which propositions the language users have *committed* themselves to for the duration of the discussion and it may therefore be regarded as their *jointly shared starting point.*[67]

How can the protagonist exploit the list of accepted propositions for his defence of an illocutionary act complex of *argumentation* performed by him? If the antagonist casts doubt on only the propositional content of this act complex, the protagonist can point out to him, if he believes it to be the case, that the proposition concerned is one that appears on the list of propositions jointly accepted. Protagonist and antagonist must then carry out a check to establish whether this is indeed the case. If it is, the antagonist is then obliged to retract his doubt about the proposition and accept the illocutionary act complex *argumentation*. The protagonist has then *successfully* defended himself against the antagonist's attack.

This method of defence on the part of the protagonist therefore consists of a *joint check* being carried out at his request, amounting to establishing whether the proposition called into question is *identical* with a proposition from the list of jointly accepted propositions. We call this method the *intersubjective identification procedure* (abbreviated IIP). If applying this procedure produces a *positive* result, the antagonist is *obliged* to *accept* the propositional content of the illocutionary act complex *argumentation* performed by the protagonist. If on the other hand it produces a *negative* result, then the protagonist is *obliged* to *retract* his illocutionary act complex.

What we earlier remarked about the conventional status of the rules for the argumentation stage of the discussion also applies to the jointly accepted propositions. In fully externalized discussions the interlocutors determine at the outset what propositions are accepted by both, but in practice these propositions almost always function as *mutually tacitly presupposed shared background knowledge*.

As long as both parties are agreed that a particular proposition is part of this shared background knowledge, it makes no difference whether or not the proposition concerned has been accepted explicitly. However, as soon as a disagreement arises in the discussion about an implicitly accepted proposition, neither of the two parties can appeal to the committedness of the other. Both parties can then easily *deny that they are committed to that particular proposition*.

The intersubjective testing procedure

The application of the intersubjective identification procedure is not the only way open for the protagonist to defend an illocutionary act complex of *argumentation* against an attack by the antagonist on its propositional content. If his options were restricted to that extent, the protagonist's argumentation would only be able to use propositions about which *agreement had already been reached at the outset*. This limitation precludes the protagonist from defending his point of view by using propositions which had not been raised in any way whatsoever when the discussion began. This is an undesirable limitation. The protagonist should also be able to call on the possibility of advancing *new* information in his defence.

To be able to use new information in a rational discussion, the discussants have to have some way of testing it. This is where the *intersubjective testing procedure* (ITP) comes in (cf. Kamlah & Lorenzen 1973:117-28). This procedure can only be used if the language users agree at the opening stage *how they will determine* whether a preposition ought or ought not to be accepted.[68]

The testing method agreed upon might, for example, consist of consulting oral or written sources (encyclopedias, dictionaries and other works of reference) or it might include the joint conduct of observations or experiments. As with the list of jointly accepted propositions, both language users must regard the method chosen as sufficient to its task.

Applying the ITP follows the same pattern as applying the IIP: the protagonist requests the application of the ITP to a proposition that has been called into question and the ITP is then carried out jointly by protagonist and antagonist. If the result is positive, the antagonist is obliged to accept the proposition (and the protagonist has successfully defended his illocutionary act complex *argumentation* against the antagonist's attack). If the result is negative the protagonist is obliged to retract the illocutionary act complex (which the antagonist has therefore attacked successfully).

It should be observed here that it is not *irrational* to express a proposition which after application of the IIP or ITP proves to be untenable, any more than it is to cast doubt on a proposition which after application of the IIP or ITP proves to be tenable. However, it *is* irrational following a negative result of the application of the IIP or ITP *not* to retract the statement in which the proposition concerned is expressed, or *not* to accept it in the case of a positive result of the IIP or ITP.

For reasons of efficiency, apart from anything else, it is a good idea to use the ITP only if the IIP has already produced a negative result, since if a proposition is one of those that are jointly accepted there is, of course, no need to apply the ITP. In some cases, indeed, to do so would be to introduce undesirable complications.

For example, what is supposed to happen if the result of the ITP is negative and the result of the IIP positive? The protagonist would then be quite justified in appealing to the IIP and the antagonist to the ITP, thus blocking the way to a resolution of the dispute.

The list of jointly accepted propositions constitutes the *common starting point* for the discussion, and this starting point is undermined by submitting propositions occurring on the list to the ITP. The question of whether a proposition ought to be on the list in the first place is one that cannot be raised in a discussion in which the proposition concerned is itself a *starting point*, but it may of course be the subject of a new discussion.

The implication of the recommended further regimentation of the protagonist's defence options is that we must include a restriction in the definition of a *successful defence of* or a *successful attack on* the propositional content of a statement by means of the IIP and ITP.

During his defence the protagonist must always ask for the IIP to be applied. If the result of the IIP is positive, the statement has been successfully defended. If it is negative, the protagonist still has an opportunity to ask for the ITP to be applied. If the result of that is positive, then the statement has after all been successfully defended and if the result is again negative the statement has been successfully attacked.

For a successful *defence* it is sufficient that *one of the two procedures produces a positive result*. For a successful *attack, both procedures must produce a negative result*. The order in which the two procedures are carried out must always be *first the IIP, then (if necessary) the ITP.*

Rule 9

a. *The protagonist has successfully defended an illocutionary act complex of argumentation against an attack by the antagonist on its propositional content if the application of the IIP produces a positive result and, if it does not, if the application of the ITP produces a positive result;*
b. *the antagonist has successfully attacked the propositional content of the illocutionary act complex of argumentation if applying neither the IIP nor the ITP produces a positive result.*

The intersubjective explicitization procedure

As established in rule 8, the antagonist may attack an illocutionary act complex of *argumentation* not only by casting doubt on its propositional content but also by calling into question its *justificatory* or *refutatory potential*. How can the protagonist *successfully defend* himself against an attack on the justificatory or refutatory potential of his argumentation, and when is the antagonist *obliged* to *accept* it?

If the protagonist adopts a positive point of view it is possible to ask whether the argument '*propositional content (of the illocutionary act complex of argumentation), therefore expressed opinion*' is valid, and if the adopts a negative point of view then we may ask whether the argument '*propositional content, therefore not expressed opinion*' is valid. To answer these questions it is as a rule necessary first to *reconstruct the underlying argument by explicitizing one or more unexpressed premises* (cf. 6.5).

To reconstruct the argument expressed in the argumentation it is necessary to use an *intersubjective explicitization procedure* (IEP). This, we believe, can be based on the same starting points as the procedure developed in chapter 6 for the explicitization of unexpressed premises. Its result must be that the language users involved in the discussion reach agreement as to which argument is expressed in which premises in the protagonist's argumentation.

Since the protagonist's argumentation is almost always framed in an argument form which is strictly speaking invalid, it is *in the protagonist's interest* for the intersubjective explicitization procedure to be performed, and it must therefore be performed jointly by protagonist and antagonist *at the request of the protagonist.*

The intersubjective reasoning procedure

If the protagonist's argument has been reconstructed with the help of the IEP this means that the argument is *valid*. If no such reconstruction has taken place, it is still necessary to check the validity of the argument. Before this is possible, however, the language users must first establish, at the opening stage of the discussion before the argumentation stage, how they are going to carry out the check.

Before *that* can be done, however, they must have *logical rules* which they can apply in order to evaluate the validity of the protagonist's argument. This may be done dialectically by, for example, using the dialogical rules of the Erlangen School and establishing whether the disputed expressed opinion is defensible in relation to the premises which together form the argumentation (cf. Kamlah & Lorenzen 1973, ch. 7). Since the important thing here is actually to establish whether the arguments put forward by the protagonist are valid, we shall call this procedure the *intersubjective reasoning procedure* (IRP). Like the other procedures, the IRP is carried out by protagonist and antagonist together *at the request of the protagonist.*

Rule 10
a. *The protagonist has successfully defended an illocutionary act complex of argumentation against an attack by the antagonist on its justificatory or refutatory potential if the application of the IEP produces a positive result and, if the IEP has not been applied, if the application of the IRP produces a positive result;*
b. *if applying neither the IEP nor the IRP produces a positive result, the antagonist has successfully attacked the justificatory or refutatory potential.*

The sufficient attack and defence of points of view

On the basis of what we have already said and using rules 9 and 10 we can now say when the protagonist has *sufficiently* defended an initial or subordinate point of view by means of an illocutionary act complex of *argumentation* and when the antagonist has *sufficiently* attacked that point of view.

For the *sufficient defence* of a point of view the protagonist must have successfully defended *both* the *propositional content* of the illocutionary act complex *argumentation* (in the manner prescribed in rule 9) *and* (in the manner indicated by rule 10) the *justificatory* or *refutatory potential* in respect of the expressed opinion to which the point of view relates.

For a *sufficient attack* on a point of view it is enough for the antagonist to have successfully attacked either the *propositional content* or the *justificatory or refutatory potential* (in the manner prescribed in rules 9 and 10). The antagonist may (as prescribed by rule 8) try to do both, but for a sufficient attack on the point of view it is enough for one of the two attempts to succeed. This is embodied in rule 11:

Rule 11
a. *The protagonist has sufficiently defended an initial or subordinate point of view by means of an illocutionary act complex of argumentation if he has successfully defended the propositional content and justificatory or refutatory potential called into question by the antagonist;*
b. *the antagonist has sufficiently attacked the protagonist's point of view if he has successfully attacked the propositional content or justificatory or refutatory potential of the ilocutionary act complex of argumentation.*

If the protagonist succeeds in defending the *initial point of view* in the prescribed manner, then that point of view is also at the same time *sufficiently* defended. A sufficient defence of a *subordinate point of view*, of course, does not automatically mean that the initial point of view has thereby been sufficiently defended.

A subordinate point of view arises when the protagonist has defended the propositional content of the illocutionary act complex of *argumentation* advanced by him in defence of the initial point of view, by means of another illocutionary act complex of *argumentation*. This last illocutionary act complex of *argumentation* counts as a *provisional* defence of the subordinate point of view. If the protagonist has successfully defended it in the way prescribed by rule 9, this only means that the subordinate point of view has been defended sufficiently, i.e. that the *propositional content* of the first illocutionary act complex has been successfully defended.

In order to defend the *initial point of view* sufficiently it is also necessary, according to rule 11, for the *justificatory* or *refutatory potential* of the *first* illocutionary act complex to be successfully defended (in the manner described in rule 10). And this, of course, is not guaranteed by a sufficient defence of the subordinate point of view alone.

Sufficient attack and defence of the initial point of view

When a discussion contains not only an *initial point of view* but also a *subordinate point of view*, the initial point of view is sufficiently defended if the subordinate point of view has been sufficiently defended (in accordance with rule 11) and if moreover the *justificatory* or *refutatory potential* of the illocutionary act complex of *argumentation* of which the subordinate point of view is a part has also been successfully defended (in accordance with rule 10). The same applies, *mutatis mutandis*, to the defence of *subordinate points of view* using *subordinate subordinate points of view*, and so on. The sufficient defence of an *initial point of view* in a discussion in which one or more *subordinate points of view* occur, can be embodied in a rule as follows:

Rule 12
a. *The protagonist has sufficiently defended the initial point of view if he has successfully defended the justificatory or refutatory potential (which has been called into question) of the illocutionary act complex of argumentation that he has advanced in defence of the initial point of view and if he has sufficiently defended all subordinate points of view;*
b. *in all other cases the antagonist has sufficiently attacked the initial point of view.*

Making the best possible use of the right to attack

Rules 9 to 12 refer to the attack and defence of points of view, but there is of course no absolute necessity for an antagonist to call into question *everything* advanced by the protagonist in the discussion. True, according to rule 8 he has the *right* to challenge both the propositional content and the justificatory or refutatory potential of *any* illocutionary act complex of *argumentation* performed by the protagonist, but he is naturally not *obliged* to do so.

It is perfectly possible – and in practice perfectly normal – for the antagonist to realize suddenly, in the middle of the discussion, that he has been wrong simply to accept the argumentation. It is also possible that to begin with he only doubted the propositional content of an illocutionary act complex of *argumentation*, but not the justificatory or refutatory potential, and that on reflection he now regrets this.

The antagonist must be given an opportunity to recover the chances he has earlier missed. He may be granted this opportunity by allowing him *throughout the discussion* to exercise the right that is his by virtue of rule 8. This supplement to rule 8 thus offers the antagonist the opportunity to *make the best possible use* of his right to attack, and that is conducive to the resolution of disputes.

Rule 13
Throughout the discussion the antagonist retains the right which he possesses by virtue of rule 8, viz. that he may call into question both the propositional content and the justificatory or refutatory potential of any illocutionary act complex of argumentation performed by the protagonist as long as the latter has not yet successfully defended it.

Making the best possible use of the right to defend

According to rule 12, for a sufficient defence of his initial point of view the protagonist is obliged to defend himself against *all* attacks by the antagonist on an illocutionary act complex of *argumentation* performed by him.

However, it is possible that the antagonist has challenged both the propositional content of an illocutionary act complex of *argumentation* and its justificatory or refutatory potential, and that in the first instance the protagonist has defended himself only against the first attack by performing a new illocutionary act complex of *argumentation*. The antagonist might then in turn challenge this new illocutionary act complex, and if the protagonist defends himself against this new attack this does not automatically imply that the first illocutionary act complex has been sufficiently defended.

The protagonist must be given an opportunity to do this even at this late stage. He can be given this opportunity by allowing him *throughout the discussion* to defend any illocutionary act complex of *argumentation* that has been attacked by the antagonist. In this way the protagonist has an opportunity to *make the best possible use* of his right to defend, and that, like the antagonist's making the best possible use of the right to attack, is conducive to the resolution of disputes.

Rule 14
Throughout the discussion the protagonist retains the right which he possesses by virtue of rule 8, viz. that he may defend against any attack by the antagonist both the propositional content and the justificatory or refutatory potential of any illocutionary act complex of argumentation that he has not already success- fully defended.

Another way of enabling the protagonist to make the best possible use of his right to defend himself is to give him an opportunity of *retracting* an illocutionary act complex of *argumentation* once performed. It is possible that in the first instance the protagonist thinks he can sufficiently defend his point of view (whether initial or subordinate) by means of a particular illocutionary act complex, but that he later realizes that this is not the case.

By retracting an illocutionary act complex of *argumentation* the protagonist removes his *committedness* to it and thus also his *obligation to defend* it. In this way it is possible for the protagonist to *correct* himself during the course of the discussion. He can then, if he wants to, replace the retracted illocutionary act complex by another which he *does* think he will be able to defend successfully.

The protagonist should have this opportunity both when he retracts an illocutionary act complex of *argumentation on his own initiative* (without its having been challenged by the antagonist) and when it *has* been called into question by the antagonist. Because his obligation to defend a retracted illocutionary act complex of *argumentation* has been *cancelled*, the protagonist can then still be in a position to conform to the requirement formulated in rule 12 for a sufficient defence of initial points of view.

Rule 15
*Throughout the discussion the protagonist has the right to retract any illocution-
ary act complex of argumentation performed by him and thereby to rescind his
obligation to defend it.*

The orderly conduct of discussions

The addition at the end of rules 13 and 14 implies that the antagonist may not
carry out attacks on the propositional content or justificatory or refutatory
potential of an illocutionary act complex of *argumentation* which the protagonist has already defended sucessfully, and that the protagonist does not
have to defend himself against attacks against which he has already successfully defended himself.

These stipulations prevent the discussion being held up by interminable
repetitions of *identical* attacks and defences. Such repetitions are pointless,
since they in no way contribute to a resolution of the dispute. The legal
principle *non bis in idem* – which we mentioned in connection with rule 5 –
applies here too.

For the same reason it is necessary to avoid all other repetitions of speech
acts performed by protagonist or antagonist, e.g. the performance of or
request for identical *usage declaratives*. Precization of a formulation already
made more precise in exactly the same way makes absolutely no contribution
to the resolution of the dispute.

In a rational discussion it is not sufficient merely to avoid useless repetitions of identical speech acts, the discussion must also follow an *orderly*
course. For this to be achieved it is necessary to have rules conducive to the
rapid and efficient resolution of disputes. These rules might together constitute a sort of *order of business* for rational discussions. The stipulations
proposed in rule 16 would, we believe, be among the first items on such an
order of business:[69]

Rule 16
a. *Protagonist and antagonist may not perform the same illocutionary act or
   the same illocutionary act complex more than once in the same role in the
   discussion.*
b. *Protagonist and antagonist must take turns in performing and illocutionary
   act or illocutionary act complex.*
c. *Protagonist and antagonist must not in the same turn perform more than one
   illocutionary act or illocutionary act complex.*[70]

7.5. RULE FOR THE CONCLUDING STAGE

At the *concluding stage* of the discussion the language user who has fulfilled
the role of protagonist at the argumentation stage either does or does not
retract the initial point of view and the language user who has fulfilled the
role of antagonist at the argumentation stage either does or does not main-

tain his doubt about the initial point of view. The language users terminate the discussion jointly by establishing the final result (and may, as a result of that, decide to start a new discussion).

The only thing that needs to be explicitly regimented at the concluding stage is when the *protagonist is obliged*, on the basis of the attacks carried out by the antagonist at the argumentation stage, to retract the *initial point of view*, and when the *antogonist is obliged*, on the basis of the defence conducted by the protagonist at the argumentation stage, to retract his *doubt about the initial point of view*. This regimentation is effected by rule 17:

Rule 17
a. *The protagonist is obliged to retract the initial point of view if the antagonist has (while observing the other rules of the discussion) sufficiently attacked it (in the manner indicated in rule 12) at the argumentation stage;*
b. *the antagonist is obliged to retract his doubt about the initial point of view if the protagonist (while observing the other rules of the discussion) has sufficiently defended it (in the manner indicated in rule 12) at the argumentation stage;*
c. *in all other cases the protagonist is not obliged to retract the initial point of view and the antagonist is not obliged to retract his doubt about the initial point of view.*

It is not necessary to have a rule to determine when the protagonist *may* retract the initial point of view and when the antagonist *may* retract his doubt about it. At all stages of the discussion both language users have the right to withdraw from their original positions. If one of the two exercises this right, the dispute is thereby at once nullified and the discussion is at an end. Of course, this sort of end to the discussion cannot be regarded as a *resolution* of the dispute *as the result of the discussion*.

The reason for not embodying this right of retraction in a discussion rule is that it stems directly from one of the basic principles underlying all the rules of discussion, viz. that language users can never be *obliged* or *forced* to advance or challenge a point of view. Language users who advance or challenge points of view do so *of their own free will*, and this means that they may also retract these points of view or expressions of doubt *of their own free will*.

Nor is it necessary to have a separate rule to indicate when the protagonist *may maintain* the initial point of view and when the antagonist *may maintain* his doubt about the initial point of view. The reason for this is that it is already *implied* by rule 17. If the *antagonist is obliged* to retract his doubt about the initial point of view, then the *protagonist* has the automatic *right* to maintain the initial point of view and if the *protagonist is obliged* to retract the initial point of view then the *antagonist* has the automatic *right* to maintain his doubt about the initial point of view. The protagonist and the antagonist must decide for themselves whether they wish to exercise this right.

After the language users have closed the discussion by jointly deciding according to rule 17 who has won it, they can if they wish decide to conduct a new discussion. This may have to do with, for example, *another* initial point of view in respect of *the same* expressed opinion, a statement expressing a proposition from the list of accepted propositions (i.e. a *starting point* of the discussion just ended), or a previously accepted *discussion rule* (so that a *meta-discussion* arises).

Whether the language users actually embark on this new discussion (and if so, what its subject will be) is something that they have to decide themselves, and cannot be regimented by rules. If they decide to go ahead, they start a *new* discussion, and this is then governed by the rules stated in 7.3 for the conduct of rational discussions (rules 4-6).

With rule 17 our proposals for rules for rational discussions are now complete. Each of them, we believe, makes it possible to fulfil a necessary condition for the resolution of a dispute. Naturally all kinds of further elaboration and precization will be necessary, together with many forms of operationalization. Together, however, they help the resolution of disputes by means of argumentative discussions, though they do not guarantee that in practice they always *will* be resolved.

The rules we have formulated relate to the performance of speech acts in argumentative discussions and indicate the conditions that the usage of language users in discussions has to meet in order to be able to contribute to the resolution of a dispute. They may therefore be regarded as elements of a code of conduct for rational discussants.

Chapter 8

Fallacies and the code of conduct for rational discussants

8.1. THE TREATMENT OF FALLACIES IN THE PRACTICAL LITERATURE

Before demonstrating that fallacies can be regarded as violations of the code of conduct for rational discussants let us begin by explaining the disadvantages of the way fallacies are approached in recent literature on argument and discussion and the problems that have to be solved in the analysis of fallacies. At the very outset it should be noted that various theoretically oriented publications on fallacies have in recent years pointed to the unsatisfactory treatment that fallacies receive in practical textbooks, while the drastic revisions that regularly appear in reprints of such textbooks precisely in those passages that deal with fallacies would seem to indicate that their authors themselves have their doubts.[71]

According to Finocchiaro it is a characteristic of treatments of fallacies that they begin with a *definition* of what is understood by a fallacy, go on to a description of *sorts of fallacy* and lay down a *classification*, and finally discuss some *examples* (1980:332). Also conspicuous, it seems to us, is that fallacies are as a rule immediately divided into *formal* and *informal* fallacies and that only the first of these categories is more or less clearly defined, while the second appears to be no more than a collection of various *faux pas*. It is with these 'informal' fallacies that we shall be particularly concerned here.

The most general definition commonly given of a fallacy is that a fallacy is an argument which *appears to be correct but is not* (cf. e.g. Barry 1980:47). A *formal* fallacy is then a fallacy whose incorrectness stems from the invalidity of the argument's logical form (cf. e.g. Carney & Scheer 1980:30). All fallacies whose incorrectness is unrelated to the logical form of the argument are then regarded as *informal* fallacies. It is therefore understandable (though not acceptable) that there is no great clarity about what exactly the *correctness criterion* is on the basis of which a fallacy is accounted an informal fallacy. Solving this problem is made even more difficult by the circumstance that the various authors all divide informal fallacies into categories in different ways and that virtually every different species of informal fallacy turns out to have an unspecified number of exceptions, the result of which is that an argument that in one case is an informal fallacy in another case is not.

Against this kind of background perhaps it might be best just to start from the *examples* of informal fallacies that are quoted in the literature. However, a disadvantage of most examples is that they are not representative of the kind of fallacy they are supposed to represent. Although they are alleged to be taken from actual speech situations, as a rule they make a rather constructed or artificial (or at any rate forced) impression. Probably this is mainly because they are presented in a sort of *standard form* which bears little resemblance to the way arguing takes place in ordinary discourse. The most obvious difference between this standard form and argumentation in ordinary discourse is that the former possesses a degree of *explicitness* that is exceptional in the latter. There are, of course, exceptions even to this rule, as we see from an interview with Cliff Richard in the *Sunday Telegraph* of 1 November 1981:

> Even before his commitment was made, Cliff Richard faced the dilemma of whether he could, as a Christian, continue to play music which other Christians regarded as a wicked incitement to temporal pleasures. With the help of Bill Latham he found the solution in a neat syllogism. 'If rock 'n roll is not of God, then it must be of the Devil', Cliff argued: 'But there's nothing in the Bible about the Devil having created anything at all. Since all things are of God, everything is basically good, and it is up to us what we make of them'.

This exceptional explicitness is reminiscent of an example in the standard form that appears in Lambert & Ulrich (1980:26-7):

(1) a. Jones maintains that socialism is wrong
    b. Jones is a rich stockbroker
    c. If Jones is a rich stockbroker and he maintains that socialism is wrong, then he is lying
    d. If Jones is lying, then socialism is not wrong
    e. Therefore, socialism is not wrong

Lambert and Ulrich present argument (1) as an example of the informal fallacy known as the *argumentum ad hominem* (though in our view there is also something to be said for regarding it as at the same time an *argumentum ad ignorantiam*). However, it is exceedingly unlikely that the argument will occur *in this form* in an argumentation in ordinary speech. More likely would be for one of the following variants to be used:

(2) a. No wonder Jones says socialism is wrong, he is a rich stockbroker
    b. Jones may say socialism is wrong, but you've got to remember he is a rich stockbroker
    c. Jones may say socialism is wrong, but what do you expect, he's a rich stockbroker

Important differences between (1) and (2) are that in (1) there is a clear *argument*, whereas there is not in (2), and that in (1) *two premisses and a conclusion have been added*. (1) is presented as an example of an *argumentum ad hominem (circumstantial)*, but (2) can only be regarded as an example of that if (2) a-c is so reconstructed that it has the form of (1). That is to say, two premisses (1c and 1d) would have to be added. However, it is doubtful whether this produces a correct analysis of (2) and, if not, how in that case (2) ought to be analysed.

The question that has to be answered positively in an analysis of each of the variants of (2) is whether a speaker who has advanced (2)a, (2)b or (2)c *can be held to (1)*. Otherwise he might unjustly be blamed for an *argumentum ad hominem*, and whoever does so can in turn be accused of creating a *straw man*. This means that (2) can only be interpreted as an informal fallacy if a particular *interpretation* has first been placed on it.

Since in ordinary discourse informal fallacies are seldom put forward in a completely explicit form, this in principle also applies to other sorts of informal fallacy. At the same time it must be borne in mind that the speaker in argumentation in ordinary speech not only regularly produces arguments lacking premisses or a conclusion but also very often fails to be more specific about the justificatory or refutatory potential that he attributes to his argumentation.[72]

8.2. UNEXPRESSED PREMISSES AND THE ANALYSIS OF FALLACIES

In introductions to logic and practically oriented publications on argument and discussion the attention that is devoted to fallacies is always justified by pointing out that the reader must learn to recognize fallacies and not to produce any of his own. One might expect, therefore, to find this diagnostic and therapeutic aim being supported by the provision of *instructions* for the solution of the *interpretational problems* arising in the analysis of fallacies in ordinary discourse. But such instructions prove to be almost wholly absent. The interpretation and analysis of argumentation suspected of containing a fallacy is a neglected subject.

There are only a very few publications in which anything much is said on this subject (e.g. Purtill 1979 and Carney & Scheer 1980) albeit that the advice given is unsatisfactory. In view of the fact that the approach these authors take gives the impression that it is perfectly in accord with the guidelines that we formulated in chapter 6, it is particularly important to go into it here and point out clearly where we think it is defective. Both Purtill and Carney and Scheer recommend the reader faced with argumentation suspected of containing a fallacy to take the argument that is invalid in the form in which it is presented, *add to it a premiss which makes the argument valid, and then examine the added premiss to discover if there is anything wrong with it*. This means that they propose to treat fallacies as *unexpressed premisses*.

According to Purtill (1979:42) this addition does not in itself present any difficulty: 'we can always make a fallacy into a *valid* argument ... by supplying further premises, which we will refer to as *Added Premises*'. According to him, the added premisses will often be singularly unacceptable or, as Carney and Scheer (1980:31) put it, 'worthless', and the reason for this is precisely the same as the reason why the original argument (assuming that it is in fact a fallacy) is worthless. It is striking that Carney and Scheer believe that challenging the *truth* of the added premiss amounts to the same as challenging the correctness of the original argumentation (1980:31). According to them it makes no difference whatsoever whether the criticism relates to the *validity* of the argument or the *truth* of the premisses.

Let us examine this approach more closely by referring to an argumentation (5), which Carney and Scheer choose as an example, and the analysis that they give of it (6):

(5) a. Most people believe that the continued growth of government cannot be stopped
   b. So continued growth of government cannot be stopped

(6) a. Most people believe that continued growth of government cannot be stopped
   b. Whatever most people believe is true
   c. Therefore it is true that continued growth of government cannot be stopped

The added premiss (6)b, according to Carney and Scheer, is an example of the informal fallacy *argumentum ad populum*, and for that reason (5) too must be regarded as an example of that fallacy. Apart from the artificiality of the example, one must applaud the fact that this analysis does not regard the invalidity of the argument expressed in (5) as *definitive*. If this were the case, almost all argumentation in ordinary speech would automatically be considered unsound, and this would be premature and erroneous (cf. Lambert & Ulrich 1980:25-7).

Carney and Scheer do not say why the listener *should be prepared* to validate an argument that is invalid in the form in which the speaker presents it, nor do they make clear what *enables* him to do so. However, these important omissions can be rectified with the help of the insights we have advanced in chapter 6.

Language users conducting an argumentative discussion with the object of resolving a dispute about an expressed opinion will find that it benefits them to observe the *co-operative principle* and *maxims* formulated by Grice. Using the maxims of *relation* (validity), *quantity* (informativeness) and *quality* (committedness) they are in principle able - that is, of course, if they make the best possible use of shared background knowledge and the information that the verbal and non-verbal contexts have to offer - to deduce the *conversational implicature* that may be regarded as the *unexpressed premiss* in the speaker's argumentation.

It is doubtful, however, whether one may always apply this procedure of explicitizing unexpressed premisses,[73] since it gives rise to *contradictions*. For this reason the method of analysing fallacies recommended by Carney and

Scheer is subject to a serious objection of principle. It demands a contradictory application of the maxims falling under the co-operative principle. On the one hand the listener assumes that the speaker is observing the co-operative principle, and on the other hand he assumes that this is not the case, since he is trying to make the argument *valid* and thus make it accord to the maxim of *relation*, but he does so by adding an *untrue* premiss, and thereby automatically attributes to the speaker a violation of the maxim of *quality*. A question that immediately presents itself here is what sort of reason the listener might have for not at once assuming that the speaker is violating the maxim of relation (validity) or is indeed no longer observing the co-operative principle at all. This is a question not asked, let alone satisfactorily answered, by Carney and Scheer.

A theoretical objection with far-reaching practical implications, finally, is that the dubious aspect of the *validity of the argument* expressed in the argumentation is shifted to the *truth or untruth of an (added) premiss*. The status of the fallacy, now localized in a particular premiss, thus becomes the same as that of any other untrue premiss, and this means that in this kind of analysis fallacies are effectively lumped together with obvious inaccuracies, mistakes, and so on.

This is to ignore the special character of fallacies that makes them so treacherous. By simply attributing the incorrectness of all fallacies exclusively to the untruth of a premiss all efforts to find a satisfactory theory are thwarted at the outset, since it is now impossible to carry out the generalization necessary to arrive at a general characterization of the various specific sorts of fallacy (cf. Lambert & Ulrich 1980:27). The truth of premisses cannot be established on logical or other general argumentation-theoretical grounds.

In contrast to Carney and Scheer, we believe that this theoretical shift has very real and important practical implications. If all fallacies are treated as untrue premisses, this means that, however useful it may be in itself, the most one can do is advise the listener to brush up his general knowledge and as far as possible to check the truthfulness of statements. This means that giving *general instructions* for recognizing and analysing fallacies is made very much more difficult, because they are either purely *ad hoc* or remain insufficient and incomplete in principle.

If fallacies are treated not as arguments with (not explicitly worded) untrue premisses, but as, for example, invalid arguments which for some reason or other give an impression of validity, it then does become possible to draw up instructions for recognizing fallacies, since the validity of arguments is in principle subject to a finite number of rules which logicians can formulate systematically (even though this has so far been done only partially). This implies that language users can in principle be taught how they should observe these rules, and that preventing fallacies is a matter of argumentative *skill*.

The central difficulty with this last approach, which in principle is the one to be preferred, is that it simply assumes that *all fallacies are invalid arguments*. But a not inconsiderable proportion of the fallacies traditionally distinguished cannot be forced into the straitjacket of an argument without drastic surgery. Indeed, with this group of fallacies it may be wondered whether there is actually any question of *argument* or *reasoning*, and whether there is actually any question of *argumentation*. Typical examples are the informal *ad baculum* and *many questions* fallacies.

The question of what fallacies are and how they may best be analysed cannot be answered sensibly, in our view, as long as the soundness of argumentation is not linked with efforts *to resolve disputes about expressed opinions by means of discussion*. When it is, fallacies can be treated as contributions to the discussion which are not conducive to the resolution of the dispute but actually hinder it or make it completely impossible.

In our view, fallacies may be regarded as *violations of a code of conduct* for rational discussants whose aim is the resolution of a dispute. The implication of this is that fallacies can be analysed as violations of the individual *rules* of that code. So in this view fallacies are not simply and exclusively linked to the *validity of arguments* but to *rules for rational discussions*.

8.3. VARIOUS SORTS OF VIOLATION OF THE CODE OF CONDUCT

We shall now try to establish what consequences violations of the rules formulated in chapter 7 may have for the resolution of disputes. We shall regard every violation which may result in the resolving of a dispute being made more difficult or even impossible as a *fallacy*, as already stated. On the one hand this view is wider than the commonly accepted view that fallacies are incorrect or invalid arguments, but on the other hand it is also more specific. It is wider because we do not link fallacies solely to the argumentation stage of the discussion in which it is established whether or not the inference made by the protagonist is correct, and more specific because we explicitly link fallacies. to the resolution of disputes.

Cases which are generally labelled as fallacies but which present problems when analysed in the traditional manner can be analysed satisfactorily with our rules. This is especially true of the *informal* fallacies, which are always the biggest stumbling-block in analysis. In 8.5 we shall examine some examples in order to show that the rules of the proposed code of conduct make a systematic analysis of informal fallacies possible.

It is our contention that *both* the protagonist *and* the antagonist can be guilty of a fallacy and that fallacies can occur at *any* stage of the discussion. We shall therefore discuss the consequences of violations of the discussion rules *for each stage of the discussion* in turn, and will indicate *by which party* the violation can be committed. For the sake of convenience we shall assume that the language user who advanced the initial point of view at the confrontation stage will take the role of *protagonist* at the argumentation stage, and the language user who challenged the initial point of view the role of *antagonist*. At *all* stages of the discussion we shall refer to them as the protagonist or antagonist respectively.

Violations of rules for the confrontation stage (I)

At the confrontation stage of the discussion disputes are *externalized*. Rule 2 lays down how this is best done by stating categorically that points of view can in principle relate to *anything*, that in principle *any* point of view can be challenged, that *anybody* may advance points of view and that *anybody* may challenge points of view. An implication of this rule is that the interlocutors may *in no way* (verbal or otherwise) obstruct one another in the exercise of this unconditional right.

The consequence of violations of rule 2 is that disputes cannot be fully externalized, and that a necessary condition for the conduct of a rational discussion cannot be fulfilled. Violations of this kind are therefore to be regarded as a serious infringement of the code of conduct.

The confrontation stage of the discussion is the first at which *usage declaratives* can be performed. If it is not clear that the protagonist has, by means of (say) an assertion, advanced a particular point of view, or if it is not entirely clear what the implications of that point of view are, then it is perfectly possible that a discussion will be initiated but there will be a good chance that the interlocutors will be talking at cross purposes. In these circumstances it is even possible for the interlocutors to believe that they have achieved the resolution of their dispute when in fact this is not the case.

It is also possible for no discussion to ensue at all, simply because the antagonist has failed to realize that the protagonist's point of view is susceptible of criticism. In that case the interlocutors believe that they are in agreement, whereas in fact this is a delusion.

Of course there is no way of *guaranteeing* that disputes are *real* and not illusory, and that the solutions are likewise *real* solutions. Rule 3 is calculated to create the necessary conditions to achieve this, but no more than that. The necessary conditions are that both parties may make their own words more precise or may amplify them (either on their own initiative or at the request of the other party) and that either party may request the other for precization or amplification of his words. The language user to whom such a request is addressed is always obliged to accede to it.

The unclarity or misunderstanding resulting from a violation of rule 3 can relate to the *illocutionary force* of an illocutionary act, but also to the *propositional content*. To make the illocutionary force clear, the language users may, for example, use *standard paraphrases* such as we introduced in 5.5. Aids of this kind are not available for the clarification of the propositional content, and this means that there can be no guarantee that no *fallacies of ambiguity* will occur in the discussion.

The *straw man fallacy*, too, is difficult to rule out. It arises either when the antagonist attributes to the protagonist a *stronger illocutionary force* than the protagonist himself intended or when the antagonist attributes to the *propositional content* of an illocutionary act by the protagonist a *wider scope* than the latter intended.

An example of the first of these occurs if the protagonist presents a particular point of view as a conclusion that on the basis of certain information is *plausible*, whereas the antagonist takes it to be a *necessary conclusion*. In other words, the protagonist advances an *inductive probability argument* and the antagonist behaves as if the protagonist has presented him with a *deductively valid argument*. If at the end of the discussion the protagonist has verified the probability claim but not the supposed claim of validity, in the antagonist's eyes he has lost the discussion whereas from his own point of view, by contrast, he has won it.

Something of the kind also happens if the antagonist attributes a wider scope to the propositional content than that intended by the protagonist. Suppose the protagonist wishes to defend the point of view that women *by and large* have a different logic from men, but the antagonist interprets his words in such a way that the protagonist, according to him, is obliged to defend the point of view that *all women* have a different logic (and this can easily happen if, for example, the protagonist says 'In my opinion women have a different logic from men'). If, then, during the course of the discussion a woman were to be mentioned who in the opinion of both protagonist and antagonist has the same logic as men, the protagonist need not necessarily abandon the position he has adopted, but in the antagonist's interpretation he has lost the discussion.

Violations of rules for the opening stage (II)

At the opening stage of the discussion the protagonist is challenged by the antagonist to defend his point of view. Rules 4-7, which relate to this stage, are designed to ensure that after the dispute has been externalized the parties together attempt to arrive at a resolution of it.

Violations of the rules at this stage in the discussion can result in the protagonist and the antagonist never getting as far as the argumentation stage because the protagonist is not challenged by the antagonist (rule 4) or refuses the challenge (rule 5), because the interlocutors are not both prepared to fulfil the roles of protagonist and antagonist at the argumentation stage (rule 6), or because the parties cannot agree on the rules for the discussion (rule 7).

For it to be certain that the protagonist and the antagonist, once the dispute has been fully externalized, will indeed embark on the argumentation stage, the interlocutors' *willingness to discuss* must also be externalized (rules 4-6) and rules for the discussion must be agreed which are acceptable to both (rule 7). As regards the first of these points it is the arrangement concerning the *burden of proof* that is crucial, whereas as regards the second the crucial point is agreeing on adequate rules relating to the *sufficient attack and defence of points of view*.

A protagonist who does not acknowledge that because he has voluntarily advanced a point of view (which has been called into question by the antagonist) the *burden of proof* with regard to that point of view rests om him, retreats from a discussion in which his point of view can be tested critically. A protagonist who tries to evade his burden of proof by passing it on to the antagonist is guilty of the fallacy of *shifting the burden of proof*. This fallacy is termed by John Locke the *argumentum ad ignorantiam* and is defined by him as follows:

> Another way that men ordinarily use to drive others and force them to submit their judgments and receive the opinion in debate is to require the adversary to admit what they allege as a proof, or to assign a better. And this I call *argumentum ad ignorantiam* (1961:278).

If either of the two language users refuses to commit himself to a system of rules for attacking and defending the initial point of view, a *regimented* discussion is, by definition, impossible. If the one party does not wish to commit himself to particular rules, then the other party is deprived of the opportunity to *appeal* to those rules. A person who wishes not to arrange rules at all may get as far as the argumentation stage, but no other language user can be obliged to enter into a discussion with such an 'uncommitted' language user. Agreeing on common rules for the argumentation stage is a *sine qua non* for rational discussions.

The situation is different when a language user, having declared himself committed to particular rules, subsequently brings them up for discussion at the argumentation stage (for example because on further reflection he finds them not so much to his liking as he had thought). The language user who does this obscures the discussion of the initial point of view. In itself, of course, there can be no objection to conducting a *meta-discussion* about the adequacy of the rules for the argumentation stage, but to *mix* a meta-discussion with the original discussion about the initial point of view is probably to bring about the undesired effect that *both* discussions have a rough passage. Indeed, the whole discussion can sometimes grind to a halt.

Violations of rules for the argumentation stage (III)

The rules relating to the argumentation stage of the discussion (rules 8-16) regulate the way in which the initial point of view may be *attacked* and *defended* and when the attack or defence is *sufficient*. Here the *intersubjective identification procedure*, the *intersubjective testing procedure*, the *intersubjective explicitization procedure* and the *intersubjective reasoning procedure* all play an important role.

These four procedures (IIP, ITP, IEP and IRP) are all of crucial importance for the rationality of the argumentation stage. We shall first discuss violations relating to the *propositional content* of the illocutionary act complex of *argumentation* performed by the protagonist (IIP and ITP) and will then move on to violations relating to the *justificatory* or *refutatory potential* of the argumentation (IEP and IRP).

With regard to the *propositional content* of an illocutionary act complex of *argumentation* performed by him the protagonist can make the mistake of performing an illocutionary act complex consisting of statements some or all of which do not appear on the list of statements expressing accepted propositions (negative result of IIP), which are incapable of being succesfully tested intersubjectively (negative result of ITP), and not accepted without question by the antagonist, yet which he still maintains.

According to rule 9 the protagonist has only defended the propositional content of an illocutionary act complex of *argumentation*, and has only defended it succesfully, when either the IIP or the ITP has produced a positive result. If the result of both is negative, the antagonist has successfully attacked the propositional content and the protagonist is obliged to retract the act complex. If he refuses, he evades a rule to which, according to the agreements reached with the antagonist, he is *committed*.

The antagonist can make the converse mistake by refusing, despite a positive result from either IIP or ITP, to accept the propositional content concerned. In that case he too evades rule 9, to which he too is *committed* according to the agreements made.

Whether it is the *protagonist* or the *antagonist* who violates rule 9, in *either* case there is little point in any further discussion since a joint resolution of the dispute is only possible if *both* parties adhere to the rules governing what counts as a succesful attack and what counts as a successful defence. Without such rules it may sometimes be possible for one party to win the other (or a third party consisting of an audience) over to his point of view, but a succesful *attempt to influence* can never be deemed to be a successful *attempt to convince by means of argumentation in a rational discussion* (cf. chapter 3).

When it comes to the *justificatory* or *refutatory potential* of an illocutionary act complex of *argumentation* it is possible for both protagonist and antagonist to violate rule 9 in ways comparable to the violations relating to the propositional content. The literature of fallacies has always paid most attention to possible errors relating to the justificatory or refutatory potential, since they are relatively easily analysed cases of *invalid arguments*.

Indeed, these errors are considered so important that as a rule they form the backbone of the *definition* given of a fallacy. Attention is thus focused unilaterally on negative results of the *intersubjective reasoning procedure* (IRP), and as a result of that the protagonist is held responsible for all fallacies.

Violations of the rule for the concluding stage (IV)

The only rule to relate to the concluding stage of the discussion, rule 17, sets out the consequences for the protagonist of a sufficient attack on the initial point of view by the antagonist and the consequences for the antagonist of a sufficient defence by the protagonist. In the former case the consequence is that the protagonist must retract the initial point of view and in the latter case it is that the antagonist must withdraw his doubt about the initial point of view.

A protagonist who in these circumstances refuses to retract his initial point of view or an antagonist who refuses to retract his challenge may up till then have taken part in the discussion entirely in accordance with the rules, but by this attitude the resolution of the dispute is nevertheless prevented even at this last stage of the discussion.

The consequences outlined above are the *only* consequences deriving from rule 17. The parties may attach to winning and losing the discussion no other consequence than the retraction either of the initial point of view or of the doubt expressed about it. If the protagonist has lost the discussion, he must, according to rule 17, retract his initial point of view.

In the simple single discussions that we discuss here, a resolution in favour of the antagonist does not automatically justify the conclusion that *the point of view opposite to that of the protagonist is thereby justified, let alone proved.* This warning is not as superfluous as it may seem, for in practice antagonists (or their supporters) are easily tempted after a successful attack to draw the conclusion that it has now been demonstrated that the protagonist's positive point of view must be rejected *in favour of a negative point of view*, or that the protagonist's negative point of view must be exchanged *in favour of a positive point of view*.

This conclusion is premature on two counts. In the first place - and this is the most important reason - a successful *attack* on a particular point of view need not necessarily, of course, coincide with a *successful defence of another point of view*. This can only be the case in a *compound discussion*, in which both language users play the part of both protagonist (in respect of their own point of view) and antagonist (in respect of the other's point of view).

In a simple discussion the sole task of the antagonist is to attack the point of view that is at issue in the discussion. He *defends no point of view* and can therefore never perform a successful (or unsuccessful) attempt to defend. Equating a successful attack on a particular point of view with a successful defence of another point of view means erroneously treating a *simple* discussion as a *compound* discussion. To do so is to be guilty of the fallacy known nowadays (departing from Locke's definition) as *argumentum ad ignorantiam*.

The second reason for calling the conclusion just mentioned premature, is that it erroneously assumes that a successful attack on a particular point of view must always result in *the adoption of the opposite point of view*. This erroneous assumption, of course, would mean that following the failure of his defence the protagonist of a positive point of view, for example, would be forced to adopt a negative point of view in respect of the same expressed opinion.

This, of course, need not be the case. In such circumstances the protagonist's only obligation is to give up his positive point of view. This *may* go together with adopting a negative point of view, but it may also amount to his taking a *zero* point of view. Where there is an alternative, to pretend that there is only one possibility is to create a *false dilemma* and to be guilty of a form of polarized thinking sometimes known as *thinking in black and white*.

If the dispute is resolved *in the protagonist's favour* the position is different. The only possible consequence of this is that the antagonist adopts the protagonist's point of view so that both language users hold the same view. If the antagonist should confront the protagonist with *another* expression of doubt, a *new discussion* is called for.

8.4. THE CODE OF CONDUCT AND THE ANALYSIS OF FALLACIES

The survey given in 8.3 of possible violations of the proposed code of conduct for rational discussants shows how the resolution of disputes *can be made more difficult by either party or both at any stage of the discussion*.

Violations of the rules relating to the *confrontation stage* (rules 2 and 3) may be committed by either *protagonist* or *antagonist*, and mean that the dispute is not properly externalized, which in turn means that one of the necessary conditions for the resolution of a dispute has not been fulfilled.

Violations of the rules relating to the *opening stage* (rules 4, 5 and 6) may also be committed by either *protagonist* or *antagonist* and mean that the language users never reach the argumentation stage, which in turn means that they never reach a resolution of the dispute.

Violations of the rules relating to the *argumentation stage* (rules 8-16) may again be committed by either *protagonist* or *antagonist* and mean that the argumentation stage, on which the resolution of the dispute depends, proceeds in an unsatisfactory manner. This may have to do with either the *propositional content* or the *justificatory* or *refutatory potential* of an ilocutionary act complex of *argumentation* performed at this stage of the discussion. Here both the *acceptability of propositions* and the *validity of arguments* are at stake.

Violations of the rule relating to the *concluding stage* (rule 17), finally, may like the others be committed by either the *protagonist* or the *antagonist* and mean that a discussant refuses to acknowkledge that the other party has won and refuses to retract an insufficiently defended point of view or to accept an insufficiently attacked point of view. The *argumentum ad ignorantiam*, which is a violation of rule 17, is an exception in that it is an infringement that can be committed only by the *antagonist*.

It seems from our analysis, therefore, that fallacies have to do with many more aspects of the discussion than one would think from the traditional definition of the fallacy as an *invalid argument*.[74] In the traditional analysis, fallacies are reduced to violations of *a single discussion rule* (rule 10) which, moreover, can be committed only by *one party* (the *protagonist*). And this is in spite of the fact, remarked on in 8.2, that the traditional analyses almost always tacitly overlook the important activity of *explicitizing unexpressed premisses*, which must always precede any analysis of fallacies as invalid arguments.

After this survey we can now summarize in a definition what we mean by a *fallacy*:

> *Any violation of any of the rules of the code of conduct for rational discussants (by whichever party at whatever stage of the discussion) is a fallacy.*

In this view, fallacies are not 'absolute' errors simply to be attributed to language users by a researcher who has penetrated the 'essence' of rationality, but violations of a well-defined system of rules for the resolution of disputes that has been accepted by the discussants jointly, so that a fallacy is a fallacy only in relation to a particular theoretical conception of rational discussions and only for language users who explicitly or implicitly agree with that conception. A major advantage of this approach is that it becomes possible when analysing fallacies to dispense with the use of vague and subjective concepts like *appearance of* validity and *seemingly* correct, which Hamblin (1970:12) regards as characteristic of the traditional analyses of fallacies, while it now also becomes possible to analyse fallacies systematically on the basis of an explicitly formulated code of conduct.

8.5. ANALYSES OF SOME FALLACIES BY WAY OF EXAMPLE

To demonstrate that fallacies which always present difficulties when analysed on traditional lines can be satisfactorily analysed using the analysis apparatus that we have developed, we shall now analyse two fallacies acknowledged as problematical: the informal fallacies of *begging the question* and the *argumentum ad hominem*.

Begging the question

The *begging the question* fallacy (also known as *reasoning in a circle* or *petitio principii*) is a clear example of a fallacy in which the 'fault' does not lie in the *invalidity* of the argument used. The clearest case of this fallacy is '*A*, therefore *A*'. This (according to the law of *identity*) is a *valid* argument, and if the argumentation in which it is used is nevertheless unsound, the unsoundness must be the consequence of something other than invalidity. In the literature of fallacies various attempts have been made to answer the puzzle of where the source of the unsoundness lies, but none of the suggested answers is satisfactory.[75]

Using the rules for discussions that we have formulated this fallacy can be analysed as follows. If a dispute exists, one language user has expressed a point of view which has been called into question by another language user. In other words, as to the acceptability of this point of view these language users are *not* agreed. To attempt the resolution of this dispute by means of a regimented discussion and for this attempt to have any chance of succes, it is necessary for the language users to take a number of propositions accepted by both of them (see rule 9) as their *starting point*. The *initial point of view* (in this case *A*) does not, of course, appear as one of the list of statements expressing *jointly accepted* propositions. If that were so, there would *be* no dispute.

When the *begging the question* fallacy is used it is natural to suppose that at a given moment in the discussion the protagonist will advance a proposition which he claims can be succesfully defended by means of the *intersubjective identification procedure*. His error is then that he uses a statement which, as he should or may have known, does *not* appear on the list of statements expressing jointly accepted propositions, so that the IIP *cannot* produce a positive result. If the statement *did* appear on the list, or were added later, the dispute would immediately be resolved, and there is no question of that in this case.

Argumentum ad hominem

We now turn to the *argumentum ad hominem*. Three variants of this fallacy are generally distinguished in the literature: the *abusive*, the *circumstantial* and the *tu quoque*.[76]

The *abusive* variant can best be described as a *direct personal attack* in the opponent is made out to be stupid, dishonest, unreliable or otherwise negative. The *circumstantial* variant is an attempt to undermine the opponent's position by suggesting that his only motive is *self-interest* and that the argumentation he puts forward is nothing but a rationalization.

The *tu quoque* variant, finally, is calculated to show up the *contradiction* that the other party in this discussion is attacking (or defending) a point of view that he himself earlier defended (or attacked). This may be a discrepancy within a single discussion, but it may also be a discrepancy between the point of view adopted by the other party in this discussion and a point of view that he has earlier defended during another discussion or on some other occasion. It is also possible that the point of view now adopted does not accord, or even conflicts, with the rest of the opponent's behaviour or with certain principles that he may be expected to observe.

Features common to all three variants are that the discussant who resorts to them (a) is not responding to the point of view or argumentation of the other party, (b) tries instead to win or compel agreement with his own point of view in some other way, and (c) does this by making the other party out to be unreliable.

The three variants differ in that the objective in each is sought after in a different way. In the *abusive* variant doubt is cast on the expert knowledge, intelligence or integrity of the other party *in general*. In the *circumstantial* variant an attempt is made to show that the opponent is incapable of making an impartial judgement *in this matter because of his personal interest*. In the *tu quoque* variant, finally, efforts are made to undermine the opponent's credibility by accusing him of being *inconsistent* if in *this* matter he adopts *this* point of view.

The first thing that should be noted is that the first two variants of the *argumentum ad hominem* can be used by either protagonist or antagonist; the second is that these two are not directly *addressed to* the other party (though they are of course directed *against* him), but to a *third* party consisting of spectators. These are *rhetorical* rather than *dialectical* tricks. However, it will be plain that *all three* variants can be used in the presence of third parties in order to *silence* the other party. The question is now to what extent the three variants, in discussions aimed at resolving a dispute between two parties, can be regarded as violations of discussion rules, and which rules these might be.

In the case of the *tu quoque* variant it is important to distinguish between inconsistencies (whether real or supposed) *within the same discussion* and inconsistencies compared with *discussions conducted previously* or with the other party's *other behaviour*. In the first of these cases the party accused of an inconsistency challenges (if the accusation is accurate) a statement that appears on the list of statements containing jointly accepted propositions. Now the very purpose of that list, as we have more than once remarked, is that these statements should function as a *common starting point* for the discussion. According to the rules for discussion that we have established, only the antagonist is in a position to cast doubt upon statements by the protagonist, and he is therefore the only one who can be accused of such an inconsistency.

Succesful argumentation will almost always be argumentation *ex concessis*, and there is nothing wrong with that. If during the course of the discussion the antagonist should nevertheless cast doubt upon a statement that is one of the shared 'concessions', he is in contravention of rule 9, which lays down the IIP as the method of defence for the protagonist, and rule 7, which prescribes that the agreed rules for the argumentation stage of the discussion (to which the IIP belongs) shall not be challenged *in the discussion itself*.

The situation is different when the inconsistency (real or otherwise) relates not to the actions of the other party in the same discussion but to discussions conducted earlier or to the further behaviour of the opponent. According to rule 2 language users have the *unconditional right* to advance *any* point of view and to cast doubt upon *any* point of view. The only *obligation*, to retract either the initial point of view or the doubt expressed about the initial point of view, stems from rule 17, since it only exists if the antagonist has sufficiently attacked the point of view or if the protagonist has sufficiently defended it.

To claim on any other grounds than these that the opponent must retract his point of view or doubt is to contravene rule 17, and an interlocutor who does so is guilty (if the claim means that the other party is accused of an inconsistency on the grounds of an earlier discussion or his other behaviour) of the *tu quoque* variant of the *argumentum ad hominem*. In the example we discussed earlier it is not the party who draws his opponent's attention to the inconsistency who makes an error in the discussion, but the language user who commits the inconsistency (given that the accusation is justified and the statement attacked is *indeed* accepted by both interlocutors).

The *abusive* and *circumstantial* variants may be regarded as violations of rules 4 and 5, according to which a language user is *always* entitled to challenge others to defend their points of view, while language users so challenged can evade their obligation to accede to the challenge *only* if they have already defended their point of view against the same challenger according to exactly the same rules of discussion and with the same starting points, or if the challenger is *not* prepared to commit himself to common rules and starting points.

The fact that the other party is an evil person or has a financial interest in a particular point of view is *not*, according to rules 4 and 5, a valid reason for not accepting his challenge. Nobody is obliged to advance a point of view to someone who for one reason or another does not appeal to him, but once one has *voluntarily* expressed a point of view one is also obliged, if so requested, to defend that point of view. The same applies, *mutatis mutandis*, to the antagonist's casting doubt on the protagonist's point of view and challenging him to defend it.

These two variants of the *argumentum ad hominem* may thus be regarded as attempts by one language user to deny his opponent the unconditional right, which is his by virtue of rule 4, to withdraw from the obligation that he has by virtue of rule 5.

In this brief discussion of the *begging the question* and *argumentum ad honinem* fallacies we have shown that it is possible using the rules we have formulated to give a satisfactory analysis of some problematical informal fallacies. Together with the examples that we gave in 8.3 during our discussion of fallacies as violations of the rules of discussion, we hope that this analysis makes clear that fallacies are not exclusively linked to the role of protagonist, nor to the argumentation stage (or one aspect of it) of the discussion.

The *argumentum ad hominem* is a good illustration of a fallacy whose analysis presents considerable difficiulties if fallacies are linked exclusively to the invalidity of the arguments expressed by the protagonist in his argumentation at the argumentation stage of the discussion. Our analysis, in which the *argumentum ad hominem* is linked to rules relating to the opening stage, gets round these difficulties. The *argumentum ad ignorantiam* (in its modern interpretation) is a good illustration of a fallacy that can only be analysed adequately if it is linked to rules relating to the concluding stage and the role of the antagonist.

Notes

1. We shall at all times refer to the language users taking part in a verbal exchange of ideas about an expressed opinion as *speakers* and *listeners*. Our observations about the contributions made by speakers and listeners apply also, *mutatis mutandis*, to *writers* and *readers*. We shall not constantly state this expressly, any more than we shall continually state whether the language users concerned are men or women, young or old, rich or poor, and so on.

2. It is possible to distinguish between various types of rule for language usage. Parret (1980), who terms the various types of usage rule collectively *strategies*, indicates in 'Les stratégies pragmatiques' how it is possible to distinguish these types from one another not only conceptually but also terminologically. In any event it is possible to distinguish between grammatical rules, rules for the performance of speech acts, rules for the conduct of conversations and rules for the performance of logical operations. The rules for the conduct of discussions that we shall formulate here are concerned with all these aspects of usage. However, we shall not make further distinctions between types of rule but will use the term *rule* as a general label for every type of usage rule that possesses the characteristics regarded by Gumb in *Rule-Governed Linguistic Behavior* as characteristic of *social* rules (1972:37-44). Our rules are not intended to be mandatory regulations which must once and for all lay down exactly what language users in argumentative discussions have to do. They should be regarded rather as *suggestions* to language users wishing to resolve differences about expressed opinions by means of argumentative discussion. As soon as better alternatives are available the rules must be replaced.

3. Cf. Kamlah & Lorenzen 1973: 86-93, 129-45.

4. In *Language and Philosophy* Hartnack points out that the concept of 'intention' is indispensable for acquiring an insight into language usage. He regards the having of intentions as a necessary condition for the performance of illocutionary acts (1972:32).

5. Janik and Toulmin (1973) point out in *Wittgenstein's Vienna* that it was Russell's view that the real logical form of propositions was concealed by the misleading grammatical cloak of the natural languages, and that this logical form was done the best justice by expressing it in the logical symbol-language of the *Principia Mathematica*. They quote Wittgenstein, who considered that Russell's chief merit lay in having demonstrated that the *apparent* logical form of a sentence need not be its *real* logical form. Cf. also Passmore (1972:424-5). Russell's view is still widely held.

6. This does not apply to the logicians of the Erlangen School. They have tried to give a *normative reconstruction* of the use of the elementary and compound statements which makes it possible to resolve disputes about expressed opinions by means of a dialogue. Important publications by this school include *Formale Logik* by Lorenzen (1970) and *Konstruktive Logik, Ethik und Wissenschaftstheorie* by Lorenzen and Schwemmer (1975). Of particular relevance to the theory of argumentation are: *Logische Propädeutik* by Kamlah and Lorenzen (1973), *Normative Logic and Ethics* by Lorenzen (1969) and *Dialogische Logik* by Lorenzen and Lorenz (1978). Barth and Krabbe (1982) continue to build on the insights of the Erlangen School.

7. This reconstruction of argumentation as a concession by the opponent does produce some peculiarities. Thus the proponent (according to the rule system of dialogical logic) acquires the right to make a counter-attack on the compound statement which was originally his own argumentation. If he exercises this right it can have far-reaching consequences for the further course of the dialogue. However, it should be noted here that this dialogue acts as a test of the

defensibility of the expressed opinion in relation to the argumentation. The dialogue takes place between the interpreters of two different dialogical roles. There is here no question of a description of an attempt to convince, such as that undertaken by one language user in respect of his opponent in the actual practice of argumentation. This view of the logical testing process is allied to Jarvie's opinion that 'logic as a theory of criticism cannot be regarded as in any sense a theory of how in practice we do, or ought, to *think* or to *reason*' (1976:331). He amplifies this as follows: 'Logic is there to help us unpack the consequences of statements we are considering, with a view to discovering inconsistencies between those statements and others, and then transmitting the falsity thus disclosed back through the system' (1976:331).

8.   There are in fact so many criticisms to be made of the approach of Perelman and Olbrechts-Tyteca (1971) that is is extremely doubtful whether their description is really good enough. See Van Eemeren, Grootendorst & Kruiger (1983:Ch. 5.6).

9.   Albert uses the term *Münchhausen-trilemma* to refer to the problem that consists in the fact that ultimately every justificationist faces a choice between (1) an infinite regression, (2) a logical circle, and (3) the breakdown of the attempt to justify at an arbitrary point (1975:11).

10.   Unlike the definition of *argumentation* that we gave in Van Eemeren, Grootendorst & Kruiger (1983), this is not a general definition that is theoretically 'neutral'. Rather, it is our own conception of argumentation, and we do not, therefore, need to provide a definition that embraces all sorts of different views of argumentation such as would be necessary in the introduction to a survey of a number of different contributions to the theory of argumentation.

11.   We have previously studied this problem in Van Eemeren & Grootendorst (1982a). Some of the essential points of the view developed there have been retained in the present study, but there are important differences in their elaboration.

12.   There are, in fact, exceptions to the principle that a speaker uttering a sentence performs an utterance act, a propositional act and an illocutionary act. Not all speech acts necessarily have a particular propositional content. Thus Searle (1970:64) calls *greetings* 'a much simpler kind of speech act' which has no propositional content. Such speech acts as *congratulation*, too, do not always have a propositional content, even though it seems to us that one will always be present implicitly.

13.   In our view the use of language is always both a form of verbal *communication* and a form of social *interaction*. We believe that the use of language is never exclusively calculated to bring about the *illocutionary effect* which means that the listener recognizes the illocutionary force of the utterance and knows to which proposition this illocutionary force applies. By means of his speech utterance the speaker will also wish to achieve a more far-reaching *perlocutionary effect* on the listener which will entail the listener reacting in a particular manner – perhaps by replying, indicating his agreement, or passing a cigarette lighter. For example, a speaker making a request of the listener will in principle achieve not only that the listener understands *that* a request is being made of him and *what* this request entails, but also that he will either perform or refrain from performing a specific (verbal or non-verbal) act, as the case may be. A warning is intended to alarm the listener, an argumentation is supposed to convince him, and so on. It is not always immediately clear what perlocutionary effect the speaker hopes to achieve on the listener with his illocutionary act, but using language would be rather pointless if there were not *some* perlocutionary effect being aimed at. We believe that clarity is improved if the analysis of speech utterances at the *illocutionary* level is linked to their *comprehensibility* for the listener, and analysis at the *perlocutionary* level linked to their *acceptability*, so that it is possible to distinguish two different complexes of problems. Comprehension and acceptance are the *minimum* illocutionary and perlocutionary effects that a speaker strives after in the listener when he performs his speech act. Seeking after illocutionary effects, *analytically speaking*, precedes the occurrence of perlocutionary effects. You cannot expect an answer from someone if you have not first made it clear to him that he is being asked a question, and you cannot expect someone to give you a light if you have not first made it clear to him that your cigarette needs lighting, and so on. Of course, this thesis needs some refinement, but all we wish to establish at this point is that problems of comprehensibility (on the illocutionary plane) are in principle *preliminary to* problems of acceptability (on the perlocutionary plane).

14.   The distinction between argumentation linked to an expressed opinion (*conclusion*) following it and argumentation linked to an expressed opinion (*thesis*) preceding it can be expressed terminologically by referring in the former case to a *prospective* and in the latter case to a *retrospective* presentation. However, the differences are not essential (cf. Van Eemeren, Grootendorst & Kruiger 1983:22-3).

15.   From a recent interview with Searle it seems that he himself realizes perfectly well that speaking a language does not consist of performing a series of *isolated* speech acts: 'Of course life isn't like that – life goes on with whole series of sequences of Speech Acts in larger chunks of conversation or discourses of various kinds.' Here Searle appears to be referring to the institutional units of language usage that we (in 2.4) call *text genres*. However, although he does not say so in so many words, he is also thinking of the functional usage units that we call *compound illocutions* or *illocutionary act complexes*: 'If I'm asked to "describe" (notice the verb there) the layout of the Piazza San Marco or I'm asked to "explain" (another illocutionary verb) the operation of the internal combustion engine, in doing either of those things, describing or explaining, I will perform a *series* of Speech Acts , and that series will have its significance not because of each isolated unit but because of the set of units that together add up to a description or an explanation. We get a series of statements, each of which is a Speech Act, but taken together, they add up to a larger unit, namely a description or an explanation' (1980:27).

16.   What we mean by a compound illocution corresponds most closely to what Kopperschmidt (following Habermas 1973:24) calls a sequence or chain ('Kette') of speech acts which is a 'pragmatic functionalization' of various (elementary) speech acts (1980:88). Unlike Schecker (1977b:75 ff.), for example, Kopperschmidt considers it erroneous to treat argumentation as a separate sort of illocution. He believes, as do we, that argumentation is a compound illocution which as a rule consists of (elementary) assertions and is comparable (at what we call a *higher textual level*) with a speech act like *answer*.

17.   Quasthoff, indeed, does not regard argumentation as a *speech act* at all. However, she appears to use the term *speech act* to be synonymous with *illocutionary act*, so that it would be wrong to conclude that she believes that arguing also (or even predominantly) takes place by non-verbal means.

18.   Our objections also apply to Searle's *amended version* of his sincerity condition. Searle continues, unnecessarily and dangerously, to rely on the concept of 'intention' by referring in the new formulation to a speaker who has the *intention* of holding himself responsible. (There is no such amendment, incidentally, in the *rules* formulated by Searle for the illocutionary act *promise*.)

19.   It is also possible to formulate the second and third preparatory conditions less rigidly by adding that the speaker must believe that there is at least a *chance* that the listener will accept the propositions expressed in the statements S_1, S_2 $(,\ldots, S_n)$ or will accept the constellation of statements S_1, S_2 $(,\ldots, S_n)$ as a justification of O. The same applies, *mutatis mutandis*, to the second and third preparatory conditions for contra-argumentation. However, we prefer a formulation which *does not specify the degree of strength of the speaker's belief*, so that the description of the conditions covers both a case in which the speaker is absolutely certain that the listener will accept and a case in which he is not so sure.

20.   Although in order to keep to Searle's scheme we have continued to refer to *sincerity conditions*, it is clear from this that our preference for the term *responsibility conditions* is indeed justified. If the speaker argues 'ex concessis', i.e. uses one or more statements in his argumentation that he knows are endorsed by the listener, it is perfectly possible that the speaker himself does not believe these statements but is only using them because he knows they will help to convince the listener. In our opinion the speaker is nevertheless for the rest of the discussion *committed* to the statements concerned because he has made himself responsible for them by the advancing of his argumentation. If the speaker does not consider himself committed to these statements to which he does not really subscribe, he is not seriously engaged in resolving a dispute about an expressed opinion together with the listener.

21.   For the corresponding consequences of 'presupposition failure', compare *The Theory of Presupposition Failure* by Harder & Kock (1976:50-9).

22.   The fact that someone is convinced may of course be due to *different* argumentation from the argumentation suggested to him, but in that case his conviction is not a normal effect of the specific attempt to convince that has been undertaken in that case.

23.   Compare the analysis of perlocutionary acts given by Gaines (1979).

24.   Barth and Krabbe (1982) have taken the rules drawn up by Kamlah and Lorenzen (1973) for the conduct of formal dialogues and have further elaborated them, made them more precise and systematized them into a dialectical system of rules for the conduct of regimented discussions. They call this system a *formal₃ dialectic*, the subscript 3 serving to distinguish *formal* in the sence of 'conforming to a particular system of rules' from other senses of the word.

25.   Distinguishing between sound and unsound *argumentation schemata* is of course one of the important tasks of argumentation theorists, and is indeed often regarded as their *only* task. The subject of the theory of argumentation is then regarded as a non-formal counterpart of the formal logic in which valid *argument forms* are distinguished from invalid ones. In the present work one of our concerns is to make plain that this is an inappropriate limitation of the field of argumentation theory (cf. esp. Ch. 4-8).

26.   An expressed opinion can of course also be *negative*, so that in this example the expressed opinion might have been that women do *not* have a logic of their own. But this has no essential implications for the rest of our thesis.

27.   The stages of the discussion that we have distinguished do not correspond to those used, without amplification, by Ballmer and Brennenstuhl (1981:85-107) in the 'Struggle Model' (nor to the phases in the 'Arguing Devices'). The rationale of Ballmer and Brennenstuhl's classification is wholly obscure.

28.   The condition that the speaker must have evidence or arguments for what he asserts also appears in Searle and Vanderveken, for example (n.d. III-12, IV-21-2, VII-12-13). The observation that from the maxim of quality the listener can claim the right to ask the speaker for argumentation is also to be found in Fogelin (1978:22).

29.   Here we see very clearly expressed the difference between how we look at *pro*-argumentation and *contra*-argumentation and the way they are treated in Naess's *pro aut contra survey*, which provides a clear overview of the chief arguments which, *according to a particular person or group*, testify for or against an assertion (1966:102). Carrying on the terminology for the parties that we have used, we might say that Naess's pro aut contra survey is drawn up by a *tritagonist* who records which arguments have been advanced for and against the initial expressed opinion, which arguments have been propounded for and against those arguments, and so on, *without connecting these arguments to the various parties in the discussion*. The two columns into which Naess divides the various arguments are not identical to a division into *arguments by the protagonist* and *arguments by the antagonist*. They indicate which arguments argue for the initial expressed opinion and which against, and which arguments argue for and against those arguments. Thus in fact the pro aut contra survey relates to a *compound dispute*, even though the initial expressed opinion is not countered explicitly with an opposite initial expressed opinion. Naess stresses that the pro aut contra survey ends with a 'conclusion' and that this 'implies, accordingly, that the arguments have all been weighed against one another' (1966:102), later saying that it is important that 'a survey should show clearly how each sentence is related to the others in the pattern of the argumentation' (1966:108). We agree that it is important for the *connection between the various arguments* to be made clear, but we also believe that it should also be made clear *which party is responsible for which arguments*, and this does not happen in Naess's pro aut contra survey. For example, it is possible for his left-hand column to contain the contra-argument C_1P_3 against the pro-argument for the initial expressed opinion P_3 without it being made clear that in a discussion this contra-argument comes from a different party from the originator of the pro-argument against which it is directed. In Naess's pro aut contra survey the left and right-hand columns contain *two separate dialogues* or *two dialogue clusters*, albeit that they are entered as monologues, i.e. without linking the arguments to two different *parties*. The *connection* between the argumentation in the left-hand column and that in the right-hand column is *ignored*. There is no *interaction* between pro-arguments on the left and contra-arguments on the right, only between pro- and contra-arguments in the (subordinative) argumentations relating to the (co-ordinate) arguments for and against the initial expressed opinion. It may

be supposed that Naess does have some such interaction in mind. In any event, in our definitions of *pro-argumentation* and *contra-argumentation* we have explicitly taken the *party-linked ordering of arguments* as one of our points of departure.

30.   Besides *multiple* argumentation, in which the premises are all individually sufficient but in which none of the premises is individually necessary to justify or refute the expressed opinion, and *co-ordinative compound* argumentation, where each of the premises is individually necessary but where the premises are only sufficient together, one might also distinguish a form of compound argumentation in which the premises are neither individually necessary nor individually sufficient, but only together necessary and sufficient. We shall not examine this more complicated possibility any further here.

31.   For reasons of practicality we shall assume here and in what follows that the subordinative compound argumentation does not also contain co-ordinative compound argumentation or multiple argumentation, though in practice this may of course be the case. But it would make the analysis more complicated than that shown here.

32.   For our classification of speech acts we have started from the taxonomy of illocutionary acts drawn up by Searle (1979). This means that we distinguish between *assertives, directives, commissives, expressives* and *declaratives*. These categories correspond to the five basic functions of language usage that we distinguished in 2.1. In the course of our thesis we shall return on some points to the division into *verdictives, expositives, exercitives, behabitives,* and *commissives* used by Austin which Searle finds inadequate (1979:8-12). The point here is that we sometimes find Austin's observations superior to Searle's. We shall make no use of classification systems such as those produced in response to Searle's taxonomy, e.g. by Bach and Harnish (1979) and Ballmer and Brennenstuhl (1981), since they do not represent an advance on it.

33.   Piel (1980) evidently also regards argumentation as an *assertive*, since he calls supporting a proposition a special form of *asserting*. However, he makes no distinction between *elementary* and *complex* illocutionary acts or between *compound* and *simple* discussions, so that his analysis remains inadequate.

34.   It is important to note that in this case we are not dealing with an *indirect speech act*. The illocutionary force of 'Let's take an umbrella' is that of a *proposal*, not of an *assertion*. However, the expressed opinion at the centre of the dispute, whether potential or actual, has exclusively the illocutionary force of an *assertion* and not also that of a *proposal* (and it is therefore not a *directive*). The same applies to the illocutionary act complex that forms the argumentation (single or otherwise) for the expressed opinion. The *argumentation* for the expressed opinion 'It is advisable to take an umbrella' is not, of course, 'or do you want to get wet?' but something like 'otherwise we shall get wet'. On the other hand in an externalized (mini) discussion of this question the speaker *can* say 'It is advisable to take an umbrella, *because* otherwise we shall get wet', but *not* 'It is advisable to take an umbrella, *because* or did you want to get wet?'

35.   Here are some more or less complicated examples of cases in which the expressed opinion or part of the argumentation appears not to be an *assertive*. The parentheses indicate the category they appear to belong to. 'I promise you, because then at least you'll believe me' (*commissive*); 'You can depend on it, because I promise you' (*commissive*); 'Congratulations, because you'll be glad it's all behind you' (*expressive*); 'The discussion is closed, since we'll never find a solution anyway' (*declarative*); 'You're fired, for the work isn't good enough' (*declarative*).

36.   There is an exception in the *usage declaratives*. See 5.4.

37.   If a discussion turns on one of the variants of (i), language user 1 (who plays the part of protagonist) must *retract* this assertion *completely* if language user 2 (who plays the part of antagonist) performs a successful attack. With (ii)a this would not seem automatically to apply. A protagonist of (ii)a can still *weaken* his original assertion to (ii)b in the event of a successful attack by the antagonist. Fogelin (1978:42-3) calls this weakening 'hedging', but he erroneously equates the *illocutionary strength* and the *propositional scope* and fails to realize that in such circumstances a *new discussion* is needed. The protagonist cannot weaken his assertion until he has first retracted it in its original form and substituted for it another assertion of *more limited scope*.

38.   If a *directive* is performed which belongs to the subclass of the *usage declaratives*, the result is an *explicative dialogue*, which we, in 2.2, have distinguished from a *problemizing dialogue* (cf. Wunderlich 1972:23).

39.   It is of course possible for argumentative discussions to contain other illocutionary acts and act complexes besides the ones discussed here, but this need not necessarily mean that it is not a *rational* discussion. For example, the language users may adorn their arguments with speech acts in which they tell anecdotes or jokes, and this may even be beneficial to the atmosphere of the discussion. However, speech acts of this kind do not constitute part of the process of resolving the dispute. A psychological study of the conduct of argumentative discussions would have to pay some attention to them, but they can be disregarded in our attempt at an analytical reconstruction of the distribution of speech acts in rational discussions. In any event it should be stressed that our reconstruction is in no way intended to prohibit these or similar speech acts in argumentative discussions.

40.   See also Van Eemeren & Grootendorst 1982b.

41.   The observation that in practice it is perfectly normal for argumentation to contain all sorts of elements which remain implicit may be found in Black (1952:22-3, 26, 66), Fogelin (1967:107), Schellens & Verhoeven (1979:2, 5) and Scriven (1976:xvi) and elsewhere. In our view it may even arouse suspicion if the speaker is over-explicit.

42.   Grice's nomenclature and arrangement of the maxims is borrowed from Kant. The maxims, some of which can be subdivided into submaxims, are formulated by Grice as follows (1975:45-6):

Quantity
1.   Make your contribution as informative as is required (for the current purposes of the exchange)
2.   Do not make your contribution more informative than is required

Quality
Try to make your contribution one that is true
1.   Do not say what you believe to be false
2.   Do not say that for which you lack adequate evidence

Relation
Be relevant

Manner
Be perspicuous
1.   Avoid obscurity of expression
2.   Avoid ambiguity
3.   Be brief (avoid unnecessary prolixity)
4.   Be orderly

43.   The view that explicitizing unexpressed premisses is one of the most difficult tasks facing language users engaged in a discussion with each other may be found expressed in Black (1952:23, 27-8, 69), Fogelin (1967:107), Fogelin (1978:182), Scriven (1976:xvi, 43, 81, 86, 163) and elsewhere.

44.   The authors calling unexpressed premisses a neglected subject include Fogelin (1967:107), Fogelin (1978:182), Lambert & Ulrich (1980:x), Quasthoff (1978:25, 30) and Scriven (1976:xvi).

45.   We shall refrain from looking at differences in the interpretation of example (1), which might produce, besides 'All Englishmen are brave', the following possible unexpressed premisses: 'Almost all Englishmen are brave'; 'Englishmen are generally brave'; and so on.

46.   Similar explanations of the fact that in practice it is not necessary to be completely explicit are given by, for example, Fogelin (1978:182), Hamblin (1970:235-45), Öhlschläger (1979:88-102), Quasthoff (1978:16) and Scriven (1976:173).

47.   The authors who make an appeal, in a general sense, to the Principle of Charity include Grice (1977:I-11), Lambert & Ulrich (1980:60) and Scriven (1976:71, 173). It is important that we point out here that Rescher, among others, subscribes to a view of the Principle of Charity that is to some extent at variance with that of its leading exponent, Davidson (1971). Following Davidson, Parret describes the principle thus: 'the generally desired (final) end of language-in-context is truth and its communicability' (1978:136).

48.   Our contention is that the listener is *in principle* faced with a dilemma in respect of the logic to be chosen, since naturally not every listener is a logician and will be able to recognize the precise nature of the options. In an explicit justification, however, reference will have to be made to the logic concerned.

49.   In subsequent publications Stalnaker several times revised his definition of *pragmatic presupposition*. These and other definitions have been collected and discussed by Gazdar (1979:103-8).

50.   Bartsch (1979:24) rightly points out that Grice gives the erroneous impression that only the *speaker* must observe the co-operative principle, whereas of course it also applies to the *listener*.

51.   It sometimes also happens that the speaker violates one of the other maxims, in which case the situation becomes appreciably more complicated.

52.   This applies, for example, to conversational implicatures like *indirect speech acts*, when it is necessary to establish the primary illocutionary force.

53.   For empirical research into the explicitization of unexpressed premisses, compare Jackson & Jacobs (1980).

54.   This necessity is naturally present if the argument concerned can *only* be validated by adding a false premiss.

55.   In 'Conversational Relevance' Dascal (1979:167) touches on a sore point: 'An account or justification of how the hearer hits upon that precise q which will ultimately establish the missing link of relevance between his reaction and the conversational demand is unavailable in Grice's theory.'

56.   Precizations of Grice's maxims have been proposed *inter alia* by Dascal (1979), Gazdar (1979), Kempson (1975) and Sadock (1978).

57.   The distinction between inference rules and premisses (whether or not implicit) has been the subject of attention from Fogelin (1967:103), Grice (1977:I-8/10), Jarvie (1976:319-21) and Popper (1974:203) among others.

58.   We use the term *indeterminate* here in the sense given to it by Crawshay-Williams (1957) in *Methods and Criteria of Reasoning*, though the meaning he gives it is slightly more specific (but not to an extent that conflicts with the sense in which we use it).

59.   According to Dascal the ideal heuristic search strategy 'triggers the whole process of searching for an implicature... it triggers the process in a certain direction; it creates, so to speak, guidelines for the search. Among other things, these guidelines suggest what kind of contextual features to focus upon, thus avoiding the need for a search through all the infinitely many faces of the "context"' (1979:168).

60.   In the drawing up of these rules we have profited from insights in the *Formal Dialectics* of Barth and Krabbe (1982). One might even say that with the code of conduct for rational discussants that we have drawn up we try to make a conceptual connection between Barth and Krabbe's Formal Dialectics which is inspired by the dialogical logic of the Erlangen School, and an analysis, inspired by the speech act theory of Austin and Searle, of language usage in discussions directed towards resolving disputes about expressed opinions. Barth and Krabbe's 'formal3 rules' are 'first order' rules, whereas the majority of our rules may be counted among the discussion-promoting rules which they (without much amplification) call 'higher order' rules (cf. Van Eemeren, Grootendorst & Kruiger 1983: Ch. 3.4).

61.   The discussion situation that arises when these preliminary conditions have been met need not always be present in practice, but neither is it a purely theoretical construction. Discussants involved in the conduct of an argumentative discussion who act as rational language users assume that in principle this condition has been met. With Habermas (1973) one might say that by taking this supposition as granted they anticipate an *ideal discussion situation*. The preliminary conditions formulated by us are actually composed of two groups. Some of them, in principle, hold good for every form of information exchange, while the others are particularly applicable in argumentative discussions. Another difference is that most of the first are founded on *practical* considerations, whereas the last are more concerned with matters of principle. These conditions must be met before there can be any question of applying rules to rational discussions. Authors who formulate no conditions in advance include Alexy (1978), for

example, though many elements of the preliminary conditions we have formulated do reappear in his 'Regeln des allgemeinen praktischen Diskurses' (Rules of general practical discourse). To some extent he waters down the demands made by Habermas of the ideal discussion situation and incorporates them in his own rules: 'The rights of equal opportunities, universality and absence of coercion can be formulated as three rules. ... The first rule relates to the initiation of discourse. Its content is as follows:

1. Any person who can speak may take part in discourses. The second rule normalizes the freedom of discussion. It can be subdivided into three rights:
2. a. Any person may problemize any assertion.
    b. Any person may introduce any assertion into the discourse.
    c. Any person may express his points of view, wishes and needs. ...

The third rule, finally, has the job of protecting discourses from coercive forces. It is:

3. No speaker may be prevented, by coercion from within or outside the discourse, from exercising his rights as laid down in (1) and (2)' (trans. fr. Alexy 1978:169).

In the *rationality norm* formulated by us the *language user* is the central figure. This answers critics of a purely product-oriented approach to rationality such as Toulmin (1969), though without degenerating into a purely process-oriented approach. At this point our view of rationality differs from that of Toulmin and Habermas as summarized by Burleson: 'Rationality has little to do with the construction of deductively entailed sets of propositions, but everything to do with the conduct of persons who engage in the unconstrained exchange of ideas. Rationality is not reducible to reasoning with abstract formal structures, but is displayed only in the attitudes and behavior of those who sincerely seek answers to questions having theoretical and practical significance. Rationality does not depend on analytically drawn conclusions, but is realized in the open and free intercourse among persons pursuing the resolution of concrete problems. Rationality, then, is manifested in the social processes through which human actors attempt to reach consensual decisions about matters of common interest' (1979:126-7). Compare also Berk's *Konstruktive Argumentationstheorie*, in which he observes that we must not only have rules of argumentation that enable us to arrive at new statements from statements already accepted, but must also have an insight into argumentations as 'a sequence of speech acts in an ideal speech situation' (trans. fr. Berk 1979:14). Habermas, Toulmin and Burleson also pay attention to the ideal discussion situation. In 'Jürgen Habermas and the dialectical perspective on argumentation' Wenzel gives the following characterization of Habermas's ideal speech situation: 'The ideal speech situation expresses, at once, the goal of critical theory and the standard of rationality against which critical discourse must be measured' (1979:93). Habermas outlines his ideas on the ideal speech situation in e.g. 'Toward a Theory of Communicative Competence' (1970), and at greater length in 'Vorbereitende Bemerkungen zu einer Theorie der kommunikativen Kompetenz' (1971).

62.   Obstructing the other party in the exercise of the right laid down in rule 2 is in fact already prescribed out by rule 1, since it would require the performance of a *non-verbal act* or of a *directive* (such as the issuing of a *threat* or *prohibition*), and according to rule 1 it is only permitted, at the confrontation stage, to perform *speech acts* belonging to the category of the *assertives* or consisting of the *commissive accept* (or its illocutionary negation). It is therefore unnecessary to state explicitly in a rule that it is not permitted to obstruct the other party in the advancing of points of view or the casting of doubt upon points of view.

63.   The same naturally applies *mutatis mutandis* to a language user who has just lost a discussion in which he has cast doubt upon a particular point of view.

64.   The traditional view of the division of the burden of proof decrees that the burden of proof rests with the person attacking a generally accepted opinion or *status quo*. Cf. Alexy (1978:244), Ehninger & Brockriede (1978:140), Rescher (1977:2, 3, 17, 25-45, 105-9) and Smith & Hunsaker (1972:139-40).

65.   Such an 'unnatural' division of roles need not necessarily mean a violation of the preliminary condition that the language users be serious, since they may have elected for this allocation of roles because they believe it is in the interests of a critical assessment. A person who advances a point of view has thought about it, we may assume, and probably knows better than anyone else what its weak points are. If he is interested in testing this point of view against

criticism (and is not chiefly concerned to avoid a loss of face), then there is much to be said for his assuming the role of critical attacker. Conversely it may be so that once the challenger assumes the role of protagonist he will realize that the point of view that he has cast doubt upon is stronger than he had supposed. That might (and in some cases must) be grounds for retracting his earlier expressed doubt. Such 'role play' certainly need not be to the detriment of the seriousness of the discussion, and may indeed be a real contribution to the resolution of the original dispute.

66.   For example, this is easily demonstrated by classical propositional logic (cf. Kahane 1973:67-70). If contradictory statements are accepted it is even possible to put up a successful defence of both a *positive* and a *negative* point of view in respect of the *same* expressed opinion (cf. Popper 1974:312-35).

67.   Unlike Alexy, one of whose ground rules is that a speaker may only assert that which he believes to be true (1978:234), we believe it is unnecessary to include a *sincerity clause* in the rules for rational discussions. It would conflict with the principle of externalization, of course, but it is also unnecessary because a serious speaker is committed to what he has said, irrespective of whether he actually believes it (cf. our remarks in 2.1 on responsibility in connection with Searle's sincerity conditions).

68.   In the form in which it is outlined here the intersubjective testing procedure can only be applied to *elementary* statements, containing no logical particles. This is in contrast to the intersubjective identification procedure, which is applicable both to elementary statements and to non-elementary ones, which may even consist of whole theories. If while defending a non-elementary statement the protagonist wishes to make use of the intersubjective testing procedure, the statement must first be *decomposed*, during which process it is possible for him to apply the rules for the use of logical particles proposed by Kamlah and Lorenzen (1973:Ch. 5).

69.   In such an order of business it is of course possible, if the discussants should require it, to regulate a great many other matters. For example, the *duration* of the discussion might be fixed in advance.

70.   The reader should be reminded at this point that one illocutionary act complex of *argumentation* is a constellation of statements and that it will in principle consist of more than one *assertive*.

71.   Among those writers who regard the treatment of fallacies as unsatisfactory are Barth and Martens (1977), Finocchiaro (1980) and Lambert and Ulrich (1980). Modifications to the way fallacies are treated appear, for example, in reprints of introductions to logic by Copi (1972), Kahane (1973) and Carney & Scheer (1980).

72.   For example, it is by no means certain whether the listener may always attribute to the speaker the belief that he is advancing a *deductively valid* argument. Ascribing to the speaker a more powerful argument than that to which he can strictly speaking be held amounts to creating a *straw man*, though this danger threatens not only in the case of *informal* fallacies but also with *formal* ones, as is illustrated by the analysis, as a formal fallacy, of the *affirmation of the consequence* given in (2) of the argumentation in (1):
1. I am not going to hoard, because then there will be a war
2. a. If there is a war, people will hoard
   b. I am going to hoard
Therefore:
   c. There is going to be a war

Another, and perhaps more likely interpretation of example (1) might be: (a) The last time I started hoarding there was a war, (b) If I start hoarding there will be a war, (c) Therefore: I shall not start hoarding, because if I did there would be a war. In this interpretation the argumentation is *compound* and contains a *hasty generalization* or the *post hoc ergo propter hoc* fallacy.

73.   An essential objection to the analysis of fallacies as unexpressed premises which presents itself straight away is that the method cannot be applied in *all* cases. For example, it does not work with the informal fallacies of *begging the question* and *argumentum ad ignorantiam*.

74.   The view that a fallacy is always an invalid argument is propounded by Woods & Walton (1981), among others.

75.   For discussions of the *begging the question* fallacy, see e.g. Woods & Walton (1975 and 1977).

76.   For discussions of the *argumentum ad hominem*, see e.g. Barth & Martens (1977) and Woods & Walton (1976).

Bibliography

Albert, H.
  1963 'Die Idee der Kritischen Vernunft. Zur Problematik der Rationalen Begründung und des Dogmatismus'. In: G. Szczesny (Hrsg.), *Club Voltaire. Jahrbuch für Kritische Aufklärung*, Bd. 1, München.

Albert, H.
  1967 'Theorie und Praxis. Max Weber und das Problem der Wertfreiheit und der Rationalität'. In: E. Oldemeyer (Hrsg.), *Die Philosophie und die Wissenschaften. Simon Moser zum 65. Geburtstag*. Meisenheim am Glan.

Albert, H.
  1975 *Traktat über Kritische Vernunft*. 3. erw. Aufl. Tübingen: Mohr. 1st ed. 1968.

Alexy, R.
  1978 *Theorie der Juristischen Argumentation*. Frankfurt: Suhrkamp.

Austin, J.L.
  1976 *How to Do Things with Words*. Edited by J.O. Urmson and M. Sbisà. Oxford University Press (2nd rev. ed., 1st ed., 1962).

Bach, K. and R.M. Harnish
  1979 *Linguistic Communication and Speech Acts*. Cambridge (Mass.): M.I.T.-Press.

Ballmer, Th. and W. Brennenstuhl
  1981 *Speech Act Classification; A Study in the Lexical Analysis of English Speech Activity Verbs*. Berlin: Springer.

Barry, V.
  1980 *Practical Logic*. New York: Holt, Rinehart & Winston (2nd ed.; 1st ed., 1976).

Barth, E.M.
  1972 *The Logic of the Articles in Traditional Philosophy*. Dordrecht: Reidel.

Barth, E.M.
  1979a *Perspectives on Analytic Philosophy*. Amsterdam: North Holland.

Barth, E.M.
  1979b 'Taalfilosofie en Taalbeheersing op Weg naar een Continuüm. *Kennis en Methode 3 (2)*, 254-266.

Barth, E.M. and E.C.W. Krabbe
  1982 *From Axiom to Dialogue*. Berlin: De Gruyter.

Barth, E.M. and J.L. Martens
  1977 'Argumentum and Hominem: From Chaos to Formal Dialectics'. *Logique et Analyse, Nouvelle Série, 20 (77/78)*, 76-96.

Bartsch, R.
  1979 'Semantical and Pragmatical Correctness as Basic Notions of the Theory of Meaning'. *Journal of Pragmatics 3 (1)*, 1-43.

Berger, P. and Th. Luckmann
    1971   *The Social Construction of Reality.* Garden City (N.Y.): Anchor Books.
Berk, U.
    1979   *Konstruktive Argumentationstheorie.* Stuttgart: Frommann-Holzboog.
Black, M.
    1952   *Critical Thinking; An Introduction to Logic and Scientific Method.*
            Englewood Cliffs (N.J.): Prentice Hall (2nd ed.; 1st ed., 1946).
Black, M.
    1963   'Austin on Performatives'. *Philosophy 38*, 217-226.
Burleson, B.R.
    1979   'On the Foundations of Rationality: Toulmin, Habermas, and the *a
            Priori* of Reason'. *Journal of the American Forensic Association 16 (2)*, 112-
            127.
Carney, J.D. and R.K. Scheer
    1980   *Fundamentals of Logic.* New York: MacMillan (3rd ed.; 1st ed., 1964).
Cohen, T.
    1973   'Illocutions and Perlocutions'. *Foundations of Language 9*, 492-503.
Cole, P. (ed.)
    1978   *Syntax and Semantics 9: Pragmatics.* New York: Academic Press.
Cole, P. and J.L. Morgan (eds.)
    1975   *Syntax and Semantics 3: Speech Acts.* New York: Academic Press.
Copi, I.M.
    1972   *Introduction to Logic.* New York: McMillan (4th ed.; 1st ed., 1953).
Crawshay-Williams, R.
    1957   *Methods and Criteria of Reasoning; An Inquiry into the Structure of
            Controversy.* London: Routlegde &Kegan Paul.
Dascal, M.
    1979   'Conversational Relevance'. In: A. Margalit (ed.), *Meaning and Use.*
            Dordrecht: Reidel, 153-174.
Davidson, D.
    1971   'Mental Events'. In: L. Forster and J. Swanson (eds.), *Experience and
            Theory.* Boston: Belknap, 79-101.
Davis, S.
    1980   'Perlocutions'. In: Searle et al. (eds.) 1980, 37-56.
Dijk, T.A. van
    1978   *Taal en Handelen; Een Interdisciplinaire Inleiding in de Pragmatiek.*
            Muiderberg: Coutinho.
Eemeren, F.H. van and R. Grootendorst
    1982a   'The Speech Acts of Arguing and Convincing in Externalized Discussions'.
            Journal of Pragmatics 6 (1), 1-24.
Eemeren, F.H. van and R. Grootendorst
    1982b   'Unexpressed Premises: Part I'. *Journal of the American Forensic
            Association 19*, 97-106.
Eemeren, F.H. van and R. Grootendorst
    1983   'Unexpressed Premises: Part II'. *Journal of the American Forensic
            Association 19*. 215-225.
Eemeren, F.H. van, R. Grootendorst and T. Kruiger
    1983   *The Study of Argumentation.* New York: Irvington.
Ehninger, D. and W. Brockriede
    1973   *Decision by Debate.* New York: Dodd, Mead & Comp. (11th pr.; 1st ed.,
            1963).

Ehninger, D. and W. Brockriede
  1978   *Decision by Debate*. New York: Harper & Row (2nd ed.; rev. of Ehninger and Brockriede 1973).
Elias, N.
  1970   *Was ist Soziologie?* München: Juventa Verlag.
Feyerabend, P.K.
  1977   'Consolidations for the Specialist'. In: I. Lakatos and A. Musgrave (eds.), *Criticism and the Growth of Knowledge*. Cambridge: Cambridge University Press, 197-231.
Finocchiaro, M.A.
  1980   *Galileo and the Art of Reasoning; Rhetorical Foundations of Logic and Scientific Method*. Dordrecht: Reidel.
Fogelin, R.J.
  1967   *Evidence and Meaning; Studies in Analytic Philosophy*. London: Routledge & Kegan Paul.
Fogelin, R.J.
  1978   *Understanding Argument; An Introduction to Informal Logic*. New York: Harcourt Brace Jovanovich.
Fowler, H.W. and F.G. Fowler
  1959   *The Concise Oxford Dictionary of Current English*. Oxford: Clarendon Press (4th ed.; revised by E. McIntosh).
Gaines, R.N.
  1979   'Doing by Saying: Toward a Theory of Perlocution'. In: *The Quarterly Journal of Speech 65*, 207-217.
Gazdar, G.
  1979   *Pragmatics; Implicature, Presupposition and Logical Form*. New York: Academic Press.
Grice, H.P.
  1975   'Logic and Conversation'. In: Cole and Morgan (eds.) 1975, 43-58.
Grice, H.P.
  1977   Some Aspects of Reason (Immanuel Kant Lectures). Stanford (Cal.): Stanford University (unpublished).
Gumb, R.D.
  1972   *Rule-governed Linguistic Behavior*. The Hague: Mouton.
Gumperz, J.J.
  1972   'Introduction'. In: J.J. Gumperz and D. Hymes (eds.), *Directions in Sociolinguistics; The Ethnography of Communication*. New York: Holt, Rinehart & Winston, 1-25.
Haack, S.
  1974   *Deviant Logic; Some Philosophical Issues*. Cambridge: Cambridge University Press.
Haack, S.
  1978   *Philosophy of Logics*. Cambridge: Cambridge University Press.
Habermas, J.
  1970   'Toward a Theory of Communicative Competence'. In: H.P. Dreitzel (ed.), *Recent Sociology 2: Patterns of Communicative Behavior*. London: MacMillan, 114-150.
Habermas, J.
  1971   'Vorbereitende Bemerkungen zu einer theorie der Kommunikativen Kompetenz'. In: J. Habermas and H. Luhmann, *Theorie der Gesellschaft*

oder Sozialtechnologie; Was Leistet die Systemforschung? Frankfurt: Suhrkamp, 107-141.

Habermas, J.
1973   'Wahrheitstheorien'. In: H. Fahrenbach (Hrsg.), *Wirklichkeit und Reflexion*. Pfullingen: Günther Neske, 211-265.

Hacking, I.
1975   *Why Does Language Matter to Philosophy?* Cambridge: Cambridge University Press.

Hamblin, C.L.
1970   Fallacies. London: Methuen.

Harder, P. and C. Kock
1976   *The Theory of Presupposition Failure*. Copenhagen: Akademisk Forlag.

Hartnack, J.
1972   *Language and Philosophy*. The Hague: Mouton.

Holdcroft, D.
1978   *Words and Deeds; Problems in the Theory of Speech Acts*. Oxford: Clarendon Press.

Holdcroft, D.
1979   'Speech Acts and Conversation'. *Philosophical Quarterly 29 (115)*, 125-141.

Hymes, D.H.
1962   'The Ethnography of Speaking'. In: T. Gladwin and W. Sturtevant (eds.) *Anthropology and Human Behavior*. Washington: Anthropological Society of Washington, 13-53.

Hymes, D.
1967   'Models of the Interaction of Language and Social Setting'. *Journal of Social Issues 23 (2)*, 8-28.

Jackson, S. and S. Jacobs
1980   'Structure of Conversational Argument: Pragmatic Bases for the Enthymeme'. *The Quarterly Journal of Speech 66*, 251-265.

Janik, A. and S. Toulmin
1973   *Wittgenstein's Vienna*. New York: Simon and Schuster.

Jarvie, J.C.
1976   'Toulmin and the Rationality of Science'. In: R.S. Cohen et al. (eds.), *Essays in Memory of Imre Lakatos*. Dordrecht: Reidel, 311-334.

Kahane, H.
1973   *Logic and Philosophy; A Modern Introduction*. Belmont (Cal.): Wadsworth (2nd ed.; 1st ed., 1969).

Kahane, H.
1976   *Logic and Contemporary Rhetoric: The Use of Reason in Everyday Life*. Belmont (Cal.): Wadsworth (2nd ed.; 1st ed., 1971).

Kallmeyer, W. and F. Schütze
1976   'Konversationanalyse'. *Studium Linguistik 1*, 1-28.

Kamlah, W. and P. Lorenzen
1973   *Logische Propädeutik; Vorschule des Vernünftigen Redens*. Mannheim: Hochschultaschenbücher Verlag (2nd ed.; 1st ed., 1967).

Kempson, R.M.
1975   *Presupposition and the Delimination of Semantics*. Cambridge: Cambridge University Press.

Kopperschmidt, J.
1980   *Argumentation (Sprache,und Vernunft, Teil 2)*. Stuttgart: Kohlhammer.

Lakatos, I.
1963/1964 'Proofs and Refutations'. *British Journal for the Philosophy of Science 14*, 1-25, 120-139, 221-143, 296-342.

Lambert, K. and W. Ulrich
1980 *The Nature of Argument*. New York: MacMillan.

Lewis, D.K.
1977 *Convention; A Philosophical Study*. Cambridge (Mass.): Harvard University Press (3rd ed.; 1st ed., 1969).

Locke, J.
1961 *An Essay Concerning Human Understanding*. Edited by J.W. Yolton. London: Dent. 2 Vols.

Lorenzen, P.
1969 *Normative Logic and Ethics*. Mannheim: Hochschultachenbücher Verlag.

Lorenzen, P.
1970 *Formale Logik*. Berlin: W. de Gruyter.

Lorenzen, P. and K. Lorenz
1978 *Dialogische Logik*. Darmstadt: Wissenschaftliche Buchgesellschaft.

Lorenzen, P. and O. Schwemmer
1975 *Konstruktive Logik, Ethik und Wissenschaftstheorie*. Mannheim: B.I.-Wissenschaftsverlag (2nd rev. ed.).

Morgan, J.L.
1978 'Two Types of Convention in Indirect Speech Acts'. In: Cole (ed.) 1978, 261-280.

Naess, A.
1966 *Communication and Argument. Elements of Applied Semantics*. Translated from the Norwegian by A. Hannay. Oslo, etc.: Universitetsforlaget/Allen & Unwin.

Nuchelmans, G.
1978 *Taalfilosofie; Een Inleiding*. Muidenberg: Coutinho.

Öhlschläger, G.
1977 'Über das Argumentieren'. In: Schecker (Hrsg.) 1977, 11-25.

Öhlschläger, G.
1979 *Linguistische Überlegungen zu einer Theorie der Argumentation*. Tübingen: Niemeyer.

Parret, H.
1978 'A Note on Pragmatic Universals of Language'. In: H. Seiler (ed.), *Language Universals*. Tübingen: Narr, 125-140.

Parret, H.
1980 'Les Stratégies Pragmatiques'. *Communications 32*, 250-273.

Passmore, J.
1972 *A Hundred Years of Philosophy*. Harmondsworth (Middlesex): Penguin Books.

Perelman, Ch.
1970 'The New Rhetoric: A Theory of Practical Reasoning'. In: *Great Ideas Today*. Chicago, 273-312.

Perelman, Ch.
1980 *Justice, Law, and Argument: Essays on Moral and Legal Reasoning*. Dordrecht: Reidel.

Perelman, Ch. and L. Olbrechts-Tyteca
1971 *The New Rhetoric. A Treatise on Argumentation*. 2nd ed. Notre Dame, etc.:

University of Notre Dame Press. 1st ed. 1969. Translated by J. Wilkinson and P. Weaver. Originally Published as : *La Nouvelle Rhétorique: Traité de l'Argumentation*, 1958.

Piel, W.
1980   'Zur Formalen Pragmatik Konstativer Performatoren'. In: C.F. Gethmann (Hrsg.), *Theorie des Wissenschaftlichen Argumentierens*. Frankfurt: Suhrkamp 165-189.

Popper, K.R.
1972   *Objective Knowledge; An Evolutionary Approach*. Oxford: Clarendon Press.

Popper, K.R.
1974   *Conjectures and Refutations; The Growth of Scientific Knowledge*. London: Routledge & Kegan Paul (5th ed.; 1st ed., 1963).

Pospesel, H.
1971   *Arguments*. Englewoord Cliffs (N.J.): Prentice Hall.

Purtill, R.L.
1979   *Logic; Argument, Refutation and Proof*. New York: Harper & Row.

Quasthoff, U.
1978   'The Uses of Stereotype in Everyday Argument'. *Journal of Pragmatics 2 (1)*, 1-48.

Rescher, N.
1961   'On the logic of Presupposition'. *Philosophy and Phenomenological Research 21*, 521-527.

Rescher, N.
1964   *Introduction to Logic*. 3rd pr. New York: St Martin's Press.

Rescher, N.
1977   *Dialectics; A Controversy-oriented Approach to the Theory of Knowledge*. Albany: State University of New York Press.

Sadock, J.M.
1974   *Towards a Linguistic Theory of Speech Acts*. New York: Academic Press.

Sadock, J.M.
1978   'On Testing for Conversational Implicature'. In: Cole and Morgan (eds.) 1975, 281-297.

Schecker, M.
1977   'Argumentation als allokutionäre Sprechakte'. In: Schecker (Hrsg.) 1977, 75-138.

Schecker, M. (Hrsg.)
1977   *Theorie der Argumentation*. Tübingen: Narr.

Schellens, P.J. and G. Verhoeven
1979   'Naar een Procedure voor de Analyse en Evaluatie van Betogende Teksten'. *Tijdschrift voor Taalbeheersing 1 (1)*, 1-24.

Schlieben-Lange, B.
1975a   *Linguistische Pragmatik*. Stuttgart: Kohlhammer.

Schlieben-Lange, B.
1975b   'Perlokution'. *Sprache im Technischen Zeitalter 53*, 319-334.

Scriven, M.
1976   *Reasoning*. New York: McGraw-Hill.

Searle, J.R.
1970   *Speech Acts; An Essay in the Philosophy of Language*. Cambridge: Cambridge University Press (2nd ed.; 1st ed., 1969).

Searle, J.R.
    1971   'What is a Speech Act?' In: J.R. Searle (ed.), *the Philosophy of Language*,
            London, etc.: Oxford University Press, 39-53.
Searle, J.R.
    1975   'A Taxonomy of Illocutionary Acts'. In: K. Gunderson (ed.), *Language,
            Mind and Knowledge*. Minneanapolis: University of Minnesota Press, 344-
            369. (Reprint in Searle 1979).
Searle, J.R.
    1979   *Expression and Meaning: Studies in the Theory of Speech Acts*. Cambridge:
            Cambridge University Press.
Searle, J.R.
    1980   'An Interview (with John Searle)'. In: J. Boyd and A. Ferrara (eds.) *Speech
            Acts Theory: Ten Years Later*. Milano: Bompiani (= Versus 26/27), 17-27.
Searle, J.R., F. Kiefer and M. Bierwisch (eds.)
    1980   *Speech Act Theory and Pragmatics*. Dordrecht: Reidel.
Searle, J.R. and D. Vanderveken
    n.d.   *Foundations of Illocutionary Logic*. Cambridge: Cambridge University
            Press (forthcoming).
Smith, C. and D.M. Hunsaker
    1972   *The Bases of Argument: Ideas in Conflict*. Indianapolis: Bobbs Merill.
Stalnaker, R.C.
    1973   'Presupposition'. *Journal of Philosophical Logic 2 (4)*, 447-457.
Strawson, P.F.
    1964   'Intention and Convention in Speech Acts'. *Philosophical Review 73*, 439-
            460.
Toulmin, S.E.
    1969   *The Uses of Argument*. Cambridge: Cambridge University Press (2nd ed.;
            1st ed., 1958).
Toulmin, S.E.
    1976   *Knowing and Acting; An Invitation to Philosophy*. New York: MacMillan.
Wald, B.
    1978   'Zur Einheitlichkeit und Einleitung von Diskurseinheiten'. In: U.
            Quasthoff (Hrsg.), *Sprachstruktur - Sozialstruktur*. Kornberg (Ts):
            Scriptor, 128-149.
Walker, R.C.S.
    1975   'Conversational Implicatures', In: S. Blackburn (ed.), *Meaning, Reference
            and Necessity*. Cambridge: Cambridge University Press, 131-181.
Webster, N. and J. McKechnie
    1979   *Webster's New Twentieth Century Dictionary of the English Language*. New
            York: Simon and Schuster (2nd ed.).
Wenzel, J.W.
    1979   'Jürgen Habermas and the Dialectical Perspective on Argumentation'.
            Journal of the American Forensic Association 16 (2), 83-94.
Woods, J. and D. Walton
    1975   'Petitio Principii'. *Synthese 31*, 107-127.
Woods, J. and D. Walton
    1976   'Ad Hominem'. *Philosophical Forum 8*, 1-20.
Woods, J. and D. Walton
    1977   'Petitio and Relevant Many Premissed Arguments'. *Logique et Analyse 20
            (77-78)*, 97-110.

Woods, J. and D. Walton
  1981   'More on Fallaciousness and Invalidity'. *Philosophy and Rhetoric 14 (3)*,
          168-172.
Wunderlich, D.
  1972   'Zur Konventionalität von Sprechhandlungen'. In: D. Wunderlich (Hrsg.),
          Linguistische Pragmatik. Frankfurt: Athenäum, 11-58.
Wunderlich, D.
  1976   *Studien zur Sprechakttheorie*. Frankfurt: Suhrkamp.
Wunderlich, D.
  1980   'Methodological Remarks on Speech Act Theory'. In: Searle et al. (eds.)
          1980, 291-312.

Index of Names

Albert 16, 194n
Alexy 199n, 200n, 201n
Austin 19-22, 25-6, 30-1, 34, 36, 47, 51-2, 54-5, 62-5, 71, 96-7, 109-10, 197n, 199n

Bach 41, 137, 197n
Ballmer 196n, 197n
Barry 177
Barth 13, 18, 67, 76, 193n, 196n, 199n, 201n, 202n
Bartsch 199n
Berger 58
Berk 200n
Black 51, 138, 198n
Brennenstuhl 196n, 197n
Brockriede 200n
Burleson 200n

Carney 177, 179-81, 201n
Cohen 30, 47, 51, 53-7, 63-5
Copi 124, 126-7, 201n
Crawshay-Williams 13, 199n

Dascal 199n
Davidson 198n
Dijk, Van 37-9

Eemeren, Van 5, 38, 67, 152, 194n, 195n, 198n, 199n
Ehninger 200n
Elias 58
Erlangen School 13, 169, 193n, 199n

Feyerabend 7
Finocchiaro 113, 177, 201n
Fogelin 8-9, 15, 36-7, 113, 122-3, 131, 146, 196n, 197n, 198n 199n

Grice 8, 42, 85, 119-21, 132-5, 137, 140, 143-4, 147, 156-7, 159, 180, 198n, 199n
Grootendorst 5, 38, 67, 152, 194n, 195n, 198n, 199n
Gumb 193n

Gumperz 38

Haack 8
Habermas 195n, 199n, 200n
Hacking 6
Hamblin 131, 189, 198n
Harder 195n
Harnish 41, 137, 197n
Hartnack 193n
Holdcroft 51-2, 121
Hunsaker 200n
Hymes 38

Jackson 199n
Jacobs 199n
Janik 193n
Jarvie 194n, 199n

Kahane 124-7, 201n
Kallmeyer 37
Kamlah 14, 167, 169, 193n, 196n, 201n
Kant 198
Kempson 199n
Kock 195n
Kopperschmidt 195n
Krabbe 13, 18, 67, 76, 193n, 196n, 199n
Kruiger 5, 67, 152, 194n, 195n, 199n

Lambert 8, 113, 122, 138-42, 178, 180-1, 198n, 201n
Lewis 60
Locke 185, 187
Lorenz 67, 193n
Lorenzen 13-4, 67, 167, 169, 193n, 196n, 201n
Luckmann 58

Martens 201n, 202n
Morgan 61, 63

Naess 13, 77, 158, 196n, 197n
Nuchelmans 129-31

Öhlschläger 129-31, 198n

Olbrechts-Tyteca 12, 16, 67, 194n

Parret 193n, 198n
Passmore 193n
Perelman 12, 16, 67, 194n
Piel 197n
Popper 6-7, 16-7, 199n, 201n
Purtill 15, 126, 128, 179

Quasthoff 37-9, 131, 195n, 198n

Rescher 124-6, 129-31, 198n, 200n
Russell 193n

Sadock 51-2, 199n
Schecker 195n
Scheer 177, 179-81, 201n
Schellens 138-40, 142, 198n
Schlieben-Lange 65
Schütze 37
Schwemmer 193n
Scriven 122, 129, 138-40, 142-3, 146, 198n

Searle 19-23, 25, 27-8, 30-2, 34, 36, 39-42, 47,
   51-2, 54-6, 58, 61-3, 65, 71, 85, 95-7, 101,
   103, 106-9, 112-3, 144-5, 194n, 195n, 196n,
   197n, 199n, 201n
Smith 200n
Stalnaker 130, 199n
Strawson 58, 64

Toulmin 32, 146, 193n, 200n

Ulrich 8, 113, 122, 138-42, 178, 180-1, 198n,
   201n

Vanderveken 101, 108, 144-5, 196n
Verhoeven 138-40, 142, 198n

Wald 37
Walton 201n, 202n
Wenzel 17, 200n
Wittgenstein 193n
Woods 201n, 202n
Wunderlich 23, 36, 48, 58, 60, 113, 198n

Index of Subjects

accept 9, 23-5, 47-51, 56-7, 69-74, 102, 154
acceptability 61, 82, 96, 194n
action schema 37-8, 65
antagonist 10, 81, 162, 188
apportioning roles 162
argument, *see* argumentation
argumentation 18, 29-35, 194n
  compound – 91-3, 146-9
  contra- 9, 15, 43, 45, 48, 196n, 197n
  co-ordinative compound – 91-3, 148, 197n
  multiple – 91, 93, 197n
  practical – 48
  pro- 9, 15, 43-4, 48, 196n, 197n
  – schema 66-7, 196n
  single – 90-1, 93, 147-8, 150
  structure of – 87-93
  sub- 90
  subordinative compound – 92-3, 147-8, 197n
  theoretical – 48
argumentum
  – *ad baculum* 182
  – *ad hominem* 178-9, 189-92, 202n
  – *ad ignorantiam* 178, 185, 187-8, 192, 201n
  – *ad populum* 180
assertive 34-6, 39, 95-8, 100-9, 111, 114, 116-7, 152, 197n, 201n
assumption
  arguer's – 139
  minimal – 138-9
  optimal – 138-9
attack 164-73
  best possible – 171
  successful – 162, 168, 187
  sufficient – 165, 169-71, 185

behabitive 197n
burden of proof 117, 161-2, 184-5, 200n

code of conduct 151-75, 182-9
commissive 71, 97, 100, 102-5, 107-8, 111, 115, 152, 197n, 200n
committedness 5, 12, 69, 71, 96-7, 113, 140-1, 144-5, 163, 172, 186, 195n

comprehensibility 61, 194n
concession 13-5
context 112, 129, 142, 147, 199n
  indeterminate – 148, 199n
constative speech utterance 21
convention 58-60, 63, 68, 163
  – of language 61-2, 64-5
  – of language usage 59, 61-2, 64
  pragmatic – 22
  semantic – 22
convince 30, 47-51, 56, 63-74
co-operative principle (CP) 119-22, 132, 156-7, 180, 199n

declaration, *see* declarative
declarative 97, 106, 108-9, 152, 197n
  usage – 109-12, 115, 152, 156-8, 197n, 198n
decomposition 201n
defence 164-73
  best possible – 172
  definitive – 165
  provisional – 164, 170
  successful – 162, 166, 168, 187
  sufficient – 165, 169-71, 185
dialectic 15-8
  formal – 196n, 199n
dialectification 15-8
dialogue 9-15
  explicative – 24, 198n
  problemizing – 24, 198n
directive 97-8, 100, 102, 104-8, 110-1, 115, 152, 197n, 198n, 200n
discussion 2
  argumentative – 2, 75
  compound – 81-2, 197n
  critical – 17
  meta- 163, 175, 185
  multiple – 81-2
  principal – 89
  rational – 18, 198n
  simple – 78, 81-2, 197n
  single – 78, 81-2
  stages of –, *see* stages of discussion

sub- 89-90
dispute 10, 75-6, 79
    compound – 80, 196n
    initial – 89, 164
    multiple – 80
    original –, *see* initial
    resolution of a – 82-3, 98-104
    simple – 80-1
    single – 80-1
    sub- 89, 164

enthymeme 124-7, 129
exercitive 197n
expositive 36, 71, 97, 100, 109, 197n
expressed opinion 5, 96, 195n 196n
    initial – 89
expressive 97, 100, 106, 108, 197n
externalization 4-7, 57, 69-74, 140, 155, 183

fallacy 68, 151, 177-92, 201n
    – of affirmation of the consequence 201n
    – of ambiguity 183
    – of begging the question 189-90, 192,
      201n, 202n
    – of false dilemma 188
    formal – 177, 201n
    – of hasty generalization 201n
    informal – 177, 182, 201n
    – of many questions 182
    – of *post hoc ergo propter hoc* 201n
    – of shifting the burden of proof 185
    – of straw man 141, 179, 184, 201n
functionalization 7-9

illocution 50
    elementary – 34, 36-8, 109, 197n
    complex –, *see* illocutionary act complex
    compound –, *see* illocutionary act complex
illocutionary act 19-20, 23-8, 51-7, 194n, 195n
    indirect –, *see* indirect speech act
illocutionary act complex 34, 37-8, 109, 111,
    195n, 197n
    – of argumentation 39-46
illocutionary indicator 31, 113
illocutionary point 96
implicature
    conventional – 132-3, 145
    conversational – 120, 132-3, 145, 148, 180
indirect speech act, *see* speech act
intersubjective explicitization procedure
    168-9, 185-6
intersubjective identification procedure
    165-6, 185-6, 190
intersubjective reasoning procedure 169,
    185-6

intersubjective testing procedure 167-8, 185-6

justify 16, 18

locutionary act 26, 52, 63-4

maxim 120, 156, 180, 198n, 199n
    – of manner 120, 156, 198n
    – of quality 120, 140-1, 146, 159, 180-1,
      196n, 198n
    – of quantity 120, 140-1, 145-6, 180,
      198n
    – of relation 120, 140, 146, 180-1, 198n
maximum argumentative interpretation 117
minimum
    conversational – 146, 148
    logical – 139, 145
Münchhausen-trilemma 16, 194n

negation
    illocutionary – 101, 152
    propositional – 101
non bis in idem 159, 173
normative reconstruction 193n, 194n

opponent 13

performative formula 21, 31, 42, 62, 64, 113
perfomative speech utterance 20-1
perlocution
    contexual – 27
    force – 27
    illocutionary – 27, 51, 63
    propositional – 27
    utterance – 27
perlocutionary act 19-20, 23-8, 50-7, 194n
perlocutionary consequence 24
    consecutive – 24, 57
perlocutionary effect 24, 26, 55-6, 69-74, 194n
    inherent – 24, 57
    minimal – 24, 194n
    optimal – 24, 194n
persuade 48-9
petitio principii, *see* fallacy of begging the
    question
point of view 5, 16, 79, 87, 89-90, 164, 166
    initial – 164-5
    subordinate – 165
premiss
    suppressed –, *see* unexpressed –
    tacit –, *see* unexpressed –
    unexpressed – 119-49, 179-82, 189, 198n
presentation
    prospective – 195n
    retrospective – 195n

presupposition 129-32, 195n, 199n
principle of charity 125-6, 129, 136, 142, 198n
principle of expressibility 113
pro aut contra survey 196n
proponent 13
propositional act 19-20, 27, 194n
protagonist 10, 81, 162, 188
psycho-pragmatic primitive 6

rationality 18, 68, 198n, 200n
rational judge 5
reasoning in a circle, *see* fallacy of begging the
   question
refute 16, 18
reject 9, 72-4
rule 193n
rules for speech acts in rational discussions
   151-75, 182-8
   general rule 151-3
   rule for the concluding stage 173-5, 186-8
   rules for the argumentation stage 162-73,
     185-6
   rules for the confrontation stage 154-8,
     183-4

   rules for the opening stage 158-62, 184-5

socialization 9-15, 140
soundness 68
speech act 20, 195n
   indirect – 22, 32-3, 52-3, 197n, 199n
   macro- 37-8
speech event 38
stages of discussion 85-8, 98-100, 109
   argumentation stage 86, 88. 99, 162-73. 188
   concluding stage 86-8, 99-100, 173-5, 188
   confrontation stage 85, 88, 99, 154-8, 188
   opening stage 85, 88, 99, 158-62, 188
standard paraphrase 114, 158
standpoint, *see* point of view
strategy 193n
syllogism 124-9

text genre 38, 195n

utterance act 19-20, 27, 194n

verdictive 96-7, 197n